Baby Names

2021

Eleanor Turner

white
LADDER

Acknowledgments

Many thanks as always to Beth Bishop and Sophie Lazar at White Ladder Press: your combined good humor and patience has helped this series endure to its eleventh edition. Thank you for sticking with me through it all.

My husband Mike has always been my biggest cheerleader and advocate, and writing this edition during the Covid-19 lockdown, surrounded by children and nowhere quiet to escape to, has proved quite the challenge. Thank you for everything you do, particularly bringing me snacks and caffeine.

And finally, everything I do and everything I write about in this book is because of my children. If I have one hope, it's that they don't grow up hating their names...because that would be mortifying as a baby names expert. Owen Henri, Jasper Hugh, Josie May and Felix Brian: you are fantastic little people and I love each of you more and more every day. Now go and put some clothes on – I don't care if there is a pandemic and we're not leaving the house for a month. Love, Mama.

First published in the United States in 2020 by White Ladder
An imprint of Hachette UK

1

Copyright © Eleanor Turner 2020

The right of Eleanor Turner to be identified as the Author
of the Work has been asserted by her in accordance with
the Copyright, Designs and Patents Act 1988.

A CIP catalogue record for this title is available from the British Library

Trade Paperback ISBN 9781910336649

Typeset in Zapf Humanist BT by Hewer Text UK Ltd, Edinburgh
Printed and bound in the United States of America by LSC Communications

Hodder & Stoughton policy is to use papers that are natural, renewable
and recyclable products and made from wood grown in sustainable
forests. The logging and manufacturing processes are expected to
conform to the environmental regulations of the country of origin.

Hodder & Stoughton Ltd
Carmelite House
50 Victoria Embankment
London EC4Y 0DZ

www.hodder.co.uk

Contents

Author's note

Baby names vary widely in spelling and pronunciation. To simplify things, this book usually lists each name only once: under the most common initial and spelling. If a name has an alternate spelling with a different initial, it may also be listed under that letter.

Information relating to statistics and trends in baby names is based on the most recent data at the time of writing.

Introduction

Goodness me – what a year we've just had! 2020 was a year of chaos and uncertainty, and for those who had a baby last year I imagine it was also filled with worry and trepidation. It made for unforgettable global headlines as society was turned on its head, and we narrowed down what was truly important to each of us and how to protect it.

In the middle of all the fear, though, babies continued to be born and names were joyfully and carefully chosen for each new life. It made for some interesting developing trends, as you'll go on to learn about in this book. My wish for you if you are expecting a baby in 2021 is a calmer, simpler year ahead and a return to normal life. I hope it also comes with a renewed sense of optimism for the next generation about to be born: may they arrive into a world with love, peace…and practically perfect names.

Inside *Baby Names 2021* you'll find out:

- Why simple names are simply perfect

- What the science says about baby naming

- What babies are being called in different countries around the world

- What names celebrities are choosing

- …and why we're so fascinated by it all!

All the weird, wonderful, trendy and sciency trivia in this book is backed up by the most recent data from the Social Security Administration, and includes all kind of interesting tidbits collected throughout the previous year. The goal is to make the decision over what to name your new baby as fun and easy as possible; so grab a pencil and a frothy coffee, dip in, and find some names you like. Use the plentiful suggestions and lists we've given you to find out whether one of them is your baby's future name.

Good luck!

Eleanor Turner

Part One

1 Current baby-naming trends

Well, that was quite a year, wasn't it? At the time of writing, 2020 will be remembered for two things: a global pandemic, and developing coping strategies for said pandemic based entirely around memes. The world pressed the pause button for several months early in the year, with businesses shuttered, schools closed and hospitals overrun. It became quite an isolated and quiet place for a while. But one thing that never stopped was the number of babies being born. Nicknamed the "Quaranteenies", babies who arrived in 2020 were born into a changed world, with families separated, faces hidden behind masks and a broken economy that is still struggling to recover. However, each one of these brand-new little lives needed to be named. And that's where this book comes in.

Typically, trends in baby names follow several familiar patterns, including recycling what was popular 100 years ago, the influence of pop culture and reinventing traditional names so they feel fresh and new. But there's nothing like a significant global event to liven things up, so I invite you to join me in an exploration of how our current baby-naming trends were impacted by the pandemic, as well as the worlds of celebrities, politics and other socioeconomic developments.

So, let's get going, shall we? Let's read up on what parents across the country are currently naming their babies, and practice arranging our faces into 'oh, isn't that lovely!' expressions as we go. If you're currently expecting a new baby, then somewhere in this little tome is the perfect name for them, and lots of other neat stuff to learn along the way.

Lovely Liam and enduring Emma

We're going to start our journey by looking at the baby names American parents chose more than any others in 2020. For the third year in a row Liam topped the boys' charts, and Emma is in first place on the girls' list for the fifth year running. More than 18,500 baby girls were given the name Emma in the latest baby names data set (released by the Social Security Administration, SSA), and nearly 20,000 were given the name Liam. Crucially, while Emma was significantly down in numbers from the year before, both managed to keep their prime positions. But why these names? What's going on with these two particular choices that holds such a strong attraction for so many new parents? Well, we have to take a look at some other factors to make that clearer.

Last year was a low year for birth statistics. Just over 3,790,000 babies were born in the United States, indicating a tiny raise from the previous year, but still among the lowest recorded birth rates in over thirty years. Fertility rates were also down (the number of babies born to each woman in her lifetime), which means that families are choosing to have fewer children, if at all.

In 2020 there were 132 babies registered as Unknown and 27 named Baby.

The Nation's Top 10

Boys	Girls
1. Liam	1. Emma
2. Noah	2. Olivia
3. William	3. Ava
4. James	4. Isabella
5. Oliver	5. Sophia
6. Benjamin	6. Charlotte
7. Elijah	7. Mia
8. Lucas	8. Amelia
9. Mason	9. Harper
10. Logan	10. Evelyn

Baby Names 2021

What this means, for our purposes, is that baby names data is getting really interesting. In the past, if you picked an unusual name it would appear somewhere at the bottom of the list, having to compete with the thousands and thousands of other folks who chose more traditional names or common spellings. Now, though, if you choose something off the beaten track it carries more weight because there are simply fewer other names to compete with. There's more shuffling in the ranks now, and names that were stalwarts from a few years ago are moving down, down, down, and others that we might not have even heard of before are up, up, up. I acknowledge that this is very nerdy, but bear with me. I promise it gets even more interesting.

Consider this: until a few years ago, either Jacob or Michael had remained the top choice for parents of newborn baby boys in the US for over fifty years. Jacob has been given to more babies over that period (4.9 million and counting), but Michael has claimed the top spot more often (forty-four times), so the fact that Liam has rocketed to the top for three years running is pretty unusual. In fact, Jacob has now been pushed down to position thirteen and Michael sits in fourteenth place, which might say more about broader baby-naming and political trends than about anything else. If the two most popular baby boy names of all time are no longer in the Top 10, then we are surely on the cusp of one of the biggest shakeups in baby names history.

At first glance, the names in the girls' list don't look very different to the year before, but that's only because of the Top 10. Once we delve a little deeper into the list, you'll see how both the boys' and the girls' lists are changing like never before. Emma, Olivia and Ava have maintained their positions in the Top 3, while newcomer Harper has pushed Abigail into eleventh place. On the boys' side, Lucas is the name responsible for pushing Jacob out of the Top 10 bracket.

The 'Name of the Year' tournament pronounced Mathdaniel Squirrel the winner of its annual competition last year. Mr Squirrel

beat out popular competitors Courvoisier Dingle, Gimadiah
Scrogum and Beanbag Amerika for the title.

There are a few themes within the Top 10 on both sides, however: Biblical names, which have dominated the American charts for years, are still very much en vogue for baby boys, and Noah, Benjamin, James and Elijah are all doing very well for themselves. However, long gone are the equivalents for baby girls such as Rebecca, Rachel and Mary. Instead, parents of little girls are far more likely to choose a name based on sound, rather than historical or religious significance.

In this tradition we now see a run on girls' names with –ah sounds at the end, which accounts for a massive eighty per cent of the Top 10 and sixty-five per cent of the Top 20. In fact, the only names to not follow the pattern are Charlotte and Evelyn.

Charlotte, once an extremely popular name in the US and appearing consistently in the Top 100 from 1908 to 1953, had dropped dramatically by 1982. However, in the last decade it's seen a sharp uptick in use, and last year popped up at number six. Of course, in the last few years it has been helped along by a certain royal princess, but it's also benefiting from the 100 year rule, which sees names coming back into fashion after a century out of the spotlight.

Charlotte has now become so fashionable that even shortened versions of it are gaining momentum: Charlie entered the Top 1,000 for baby girls in 2005 and in subsequent years has leaped nearly 800 places to 152nd place. Charlie has also remained a steady favorite for parents of little boys, as it has climbed nearly 250 spots since the year 2000 in the boys' charts, landing last year in position 218.

A name fit for a Duchess

The name Meghan has had a huge resurgence thanks to the popularity of Duchess Meghan Markle. A mere 162 babies were given the name Meghan back in 2017, but last year it appeared in 703rd place—an astonishing climb considering its last heyday was back in the 1990s. In fact, it was the highest-climbing girls' name in 2019, moving up more places in the charts than any other name. Meghan is a Welsh name meaning 'pearl.'

The struggle is real

Let's look a little further into what's happening down the lists. I mentioned previously that while the Top 10 for both boys and girls has remained essentially unchanged, things get really interesting once you delve a bit deeper. Names in the Top 100 have seen huge amounts of shuffling within the ranks, with names such as Jayden falling like crazy—even though a few years ago it was the fourth most popular boys' name in the country—while others, such as Luna and Aurora, are skyrocketing.

I think there are two separate things going on here, and the combination is causing this simultaneous effect of the top names going largely unchanged every year, while the ones chasing the rear shuffle up and down like a deck of cards.

Let's start with reason number one: Americans love traditional names. Noah and William have appeared in the Top 20 boys' names every year since 2008, and the girls' names Emma, Ava, Sophia and Isabella have also stayed put. The world has changed a lot since 2008, but apparently our predominantly traditional taste in names has not.

There are a couple of theories as to why a large number of us are giving our kids the same names, year after year. Personally, I think the global pandemic of 2020 was a huge contributor last year, and bounces nicely off the trend in recent years for minimalism and everything Marie Kondo has taught us about simplifying our lives. In 2020 the world was extremely chaotic thanks to Covid-19, and women experienced their pregnancies in extraordinary circumstances. Births happened in isolation, new grandbabies had to meet their grandparents behind protective glass, and the communities we surround our mothers with after a birth suddenly all evaporated. Is it any surprise that amidst this chaos and uncertainty parents chose names that are very traditional? Tradition, stability and familiarity bring comfort, and that was extremely needed in 2020.

Continuing this theme is that parents are choosing names they've heard for so long that they feel safe and familiar. Just take a look at the Top 10 (the first five spots for baby girls end in –a), or the highest climbers (six of the ten biggest climbers for baby girls end in either –a, –ie, –y or a similar sound—see page 32). Most names ending –a or –e/–y are immensely popular for little girls right now, and that's because we simply love the sound they make.

While most of us wanted to forget about the pandemic of 2020 entirely, others took the more…permanent approach of memorializing the event. India was the first country to announce babies born with virus-themed names, when boy and girl twins Covid and Corona were born in March of that year. Manila then followed suit, with babies named Covid Bryant (after basketball legend Kobe Bryant) and Covid Rose, and then India came through again with a baby boy named Lockdown.

All of this is to say that there's a comfortable pattern to the way large numbers of us name our children that has prevailed for over 20 years now, and other old-fashioned names, such as Eleanor, Henry, James and Josephine, have climbed the popularity ranks in the Top 100 lists, along with their alternate spellings of Ellie, Harry, Jack and Josie.

Reason number two: Americans also love to buck tradition and do their own thing (looking at you, Revolution of 1776).

Despite our oh-so-traditional leanings when it comes to the names coasting at the top of the charts, research shows we are actually seeing more variation than ever before in the rest of the list. In the 1950s, the Top 25 boys' names and the Top 50 girls' names were given to half of all babies born in that decade. Think about that for a moment: half of all babies born in the 1950s were given one of either 25 boys' names or 50 girls' names. That's astonishing.

To reach the same figure now, you would have to include the Top 149 boys' names and the Top 196 girls'. That's everything from Liam (1st) to Amir (149th), and Emma (1st) to Everleigh (196th). In fact, if you look over the last decade, the percentage of babies given names in the Top 1,000 gets smaller every year: ten years ago 73.08 per cent of registered births appeared in the Top 1,000 names, but in 2019 it was only 72.72 per cent. This means there is a far greater variety of names, spellings and pronunciations than ever before, even though the names at the very top of the charts remain traditional and stable.

> Some of the US's quirkiest baby names over the last year have included Clever, Glory, Polo and Power for boys; and Ian, Leeloo, Sovereign and Stone for girls.

One explanation for this is that parents have begun to give their children names more unusual than their own. A parent who was one of a dozen Jennifers in their class in the 80s or 90s might not want the same experience for her children. Alternatively, a parent who has a slightly unusual name and enjoyed that experience growing up might feel confident about giving their offspring an even more unique name.

There's also a massive trend for taking a name that sounds pretty traditional, but adding a creative twist with the spelling to make it more modern. Examples of this include Kinsley, Madelyn, Jaxon and Kayden. In fact, substituting letters is probably the biggest trend of all in 2020, but because it results in such unique spellings, all the names in this trend get buried near the bottom of the charts. Collectively, however, there are thousands of names where a C has been substituted for a K, or an I for a Y, and they make up a huge proportion of the data set. For more on how to get creative with spelling but not make it look like you're a toddler playing with letter fridge magnets, see page 57.

Statistical stuff

	Boys	Girls
Individual names registered	14,004	18,029
Total registrations	1,800,392	1,513,104
Top names	Liam (19,837 babies)	Emma (18,688 babies)
Babies with names in Top 10	143,173	138,766
Top 10 names as percentage	7.9% of all names	9.2% of all names
Highest climbers	Genesis (up 608 places)	Meghan (up 701 places)
Biggest fallers	Aaden (down 232 places)	Audrina (down 322 places)

Every year, the SSA releases a report on the biggest climbers and fallers, and most years these names tend to be the quirkiest. The names at the top of these lists have the greatest jumps in popularity, although it doesn't necessarily mean they are widely used across the USA. In fact, it's the opposite. The biggest climbers are always those further down the charts— if ten families chose a name last year, but then twenty families choose it this year, that's an increase of 100 per cent. The same percentage increase for Liam would need an additional 19,800 families to choose the name. So a rarely-used name can jump several hundred spots in a single year, despite only having a handful of families choosing it for their little ones. Here's a short breakdown of the Top 10 game-changers:

Biggest winners		Biggest losers	
Boys	Girls	Boys	Girls
Genesis	Meghan	Aaden	Audrina
Saint	Dior	Dilan	Courtney
Baker	Adalee	Craig	Angelique
Kairo	Palmer	Mike	Annabelle
Watson	Oaklynn	Harper	Marjorie
Kenzo	Haisley	Darrell	Marissa
Jaxtyn	Kelly	Ayan	Elsa
Kylo	Novah	Maxton	Jessa
Dakari	Yara	Trent	Kenley
Karsyn	Ensley	Jessie	Kadence

So why do names increase or decrease so dramatically in a single year? I mean, look at what happened to Kylo, which was the second biggest loser on the charts last year and now finds itself as the eighth-highest climber. Well, this is probably down to the release of the final installment of the Star Wars franchise *The Rise of Skywalker* on the Disney+ streaming platform, along with the second series of *The Mandalorian*. Disappointingly, the name Mando wasn't given to any babies in either 2019 or 2020, but Rey, Finn and Leia all managed to climb up the charts for the second year running.

There's also an interesting new pattern of how we're adopting unusual spellings for our favorite names. Novah, (from Nova), Jaxtyn (from

Jackson), Karsyn (from Carson) and Kairo (from Cairo) are all versions of more common names that parents are keen to get creative with. Certainly if you look at the Biggest losers list you'll see a similar pattern in reverse, with common spellings such as Marjorie, Darrell, Courtney and Marissa falling out of fashion. It will be interesting to see what happens to those names in 2021, and whether their counterparts of Margery, Daryl, Kortney and Maryssa will rise up the ranks in their place.

Just like everything else, names fall in and out of fashion. The popularity of names tends to ebb and flow, and in the case of Elsa it may be that even though *Frozen 2* was released on Disney+ in 2020, because it was so popular in 2013 and 2014, parents have been turned off it entirely. It placed at a peak of 286th position in 2014, but with no confirmed *Frozen 3*, Elsa may have had its time in the sun already (or frozen tundra, I suppose).

Trendy or tired?

One recurrent theme that's lasted for a few years now, and indeed will probably continue to last for another few more, is to use names that were considered deeply unfashionable a generation or so ago. Think names like Esther, Mae, Benedict and August, all of which are stoically climbing the charts again.

The reason for this is pretty simple: rather like the fashion of clothing that comes in waves or cycles, names drop in and out of popularity. The names of our parents' generation have been used (or overused) so often, so recently, that they are all but disappearing, while the names of our grandparents' are suddenly unique and cool again. Even the names of the 1990s and early 2000s are fading away, to be replaced by Theodore, Lucas, Helena and Ann.

Another trend that's been on the rise for a few years and will only continue to develop is the use of nicknames as full names. This started

Royal Baby Boom?

The British royal family has always been a source of inspiration for new parents on both sides of the pond: from Princess Charlotte to Archie Harrison, we've been obsessed with royal baby names for years now. At the time of writing there are predicted to be a possible four new royal babies joining the family in late 2020 and 2021. Prince Andrew's daughters Beatrice and Eugenie are expected to announce they're expecting following their recent marriages; and the bets are on for another baby for Prince Harry and Meghan Markle, and even a fourth child for Prince William and Kate Middleton. Tradition dictates that any names chosen will likely be staunchly traditional for Prince William's child as they will be closer in line to the throne, but likely to be less formal for Prince Harry, Princess Beatrice and Princess Eugenie's children.

long before the birth of new royal baby Archie, but he can certainly be credited with continuing the fashion. And in 2020 the hottest nicknames-as-names were somewhat surprising: how about Wells, as a nickname for Maxwell? This was the fastest-rising nickname of last year, jumping 200 spots. Other trendy options included Sunny, Gus, Sylvie and Dani.

This trend isn't exactly new though. Over in the UK it's been one of the most popular ways to pick a baby name for close to a decade. In fact, it's one of the few ways culture shifts across the Atlantic in this direction; usually pop culture blasts its way from west to east thanks to Hollywood and the music industry, but when it comes to names we've all agreed that the Brits seem to know what they're doing. Other trends happening across the pond right now include gender-neutral choices (Alex, Max, Charlie), 'sweet-sounding' names (Freya, Maisie, Zara), and using hyphens (Lily-Mae, Alfie-James, Ella-Rose). Watch out for these fashions to catch on here too.

Entertain us, baby

Everything from films and TV to books and blogs shapes the world of baby names, and even during a global pandemic this didn't change.

In an unprecedented twist of fate, many blockbuster films set to release last year had to push back their premiere dates as movie theaters closed their doors for half the year. There was therefore slightly less of an impact on baby names from the entertainment industry than in years past, but 2021 looks set to make up for it in droves as the entertainment industry ramps up speed again.

However, one tactic studios used during the country's lockdown was releasing movies straight to home rental via streaming services, and this certainly helped keep our attention. *Trolls: World Tour* was one such flick, and the name Poppy, which had never charted on the SSA's Top 1,000 names before the first film's release in 2016, continued to climb another 100 spots in 2020 after we all sat watching the sequel at home munching microwave popcorn.

> Did you know Chandler used to be one of the highest-climbing names in the USA in the 1990s, thanks to *Friends*? Once at a peak of position 151, since the series ended in 2004 it's hovered in the mid-400s and fell to a low of 505th place in 2018. However, with a reunion special planned for 2021 exciting things could happen again for Mr. Bing!

Mulan, Disney's real-life update of the celebrated animated original, was another big-screen movie to be affected by the coronavirus outbreak, when its release date was pushed back from spring to summer. The name Mulan last peaked in 1998 following the cartoon's release, but suddenly appeared again in 2020 with fifty-three babies given the name. Another casualty to the cause was *A Quiet Place Part II*, moving from spring to fall. The name Evelyn, which has been gaining in popularity since the 1980s, received a boost from the original *A Quiet Place* in 2018, and again in 2020 with the sequel. Finally, *Wonder Woman 1984* was an extraordinary film that followed the enduring adventures of Diana Prince, an Amazonian princess who once again saves the world. Diana, a name that has been slowly falling in popularity since the 1997 death of Princess Diana, saw a new spike in 2020 to regain its place in the Top 200.

Another big movie in 2020 was the remake of Leonard Bernstein's *West Side Story*. Directed by Steven Spielberg, this mammoth musical blockbuster brought 1950s New York back to life, and with it a whole host of wonderful names. Names to attract our interest included Valentina, Riff and Anita—played by original 1961 cast member Rita Moreno. Moreno's birth name is Rosa Delores Alverío Marcano, but she was nicknamed Rosita at a young age. When Hollywood beckoned she shortened it to Rita and adopted her stepfather's last name to become the legend she is today. Impressively, all three of her names are currently trending: Rosa, Rosita and, to a lesser extent, Rita.

Influences on boys' names kicked off with *Top Gun: Maverick*, the sequel to 1986's original *Top Gun*. The name Maverick has made extraordinary gains in the years since the original's release and 2020 saw it place in 78th position—the highest it's ever been. Miles, the name of incomer actor Miles Teller, has followed a similar pattern, and is now in 98th place—like Maverick, the highest the name has ever placed. *Artemis Fowl*, a Disney production based on the Eoin Colfer YA fiction books of the same name and originally planned for a blockbuster spring release in theaters, instead joined Disney+ for home streaming in the summer. Artemis wasn't a familiar name for most of us until 2020, but it suddenly appeared in the charts, with thirty-five babies registered with the name. Who knows what might have happened had the movie been able to hit the big screen properly?

And finally, *No Time to Die*, the final James Bond movie for star Daniel Craig, was released just as 2020 ended. Both James and Daniel remain hugely popular in the USA, with James sitting in fourth place and never having been out of the Top 20 for the last 120 years. Daniel, meanwhile, has never been out of the Top 50, but has been falling in the last decade or so. It will be interesting to see if Daniel will perk up again in 2021, as the film came out a little too late in the year to really flex its muscles.

Small-screen style

Surely I wasn't the only one eagerly anticipating the second season of *The Umbrella Academy*, which hit our screens in all its time-twisting glory in 2020. Actually, I know for a fact I wasn't, because judging by the impact the show has had on baby names in recent years, there were a lot of expectant parents watching it too. Vanya, Diego and Ben all moved up the charts in 2020, although Luther and Klaus actually fell. Maybe that's more suggestive of there being no *Luther* series released in 2020 though, and less about *The Umbrella Academy's* favorite resident strongman?

Another big-hitter was *Little Fires Everywhere*, starring Reese Witherspoon and Kerry Washington. While the name Mia actually fell a single place to land in the seventh spot, Elena pushed up a few. In addition, Reese, which had been declining for a few years, is back on the rise for baby girls. Likewise, season three of HBO's *Westworld* hit our TVs in 2020, and with it came renewed interest in the name Maeve. Played by Thandie Newton, the character Maeve has seen her name soar since 2016 when the show was first broadcast, climbing over 600 spots in just a few short years.

> One glorious distraction from the pandemic came in the form of cult documentary series *Tiger King*. It spurred memes galore… and also inspired some baby names. In 2020 there were 39 babies called Tiger, 345 called Joe, but only 10 called Carole. Disappointingly, none were called Sardine.

And finally, *Twilight* was back! Do you remember how mad we all went for the name Bella back in the day, watching it soar from not even being in the Top 1,000 in the year 2000 to now the 48th most popular girls' name in America? Well, after the 2020 release of Stephenie Meyer's fourth book, *Midnight Sun*, everyone's ears perked up again over the names Bella,

Edward and Jacob. Stay tuned to see how they impact 2021 data, as the book came out mid-year and didn't have much time to truly make its mark.

The sporting year

The Covid-19 pandemic took a lot from us in 2020, including thousands of loved ones, millions of jobs and the entire world's sense of security. It also took away many of our favorite pastimes, such as major sporting events and entire seasons of following our beloved teams. This strange set of circumstances meant that very few events happened in 2020, and in turn, that meant that there were very few opportunities for sporting events to have an impact on baby names.

> Did you know the USA invented over 1,100 new names last year?
> That's right: 1,100 brand new spellings appeared on the SSA's data
> lists, proving that American parents have quite the imagination.

Normally at this point in our annual edition of *Baby Names* we would be delving deep into the rising stars of the Summer Olympics, or the results of the MLB's World Series. But sadly none of those events have happened yet, with decisions made to postpone everything until 2021. Delightfully, it does mean we still have an opportunity to see how the names of sports stars impact baby names, but we'll just have to wait another year for most of them to become winners. Ho hum.

One event that managed to sneak in right before the country closed everything down was the Super Bowl. Stars of the NFL always make an impression, and the Kansas City Chiefs' Patrick Mahomes, MVP winner of Super Bowl 54, proved that once again. The name Patrick showed a slight uptick in 2020, although it has a long way to go before once again reaching its previous peak of position thirty way back in 1968. Football legend Peyton Manning has seen literally thousands of babies given his name; there were almost 1,000 baby boys and a whopping 2,800 baby girls called Peyton in the most recent SSA list.

There is a long history of successful athletes creating baby name trends: Jackie Robinson, the first African-American baseball player to play professionally, and one of the great legends of the sport, increased the popularity of both the name Jack (for boys) and Jackie (for girls) during the peak of his fame in the US. He can be credited, in large part, for the continuous popularity of these names even in the twenty-first century. Likewise, gymnast Simone Biles, who continues to make us collectively gasp every time she hits her floor routine, was single-handedly responsible for the return of the name Simone following the Summer Olympics in 2016.

Celebrity power

Ah, celebrities. Love them or hate them, you have to agree that it's hard to ignore them…especially when it comes to baby names. Normally celebrities can be relied upon to deliver us some epically awful names for their children, which is why this year's announcements have been somewhat disappointing! Now don't get me wrong: there are one or two names on our list that are truly jaw-dropping, but by and large it looks as though celebrities are following the trends of the rest of us and sticking to fairly traditional choices.

> Comedian Amy Schumer legally changed her infant son's name in 2020 from Gene Attell Fischer to Gene David Fischer, after 'helpful' online commentators pointed out that Gene Attell sounded a lot like 'genital'. Oops. Attell was chosen as a tribute to a family friend, so Amy and her husband Chris Fischer switched their little boy's name to the friend's first name of David instead.

Some of the completely normal names on the list this year include Charlie, Isaac, Isaiah, Lucia and Wyatt, to name just a few. Enrique Iglesias and Anna Kournikova chose the eternal favorite Mary for their baby girl, nicknaming her the Russian version Masha in homage to Kournikova's heritage; and British Prime Minister Boris Johnson and Carrie Symonds

Celebrity Babies in 2021

Alexander Denison (Will Arnett and Alessandra Brawn)

Birdie (David Tennant and Georgia Tennant)

Charlie Elena (Alex Morgan and Servando Carrasco)

Goldie 'Gogo' Patricia (Carson Daly and Silvi Daly)

Isaac Menelik Giovanni (Ashley Graham and Justin Ervin)

Isaiah (Christina Milian and Matt Pokora)

Lucia Marisol (America Ferrera and Ryan Piers Williams)

Lyra (Michael Sheen and Anna Lundberg)

Mary/Masha (Enrique Iglesias and Anna Kournikova)

Pace (Diplo and Jevon King)

Raddix (Cameron Diaz and Benji Madden)

Slash Electric Alexander (Amber Rose and Alexander Edwards)

Vanja (Chloe Sevigny and Sinisa Mačakovič)

Vittoria Genghis and Lozen Orianna Judith (Hope Solo and Jerramy Stevens)

Wilfred Lawrie Nicholas (Boris Johnson and Carrie Symonds)

Winter Mercy (Alanis Morissette and Mario Treadway)

Wyatt Morgan (Anderson Cooper)

X Æ A-12 (Elon Musk and Grimes)

chose Wilfred Lawrie Nicholas, after two family members and the NHS doctors who saved the Prime Minister's life during his hospitalization with Covid-19.

So what is this particular batch of celeb babies to do with their normal, traditional names? I would argue that these saner choices are reflective of the greater general trend of parents continuing to embrace older, more traditional names. Although the thought has simultaneously occurred to me that perhaps our perception is just skewed, and maybe Alanis

Morissette's choice of Winter Mercy for a baby boy doesn't seem half as crazy as it should, because we've had decades to get used to celeb offspring: think sixteen-year-old Apple Martin, sixteen-year-old Pilot Inspektor Lee and six-year-old North West.

> There was a sharp uptick in the numbers of babies called Kobe in 2020 in the USA charts, after the death of basketball legend Kobe Bryant.

Anyway, let's dig in to some of the weirder names, shall we? One of the more unusual names on the list is Slash Electric Alexander, the moniker awarded to the son of model Amber Rose. Explaining that their son 'is a rockstar', Amber Rose's partner Alexander 'AE' Edwards commented that his baby boy also shares his name. I suppose if you're going to go with Slash Electric for a first name, balancing it with the more modest Alexander helps keeps things palatable.

Another unusual choice is Birdie, from David and Georgia Tennant, also parents to Ty, Olive, Wilfred and Doris. Birdie's name was accidentally dropped by the couple's eldest son Ty, when he gave a shout-out to each of his siblings during an appearance on a popular British morning show. Coincidentally, Birdie happens to be the name Jessica Simpson gave to her daughter in 2019, and it was given to 169 other baby girls in the USA in 2020.

Let's move on to Raddix, the name selected by Cameron Diaz and Benji Madden for their newborn daughter in 2020. Diaz and Madden shared with friends that they created the name from two of their favorite words: 'rad' and 'dix', with dix apparently being a translation of 'new beginning' in a philosophical belief system shared by the couple. So there you go— if you're truly stuck for a name, just follow their lead and make one up! In 2021 anything goes.

If we want to dig a little deeper, my personal long-held theory behind unusual celebrity choices is that being a celebrity often demands a unique name, so that people know instantly to whom that news headline or Academy Award belongs. Celebrities are probably just being smart in this regard: give a baby a unique name from birth and you've already started their brand. Job done. I do draw the line at saddling a child with a name that the world laughs at though: isn't being a child of celebrity parents and constantly in the spotlight hard enough?

Finally…it would be remiss of me not to mention the most talked-about name choice of all. Tesla founder Elon Musk and his partner musician Grimes were caught in the middle of some of the madness when rumors abounded that they were naming their unborn child Influenza Musk, in keeping with the global pandemic theme of 2020. However, this was only a prequel to the main event, when it was announced they'd actually chosen X Æ A-12. The couple explained it was a combination of letters and sounds related to love, artificial intelligence and an airplane model. Of course. However, as Californian baby name law prohibits the registration of names that use characters other than the standard twenty-six characters of the English alphabet, it's likely the couple's child won't be saddled with this choice for long.

State differences

What's interesting about US baby name statistics is that there is such variety in the popularity of names across different states and territories. Olivia was a favorite name for baby girls in almost every state, and only the good people of Vermont chose not to honor it.

However, only twenty states chose Liam for their top spot and a mere eight picked Noah. This is in contrast to the national lists, in which Liam appears in first place and Noah in second. Also, looking at the other top-spot winners at state level can be a helpful predictor of which names might be the national favorites in years to come, so it's possible that either Oliver or William will be at the top of the charts in 2022 or 2023.

It seems as though geography can have a major impact on baby-naming decisions, and population density can certainly change the rankings. States with smaller populations, such as Wyoming or Vermont, usually have slightly different names making up their Top 5 each year. Nebraska, for example, has Jack for baby boys, which isn't found in any of the other states listed, and Minnesota has Theodore. The reasoning for this is simple: fewer babies born means each baby name chosen carries greater weight. For Aurora to make the number one spot in Alaska it needed only 45 parents to choose it; to have the same impact and overtake Emma in New York, it would need over 1,100. Likewise, only 45 babies were called Easton in North Dakota, but it still claimed fifth place.

There are some surprising entries here too. In the south-west, particularly those states along the Mexican border, Sebastian has appeared in an unusually high proportion of lists. It ranks only eighteenth nationwide, but sits in the Top 5 for Arizona, California, Nevada and Texas. Liked by both English and Spanish-speakers, it's a firm favorite among all border state parents – so watch out for this one to appear in the national Top 10 in the next few years.

The most popular baby girl name given in any mainland US state was Emma in California, with over 2,700 registrations. Likewise for boys it was Noah, also in California, with some 2,500 registrations. The names with the fewest picks but still able to claim a top spot were Oliver and Amelia in Wyoming, with only 33 and 26 registrations apiece. So find your state in the following lists—and make sure your baby won't have another ten Emmas or Liams in their class!

Top 5 baby girl names by state

State	Rank 1	Rank 2	Rank 3	Rank 4	Rank 5
Alabama	Ava	Olivia	Harper	Emma	Amelia
Alaska	Aurora	Amelia	Charlotte	Olivia	Sophia
Arizona	Emma	Olivia	Mia	Isabella	Sophia
Arkansas	Ava	Olivia	Emma	Amelia	Harper
California	Emma	Mia	Olivia	Isabella	Sophia
Colorado	Olivia	Emma	Charlotte	Evelyn	Isabella
Connecticut	Olivia	Emma	Isabella	Charlotte	Ava
Delaware	Ava	Isabella	Charlotte	Olivia	Sophia
Dist. of Columbia	Ava	Olivia	Elizabeth	Emma	Charlotte
Florida	Isabella	Emma	Olivia	Sophia	Mia
Georgia	Ava	Olivia	Emma	Amelia	Isabella
Hawaii	Emma	Isabella	Aria	Mila	Olivia
Idaho	Olivia	Emma	Evelyn	Harper	Charlotte
Illinois	Olivia	Emma	Ava	Isabella	Sophia
Indiana	Emma	Olivia	Amelia	Charlotte	Ava
Iowa	Harper	Evelyn	Emma	Charlotte	Olivia
Kansas	Olivia	Emma	Charlotte	Evelyn	Ava
Kentucky	Emma	Olivia	Ava	Harper	Amelia
Louisiana	Ava	Olivia	Emma	Amelia	Harper
Maine	Charlotte	Amelia	Emma	Harper	Olivia
Maryland	Ava	Olivia	Charlotte	Emma	Sophia
Massachusetts	Emma	Olivia	Charlotte	Sophia	Isabella
Michigan	Olivia	Ava	Emma	Charlotte	Amelia
Minnesota	Evelyn	Olivia	Charlotte	Emma	Harper
Mississippi	Ava	Olivia	Emma	Amelia	Skylar
Missouri	Olivia	Emma	Charlotte	Harper	Ava
Montana	Harper	Olivia	Emma	Charlotte	Abigail
Nebraska	Olivia	Emma	Evelyn	Charlotte	Harper

State	Rank 1	Rank 2	Rank 3	Rank 4	Rank 5
Nevada	Emma	Isabella	Olivia	Sophia	Ava
New Hampshire	Olivia	Charlotte	Emma	Ava	Amelia
New Jersey	Emma	Isabella	Olivia	Mia	Ava
New Mexico	Isabella	Sophia	Mia	Emma	Olivia
New York	Emma	Olivia	Isabella	Sophia	Mia
North Carolina	Ava	Emma	Olivia	Charlotte	Harper
North Dakota	Olivia	Emma	Harper	Charlotte	Amelia
Ohio	Ava	Emma	Olivia	Amelia	Harper
Oklahoma	Emma	Olivia	Ava	Isabella	Harper
Oregon	Emma	Olivia	Evelyn	Charlotte	Amelia
Pennsylvania	Emma	Olivia	Ava	Charlotte	Sophia
Rhode Island	Amelia	Olivia	Emma	Sophia	Mia
South Carolina	Ava	Emma	Olivia	Charlotte	Harper
South Dakota	Harper	Emma	Olivia	Charlotte	Ava
Tennessee	Emma	Ava	Olivia	Harper	Amelia
Texas	Emma	Isabella	Olivia	Mia	Sophia
Utah	Olivia	Charlotte	Emma	Evelyn	Lucy
Vermont	Harper	Charlotte	Evelyn	Emma	Nora
Virginia	Ava	Olivia	Emma	Charlotte	Sophia
Washington	Olivia	Emma	Evelyn	Amelia	Charlotte
West Virginia	Emma	Olivia	Ava	Harper	Amelia
Wisconsin	Evelyn	Emma	Olivia	Harper	Charlotte
Wyoming	Amelia	Emma	Elizabeth	Harper	Olivia

Top 5 baby boy names by state

State	Rank 1	Rank 2	Rank 3	Rank 4	Rank 5
Alabama	William	James	John	Elijah	Noah
Alaska	Oliver	Logan	Liam	Benjamin	Michael
Arizona	Liam	Noah	Sebastian	Benjamin	Oliver
Arkansas	Noah	Elijah	William	Liam	Oliver
California	Noah	Liam	Sebastian	Mateo	Ethan
Colorado	Liam	Oliver	William	Noah	Benjamin
Connecticut	Noah	Liam	Benjamin	Logan	Lucas
Delaware	Liam	Noah	Mason	Logan	James
Dist. of Columbia	William	James	Henry	Alexander	Benjamin
Florida	Liam	Noah	Lucas	Elijah	Logan
Georgia	William	Noah	Liam	Elijah	James
Hawaii	Liam	Noah	Elijah	Logan	Ethan
Idaho	Liam	Oliver	Henry	William	James
Illinois	Noah	Liam	Oliver	Benjamin	Alexander
Indiana	Oliver	Liam	Noah	Elijah	William
Iowa	Oliver	Liam	Henry	William	Owen
Kansas	Liam	Oliver	Henry	William	Mason
Kentucky	William	Liam	Elijah	Noah	Grayson
Louisiana	Noah	Liam	Elijah	James	William
Maine	Oliver	Liam	Owen	Wyatt	Henry
Maryland	Liam	Noah	William	Dylan	Ethan
Massachusetts	Benjamin	Liam	James	Lucas	William
Michigan	Noah	Oliver	Liam	Benjamin	William
Minnesota	Henry	Oliver	William	Liam	Theodore
Mississippi	John	William	Noah	Elijah	James
Missouri	Liam	Oliver	William	Henry	Noah
Montana	Liam	William	Noah	Oliver	Henry
Nebraska	Liam	Henry	Oliver	William	Jack

State	Rank 1	Rank 2	Rank 3	Rank 4	Rank 5
Nevada	Liam	Noah	Sebastian	Elijah	Daniel
New Hampshire	Oliver	Jackson	Mason	Liam	Henry
New Jersey	Liam	Noah	Jacob	Michael	Matthew
New Mexico	Noah	Liam	Elijah	Mateo	Logan
New York	Liam	Noah	Jacob	Lucas	Ethan
North Carolina	Noah	William	Liam	James	Elijah
North Dakota	Oliver	Henry	Owen	Hudson	Easton
Ohio	Liam	Noah	William	Oliver	Owen
Oklahoma	Liam	Noah	William	Oliver	Elijah
Oregon	Oliver	William	Benjamin	Henry	Liam
Pennsylvania	Liam	Noah	Benjamin	Mason	Michael
Rhode Island	Liam	Noah	Benjamin	Alexander	Oliver
South Carolina	William	James	Noah	Elijah	Liam
South Dakota	Grayson	Henry	Liam	Owen	Oliver
Tennessee	William	James	Liam	Noah	Elijah
Texas	Liam	Noah	Sebastian	Mateo	Elijah
Utah	Oliver	William	Liam	James	Henry
Vermont	Oliver	Liam	Owen	Levi	Benjamin
Virginia	William	Liam	Noah	James	Alexander
Washington	Liam	Oliver	William	Noah	Henry
West Virginia	Mason	Liam	Elijah	Grayson	Owen
Wisconsin	Oliver	Liam	Henry	William	Logan
Wyoming	Oliver	Logan	Jackson	Lincoln	Wyatt

Canada's choices

Canada doesn't have a central database that tracks all baby name statistics across the country. Instead, each Canadian province issues its own data every year, and because some provinces are less populous than others, the information can get very specific. Alberta publishes every name given to every single baby, as does Prince Edward Island. In 2020 the most popular name in Alberta was Liam, with 225 registrations, but there were only 6,240 names in total; that's fewer than half of *all* the children called Liam in the United States last year!

However, even though Canada (very politely) declines to publish a central list of all baby names registered each year, there were still some identifiable national trends in 2020. For girls, Olivia, Emma and Charlotte were clear winners; and for boys, Liam came first most frequently, with William and Jack close behind.

Girls

Province	Rank 1	Rank 2	Rank 3	Rank 4	Rank 5
Alberta	Olivia	Emma	Charlotte	Emily	Ava
British Columbia	Olivia	Charlotte	Emma	Ava	Sophia
Manitoba	Emily	Eva	Charlotte	Olivia	Emma
New Brunswick	Emma	Olivia	Charlotte	Amelia	Avery
Newfoundland and Labrador	Charlotte	Lily	Emma	Olivia	Layla
Nova Scotia	Charlotte	Olivia	Amelia	Emma	Abigail
Ontario	Olivia	Emma	Charlotte	Amelia	Ava
Price Edward Island	Charlotte	Evelyn	Olivia	Ella	Lucy
Quebec	Emma	Alica	Olivia	Lea	Charlie
Sasktachewan	Olivia	Emma	Harper	Ava	Sophia

Boys

Province	Rank 1	Rank 2	Rank 3	Rank 4	Rank 5
Alberta	Liam	Oliver	Noah	Ethan	Logan
British Columbia	Oliver	Liam	Lucas	Ethan	Noah
Manitoba	Liam	Lucas	William	Noah	Ethan
New Brunswick	William	Liam	Noah	Oliver	Jack
Newfoundland and Labrador	Jack	William	Liam	Greyson	Jackson
Nova Scotia	Jack	Owen	Noah	Benjamin	Liam
Ontario	Liam	Noah	Lucas	William	Benjamin
Price Edward Island	Liam	Benjamin	Carter	Hunter/ Oliver	William/ Wyatt
Quebec	William	Logan	Liam	Thomas	Noah
Sasktachewan	Liam	Oliver	Benjamin	Noah	Jacob

Perfect prophecies

Before we get into how next year's names are stacking up, let's revisit a few of the trends we predicted from last year and see whether we were right!

- Vintage names: we predicted that extremely old-fashioned names would start appearing in 2020, perhaps names from as far back as the Pilgrims. Examples such as Temperance, Constance, Solomon and Elias all saw slight increases in rank last year—especially Elias, which was one of the names on the 1620 *Mayflower* passenger manifest and saw a jump up to position 67 four hundred years later.

- Names from the Roaring Twenties: Oh yes, this is definitely a predicted trend we got right. Names such as Violet, Clara, Jack and Arthur are still climbing. This is one fashion that won't be going away any time soon.

- Furthermore, what comes up must come down. We predicted that names from the mid century such as Jessica, Tammy and Brian would continue their fall, and this is still very much the case. Names that were fashionable in the 1960s–80s are no longer interesting to today's modern parents, but give them time. In another half-century they'll once again be the hottest new thing.

- And finally, more international influences: This is a trend that started in late 2018 and continues to grow. Last year we called out names from Europe and Africa specifically, including Acacius, Cyrene, Lior and Sena, and all those names crept further up the charts in 2020.

The worst baby names ever

Website Cafemom published a list of their members' most hated baby names of 2020. Does the one you love to hate the most make the list?

Addisyn

Bethenny

Brayden

Diesel

Donald

Everly

Gracelynn

Khaleesi

Kingslayer

London

Psalm

Scooter

Reasons provided included an overuse of recent trends substituting vowels for the letter –y, avoiding pop culture names, and steering clear of anything political given the uproar of the last year.

---

2 Predictions for the coming year

Future trends

So, we've covered all the happenings from 2020, but how about what comes next? What trends are coming up in 2021 and how do we know they're coming?

One of the major events from 2020 was the attention the world paid to the Black Lives Matter movement, which kicked into high gear through a series of protests in the early summer. It's very likely that this will have an impact on baby names too, as babies conceived during this time period and born in early 2021 may be given names with associated significance, such as Breonna, George, Christian and Ahmaud. The founders of BLM could also see their names trend: Alicia, Patrisse and Opal—especially Opal, as it fits into the recent popularity of jewel names that we love and return to again and again.

> In 2020 the home page of the website BabyNames.com listed the names of many Black lives that have been lost to systemic violence, with the heading 'Each one of these names was somebody's baby'.

In addition, as we mentioned earlier in the book, babies conceived during the Covid-19 lockdown will be born into a changed world in 2021. It's not surprising therefore that they may be given names we will come to associate with this unexpected time in our lives. How about names direct from all the shows we binge-watched on Netflix, like Marty (from *Ozark*), Carole (from *Tiger King*) and Maggie (*Space Force*)? Or pandemic-themed names, such as Corona, Corazon and Covid? (See page 9 for real-life examples of these.)

More likely, the larger trends will probably remain the same as in 2020, with parents choosing pared-down names that simplify life again after the chaos of the last year. Liam and Olivia, William and Emma: keeping things simple and easy sounds like the ideal way for a baby to start life in 2021.

> According to ABC News, the smash-hit musical *Hamilton*, based on the life of US Founding Father Alexander Hamilton and released on streaming services in 2020, gave rise to an increase in the number of babies given the name. This follows the trend of naming babies after US historical figures, such as Lincoln and Madison.

Predicted 2021 baby names

Boys		Girls	
1. Liam	6. Benjamin	1. Olivia	6. Charlotte
2. William	7. Elijah	2. Emma	7. Amelia
3. Noah	8. Mason	3. Ava	8. Mia
4. Oliver	9. Alexander	4. Sophia	9. Emily
5. James	10. Logan	5. Isabella	10. Evelyn

For girls' names, it's certain that those ending in –a/–er will continue to dominate the Top 20 for at least a while longer. There are currently thirteen names in that group that end in –a/–er, and of those thirteen, six moved up places from the year before (Aria, Camila, Ella, Harper, Mia and Mila); six stayed put (Amelia, Ava, Emma, Isabella, Olivia and Sophia), and only one moved down (Sofia). Other similar-sounding names in the Top 20 include Avery and Emily, which presumably means that names ending in –y or –ie sounds will also stick around for a few more years. To top it all off, two of

the Top 20 names are so similar they're essentially the same name with a different spelling: Sophia and Sofia. In fact, there are only five names that don't fit into one of the –a or –y/–ie molds—Abigail, Charlotte, Elizabeth, Evelyn and Scarlett—and all of those are such 'classics' that they, too, have grown considerably in popularity over the last ten years.

With boys' names, trends are a little harder to predict. However, there are definitely names that sound very similar in the Top 20, such as Aiden, Benjamin, Ethan, Jackson, Liam, Logan, Mason and William, so expect to see names ending in -n/-m sounds also to be big in 2021. Also, names beginning with J or M are pretty big right now (Jackson, Jacob and James; Mason, Matthew and Michael), and if you really want to dig deep, a great many of the names in the boys' list are straight from the Bible: Alexander, Benjamin, Daniel, Elijah, Ethan, Jacob, James, Lucas, Matthew, Michael and, of course, Noah. There is a great deal more shuffling in the ranks going on in the boys' names list, with huge differences over the last ten years—especially in names listed outside the Top 10. Therefore, it's probable that parents expecting baby boys in 2021 will be following trends such as traditional or religious names instead.

> According to naming website Nameberry, Luna is predicted to be big for baby girls in 2021. Currently in 23rd place, Luna has jumped an impressive 400 places in the last decade thanks to character Luna Lovegood from the *Harry Potter* series and Chrissy Teigen's baby girl born in 2016.

Finally, continuing the theme of simple and traditional names, two-syllable names will trend in 2021. A staggering number of names in the Top 100 for girls and boys (over fifty per cent) keep things easy with just two syllables, and it's not a trend to disappear overnight. Choose from the classics (Aaron, Jose, Nora, Sarah) or the more modern (Hudson, Jaxon, Paisley, Piper): either way, you'll be bang on trend.

In general, US parents prefer to give their children full-length names rather than shortened versions or nicknames, although, as mentioned previously, this trend may be declining. Elizabeth (13th) appears higher

Most popular biblical names

According to data from the SSA, these are the most popular names taken from the Bible for the last 100 years:

1. James
2. John
3. Michael
4. David
5. Mary
6. Joseph
7. Thomas
8. Christopher
9. Daniel
10. Matthew

up the charts than Ellie (37th), but the gap is closing compared to last year, as Ellie has climbed several spots but Elizabeth has stayed put. We do see this over and over again: Jacob (ranked 13th) is more popular than Jake (262nd); Abigail (11th) is higher than Abby (475th); and Eve (442nd) is much further down the charts than Evelyn (10th).

However, in some cases, a short version or a nickname actually now ranks higher than the traditional name it's taken from. The name Ella (15th last year), for example, is a shortened version of Eleanor (32nd), while Leo (50th) is a shortened version of either Leon (238th) or Leonardo (92nd); both of these shorter names are certainly more widespread than the longer ones. In parts of Europe this is particularly fashionable right now, so perhaps in 2021 we will see more of a European flair to our baby-naming game.

The website Synesthesia.me will take your baby's name and translate it into colors, using an algorithm based on a phenomenon where some people see color instead of letters and symbols.

Goings-on in 2021

As the pandemic was unfolding, it was hard to keep track of all the events that were cancelled in 2020. However, many of them were

Liberal Lena or conservative Kim?

What about the theory that you can tell the political leanings of a family by the name a parent gives their child? Well, in a study conducted at the University of Chicago, researchers noticed that parents with more liberal leanings tended to give names that contained softer sounds, like –a and –l. Examples included Ella, Sophia, Liam and Lena. Parents with more conservative views chose names with harder or stronger sounds, like –d, –b, –t and –k. Examples of those names were Kurt, Kim, Donald and Bryce. However, the researchers also noted that the level of education each parent obtained had as much of an impact as their political viewpoint: well-educated parents chose unusual names, but with traditional spellings (such as Atticus or Finnegan), and less educated parents chose traditional names with more unusual spellings (such as Andruw instead of Andrew). So, while it's true that politicians and political stances definitely affect baby name trends, it might have quite a lot to do with levels of education as well.

simply postponed until 2021, so we will still have ample opportunity this year to see how they can impact baby names. For that reason, 2021 is predicted to be the kind of year where we all get a bit wild. Between the Summer Olympics, Euro 2021, the US Open and the Women's Rugby World Cup, plus all our usual domestic sports seasons starting up again, it is going to be a hectic twelve months. And the fallout will naturally affect baby names, because let's face it: pretty much everything else does.

In 2021 there will be a number of major sporting events, and athletes who perform well at them will no doubt become inspiration for new parents. The Summer Olympic and Paralympic Games will finally take place in Tokyo, Euro 2021 is being held in a cool dozen different European cities, and of course there's the reinstatement of the usual smattering of annual events such as the Super Bowl, World Series and tennis at Wimbledon. When we lost basketball legend Kobe Bryant in early 2020 there was a surge in babies called both Kobe and Bryant, and in past Olympic years there's been a pattern of babies named after gold medal winners, such as Simone Biles. Watch out for at least some sports-star names to pop up in 2021 if history is anything to go by.

Incidentally, there is a chance that not only sports stars themselves, but also the names they choose for their own children might prove influential. It wouldn't be the first time: Dallas Cowboys defensive end Datone Jones chose the name Laila for his baby girl, citing a great admiration for boxer Muhammad Ali and Ali's daughter Laila Ali; and Arizona Cardinals cornerback Patrick Peterson chose the name Paityn for his little girl, after NFL quarterback legend Peyton Manning. Watch out for athletes who perform well at the Olympics and Super Bowl, and possibly even what they name their children!

> The *New York Times* archive of birth announcements is a joyful snapshot into the history of names. While we think of the mid-20th century as being extremely traditional and rigid, the *Times* shows us that isn't always the case. In May 1964, for example, there was an Amalia, Bettina, Edythe, Felisse and Hone in among the more stoic names of the 1960s such as Andrew, Kenneth, Michael and Susan.

So what of politics? If nothing else, you can't say that 2020 wasn't an eventful year for our country, with Biden and Trump battling it out for the Presidency. At the time of writing the Presidential election has not yet taken place, but one thing is for certain: 2021 is going to be an interesting year regardless of the results.

Still, the real question is, how will political events and headlines this year affect the names we give our babies? Few parents are turned on to the name Donald (it's currently at its lowest rank since records started to be kept), and even though the name Melania jumped up a massive 720 spots in 2018, it had actually fallen completely out of the Top 1,000 by 2020. Joe

Biden's full name of Joseph has fallen a little in the last few years (currently 23rd) and hasn't ranked in the Top 20 for a while, while his wife's name Jill has continued a steady decline since its peak in the 1960s. There is a good explanation for this though, and it comes down to when these candidates were born. Basically, it takes so much money to run for President now that you have to be an older politician to have accumulated enough money and support to even attempt a campaign (both Presidential nominees were in their 70s during the election). It stands to reason, therefore, that the names of candidates are aging as fast as the people. Babies born in the 1940s won't see their names come back into fashion until at least 2035 thanks to the 100 year rule, so while these men may have a lot of fans out there from both ends of the political spectrum, it's unlikely that there will be thousands of babies named after them. At least, not for another few years.

The idea that we don't name our children after our politicians isn't new, mind you. Neither Barack nor Obama appeared in the Top 1,000 at any point during the former President's two terms, and despite the name Hillary scoring high in the years preceding the 2016 election, it hasn't appeared there again since. However, Barack Obama's daughters are named Malia and Sasha, and the name Malia jumped a whopping 350 places the year Obama was first elected and has continued to grow in popularity ever since. Sasha, which was already fairly common, also jumped a further 100, although it's been steadily falling since the Obamas left the White House.

There's always the chance of a regal influence, particularly with celebrities such as the Kardashians and Lil' Kim choosing names like Reign and Royal. Queen Elizabeth II is Britain's longest-reigning monarch, since she has been on the throne longer than the 63 years and seven months Queen Victoria reigned. It's possible, although extremely unlikely, that she will choose to step down for her eldest son Prince Charles, sparking renewed interest in both her name and his. The name Elizabeth is in 13th place in the US right now, and has held firm in the Top 20 for over 50 years. Victoria is in 21st place, and it too has been in about the same place for decades. Both are considered such classic names that it's hard to imagine them disappearing entirely.

> A law in Sonora, Mexico, states parents cannot give their babies names that are defined by authorities as 'derogatory, pejorative, discriminatory or lacking in meaning.' Names on the published list include Twitter, Burger King, Hitler, Facebook, Harry Potter, Escroto (Spanish for scrotum) and Batman.

America's unique choices

According to the website BabyCenter.com, parents are choosing some pretty imaginative names. Users recently registered the following names for their children:

Boys	Girls
Adonis	Blakely
Atlas	Emersyn
Chanler	Nyla
Chavis	Ximena
Jax	Zuri

Showbiz babies

As always, pop culture will probably be the most prominent influence on baby names in the coming year. Celebrities with new arrivals include Jude Law and Phillipa Coan, Kel Mitchell and Asia Lee, Rooney Mara and Joaquin Phoenix, and Ryan Murphy and David Miller. If history is anything to go by, the names these couples pick will be highly scrutinized and influential on the rest of us.

Frankly, I'm expecting big things from the names on this list. Come on Jude Law…this is your sixth baby now, and you've already given us such diverse names as Rafferty, Iris, Rudy, Sophia and Ava. I think you can go a little wild for baby number six. Or how about baby number one for actors Joaquin

Phoenix and Rooney Mara? Joaquin changed his name to Leaf for a while as a child, following the nature-themed names of his famous siblings (River, Rain, Liberty and Summer), so can we expect this kid to be called Sunshine or Poppy? I do hope so. Even Kel Mitchell named his first daughter Wisdom. Maybe his second child will be called something equally smart.

The year 2021 is going to be pretty interesting for film and television. In addition to the planned releases, there are dozens of mega hits that were originally due to be released in 2020 that never made it (thank you again, pandemic…sigh…). Included in the lineup are a third *Fantastic Beasts* film starring Eddie Redmayne; *Cruella*, a prequel to *101 Dalmatians*; *Jungle Cruise*, a family action adventure based on the Disneyland ride; Marvel's *Thor: Love and Thunder*; and the much-anticipated *Avatar 2* and *Matrix 4*. So get down to the movie theater before your baby arrives to catch them all!

If your love for all things Mickey Mouse knows no bounds, how about doing what one couple did and naming your baby Disney? Jade and Joshua Jeanes picked the unusual name for their daughter in 2020, and have said if they have a future son he will be named Sonic.

Most popular names of all time

Boys	Girls
1. James	1. Mary
2. John	2. Patricia
3. Robert	3. Jennifer
4. Michael	4. Linda
5. William	5. Elizabeth
6. David	6. Barbara
7. Richard	7. Susan
8. Joseph	8. Jessica
9. Thomas	9. Sarah
10. Charles	10. Karen

Names that are featured in these films stand a good chance of influencing baby names if past trends are repeated. *Avatar 2*, for example, will almost definitely spike interest in the names Zoe and Zoey again, given the popularity of lead actress Zoe Saldana. Both of these names have been on the rise since the release of the original *Avatar* movie in 2009, and Zoey now stands in 29th place, so it could easily climb even higher. It's also entirely possible the sequel will introduce a new generation to names such as Neytiri and Jake, although the likelihood of anyone being named Na'vi is perhaps a bit of a stretch.

Most excitingly, for those of us old enough to remember the initial trilogy, *Matrix 4* will be on the big screen in 2021. The popularity of the name Keanu has risen dramatically since the announcement of the fourth installment, jumping nearly 100 spots last year after a few years languishing further down the charts. And the name Neo, which didn't exist on the charts prior to the first film's release in 1999, still had 140 babies given the name last year. It's expected that both names will spike again in 2021.

As for the influence the small screen could wield on our collective baby-naming psyche, Baby Yoda is a good place to start…right? Okay, so *technically* this adorable bundle isn't Baby Yoda, and *technically* he (she? We don't know!) doesn't have a name other than 'The Child', but there has been mega interest in *The Mandalorian* series nonetheless. First streamed on Disney+ in 2019 and then followed up with a second series in late 2020, the show made stars out of its cast. Names such as Gina and Pedro have seen a boost in popularity—particularly Pedro, which was on the decline for a while but

Big and small screen baby names

Boys	Girls
Eddie	Arwen
Jake	Gina
Keanu	Kim
Neo	Morwen
Pedro	Neytiri
Pippin	Zoe
Sam	Zoey

seems to be making a bit of a comeback. Stay tuned for a third series in 2021 or 2022 to see if it continues.

> A UK mother challenged the friendship of her sister when she named her infant son after Darth Vader, saying, 'It's not about *Star Wars* at all, just really love the name Anakin Skywalker, it has good sonics. I'm sure people won't care if he's called Anakin.' The name choice started an internet war between the two sisters, which then went viral.

Another big streaming hit set to air in 2021 is Amazon Prime's *Lord of the Rings* series. Set before the events of the books and movies, the show is bound to renew interest in all things *LOTR*-related, including the names. How about Pippin or Arwen, Sam or Morwen? I'd steer clear of Frodo and Legolas though, personally.

Reality series will continue to invade our homes in 2021 too. There are so many to pick from that it's impossible to talk about them all, so let's avoid mentioning *Love Is Blind* and *Tiger King*, and focus on two reality show family dynasties instead. Kim Kardashian West named her son

---

Fictional characters with hidden meanings in their names

Bran Stark (*Game of Thrones*)—Bran is an old Welsh name from the word for "raven".

Darth Vader (*Star Wars*)—darth is related to "dark" or "death"; vader is Dutch for "father".

Frodo Baggins (*The Lord of the Rings*)—from fród, meaning "wise by experience" in Old English.

Katniss Everdeen (*The Hunger Games*)—from the katniss plant, meaning "archer" in Latin.

Nyota Uhura (*Star Trek*)—from the Swahili term for "star freedom".

Remus Lupin (*Harry Potter*)—Remus was an ancient Roman orphan raised by wolves; lupinus is the Latin word for "wolfish".

Psalm in 2019 and seven parents promptly followed suit in 2020. Kim and singer/rapper Kanye West named their other son Saint and their daughters North (also known as Nori, which is a lot cuter) and Chicago, although Kim confessed at the time that she wishes she had used a single-syllable name for Chicago so all four children's names match. Apparently Chicago is often called Chi at home instead. The names North and Saint both picked up steam last year, with 16 babies called North and an impressive 262 called Saint (that's a 75 per cent increase for that name), and even Chicago was given to 11 kids! Other Kardashian Kid names include Dream, Stormi, True, Mason, Penelope and Reign, although both Kourtney and Khloe shut down pregnancy rumors about expanding the brood in 2020.

And finally, the Duggar family. Originally comprised of just Jim Bob and Michelle, this enormous reality-show family now boasts nineteen children and nineteen grandchildren, with another two or three on the way (I've lost count, to be honest). The original nineteen all have names that start with the letter J, and some of the grandchildren have followed the same trend. Eldest son Josh's six children all have names beginning with M, and several other children have confessed they will be following the pattern as their own families grow. Now that America's love affair with the Duggars seems be on the wane (ratings fell dramatically for the spin-offs last year), will the idea of using the same initial for each of your children also lose some steam?

3 How to choose a name

Your baby-naming checklist

Naming a baby should be, above all, a fun experience. I encourage you to think carefully about your final decision because it does have real-life implications, but there's no reason why careful consideration cannot be combined with enjoyment. Here are some nice ideas to get the old brain cells working.

- Fall in love with the name(s) you've chosen. Pick a name that makes you smile because, if you love it, hopefully your child will too.

- Don't listen to other people. Sometimes grandparents and friends will offer you baby-naming "advice", which may not always be welcome. If you've got your heart set on a name, keep it a secret until after the birth. Trust your own instincts: they will come in handy later.

  Norwegian and Portuguese baby-naming laws are so strict that parents there are only allowed to use names that appear on approved lists. Parents who break this law have been fined and even jailed! Banned names in Norway include Gesher (meaning bridge), and anything that could be mistaken for a last name.

- Find a name with meaning. Having a name that has a backstory helps your child understand their significance in the world, so whether you name them after a religious saint or prophet, an important political figure, or a hero in a Greek tragedy, ensure they know where their name came from. They may just be inspired to be as great as their namesake.

- Have fun. Picking out names should be fun. Laughing at the ones you'd never dream of choosing can really help you narrow it down to the ones you would. You can also experiment with different spellings, pronunciations or variations of names you like, or go to places where you might feel inspired.

- Expand your mind. Don't rule out the weird ones just yet! As a teenager I went to school with a girl named Siam. Her parents had conceived her on a honeymoon trip to Thailand and gave her the country's former name. She loved growing up and having an unusual name, as I'm sure Penelope Scotland (Kourtney Kardashian and Scott Disick's daughter) and Winnie Fallon do too. (Jimmy Fallon's daughter is named after the New Hampshire lake where he proposed to his wife.)

  The shortest baby names are only two letters long (Al, Ed, Jo and Ty), but the longest could be any length imaginable. Popular eleven-letter-long names include Bartholomew, Christopher, Constantine and Maximillian.

- Try it out. While you're pregnant, talk to your baby and address it using a variety of your favorite names to see if it responds. There are numerous stories of names being chosen because the baby kicked when it was called Charlie or Aisha, but was suspiciously silent when it was called Dexter or Mildred, so see if it has a preference! Try writing names down and sticking them to your fridge, practicing a few signatures, or saying one out loud enough times to see if you ever get sick of it.

- Do *not* pick the name of an ex. No matter how lovely you think your ex's name is, it would take a very understanding partner to allow you to pick it for your baby. Just steer clear of any names you know will cause problems to other people, paying particular attention to your partner and loved ones.

- What if you can't agree? This is probably the trickiest problem to solve in the baby-naming process. It's wise to research a number of names you and your partner are both interested in and make a point of discussing your reasons for liking or disliking them long before the baby is due to be born. The labor and delivery room is probably not the best place to argue as you'll both be tired, emotional and at least one of you will be in pain. Avoid sticking to your guns on a name one of you really isn't happy with because it might lead to your baby being caught in the middle.

- Compromise is the name of the game. You could try compromising and picking two middle names so you both have a name in there that you love; or you could each have five names you're allowed to "veto", but no more. Whichever way you go about it, it is important that you both eventually agree on the name you are giving your baby, even if it means losing out on the one you've had your heart set on.

> Comedian Jason Gardner presented his expectant sister and her wife with a $50 bill, telling them they could keep the money if they gave their child one of 2,000 "names" he'd compiled in a list. The list included such delights as Banana, Ferngully, McChicken and Unibrow. Sadly, the couple did not go with any of them.

Think to the future

One important aspect of naming your child is thinking ahead to their future. Will the name you've chosen stand the test of time? Will names popular in 2021 remain well-liked in 2061? Will they be able to confidently enter a room and give a crucial business presentation with an awkward or unpronounceable name? Will they be able to hand their business card over to a potential client without that client looking bemused? Even sooner, can they survive the potential minefields of elementary school and junior high with a name that could easily be shortened to something embarrassing? Would you want to try catching criminals as Sheriff Apple Blossom or have other politicians take you seriously with a name like Senator Fortune Scarlett? You don't want to give your child a name they just cannot live with for the rest of their life, so make your choice based on what's appropriate for an adult as well as a child.

Popular names from the past

Boys	Girls
Abraham	Agatha
Arthur	Bertha
Edmund	Clara
Emmett	Edith
Franklin	Gladys
Gilbert	Mabel
Jasper	Pearl
Neville	Theodora
Percival	Wilhelmina
Vincent	Winifred

To make this easier you might want to choose a longer name that can be shortened or extended as your child desires.

If your child doesn't like the name you've given them because their first and last names make a funny combination, they may choose to use just their first name professionally as an adult. An old colleague of mine goes by 'Shiney' only—omitting her last name on business cards and emails because it's a euphemism for male genitalia.

Buzzfeed.com recently ran an article on funny names of real people who worked in retail. Serving us in stores around the world are Porsche Keys, Crystal Metz and Harry Bush, among others. Imagine one of those names coming over the intercom when you're shopping? A few of the stories also came from people who explained the reasons their parents gave them unusual names: one was named after a sports stadium, one after their grandmother's cat and another after a female IRA terrorist. At least they have origin stories, I guess!

Around the same time another article appeared, listing all the reasons why having an unusual name is a hassle—examples given were not ever being able to find your name on novelty souvenirs, coffee shop baristas not knowing how to spell or pronounce your name for your order, and other people giving you "fun, new" nicknames because they can't be bothered with your given name.

Stereotypes—true or false?

Will the name you choose actually affect your child's life? Will names that seem clever make your child brainier? Will names with positive meanings make your child a happier person? The answer is...possibly.

Anthroponomastics is the term used for the study of personal names, and it's a field that continues to intrigue and amaze us. Research has also indicated that certain names are more likely to provoke strong responses in people. One study analyzed the number of stickers given to children as rewards for good behavior. Children named Abigail and Jacob were more likely to be praised for being well-behaved than children named Beth and Josh; and children who did not shorten their name or go by nicknames were more likely to be better behaved, too.

Ivy League names

Alcott	Graydon
Arthur	Katherine
Beatrice	Martha
Caroline	Robert
Charles	Victoria

Another thing you should consider is how your child's name will be perceived by the outside world. Typically, judgments are passed on a person before they are met, and made purely based on their name, such as at job interviews or in school. A survey of 3,000 teachers found that 49 per cent of them make assumptions about their pupils based on their names alone. Topping the 'naughty' charts were Callum, Connor and Jack for boys; and Chelsea, Courtney and Chardonnay for girls. On the other hand, the names in the 'clever' category were Alexander, Adam and Christopher for boys; and Charlotte, Elizabeth and Emma for girls.

A study by the University of Hertfordshire in the UK asked members of the opposite sex to rate names according to attractiveness, luck and success. The top names were James and Elizabeth, which authors concluded was a result of them being traditionally royal names, and therefore aspirational and associated with intelligence and success. However, the lowest-ranked name for sexiness was George, which is also traditionally royal…and I'm fairly certain fans of George Clooney would dispute the results anyway.

Along the same lines, a study conducted by the Hebrew University of Jerusalem in 2017 found that we subconsciously act like stereotypes of our names, and that other people can pick up on it. They asked students to guess the names of faces they were shown, and the students were able to correctly match them twice as often as expected. So think carefully about the names on your favorites list, and consider what types of personalities tend to have these names. If you don't like the answers, it might be time to reconsider. (But you can probably relax: Herbert was the name suggested to be most associated with an idiot and only 80 baby boys were given that last year, so you're probably safe.)

An article from the BBC *Science Focus* magazine last year noted that there are also people who have entered (or fallen in to) professions that match their name. The phenomenon, called 'nominative determinism', helps explain world-class athletes such as Usain Bolt, dentists such as Dennis Smiler from Los Angeles, and one of the academic researchers for the article itself being called Richard Wiseman. So that might be a cool trick to consider for your child's future: pick a first name that encourages them to be successful in their career endeavors, or a superstar athlete. No pressure at all.

A survey carried out by the National Centre for Social Research found that the more unusual the name, the less likely a candidate is to be called for a job interview. Whether or not this fact would affect a child's development and future career is yet to be determined, but it is something to consider. Along the same lines, another US-based study found that African-American girls given names such as Ebony tended to be more successful in later life and finish university, but the name was rarer among working-class Black families. As a result, young women called Ebony were held in higher regard as adults regardless of their socioeconomic standings, and more likely to be called back for job interviews, because an assumption was being made about their name right from the start.

And finally, a recent university study suggests that names are particularly important for language development in early childhood. Apparently, a child's name is one of the first words they can identify (probably from all that cooing into the cot that goes on when they're born), and they use it to learn how to construct and deconstruct sentences. Their name anchors the sentence spoken to them, enabling them to pick out other familiar words and sounds, and put them all together to identify the meaning of the entire thing. Brainy stuff!

Inspirational names		Aspirational names	
Destiny	Joy	Armani	Ferrari
Happy	Peace	Aston	Jaguar
Heaven	Serenity	Bugatti	Mercedes
Hope	Unique	Chanel	Porsche
Innocence	Unity	Dolce	Prada

Eccentric names

There are lots of advantages to having an eccentric name. For one thing, people will never forget your child's name, and if they do something influential with their life their name could become an inspiration for other parents. On the other hand, a quirky name often requires a quirky personality. If you don't think your genes could stand up to a name like Satchel or Zizi, perhaps it's time to think of one a little more run-of-the-mill.

Satirical website the *Daily Mash* published an article in 2020 with the headline, "Most popular baby names now just random jumbles of letters." Sometimes it does feel that way, doesn't it?

An eccentric name often says more about the parents than the child, and their own personalities may affect the personality of their child in a significant way. A conventional family that names its baby John will probably find he becomes a conventional child, whereas a quirky family that names its baby Zanzibar will find he develops a quirky personality. The name itself is not the leading factor; it's the eccentric or conventional behavior encouraged by the parents who chose the name that's important.

Children who are told they have inherited an ancestor's name or are named after an influential character from history might be more driven and focused than children who are told, disappointingly, 'We just liked the sound of it.' As a parent, therefore, it seems it's okay to pick an unusual name if you have a story or reason behind it. So naming your child Atticus (after Atticus Finch from Harper Lee's *To Kill a Mockingbird*, known for being a strong and moral character), or even Harper (which is now the ninth most popular name in the country), may not be a bad idea...

When it comes to the name Lucifer, America and Germany think differently. While German officials once intervened in a request to name a child after Satan, in the USA twenty-four babies were recorded as receiving that moniker in 2020.

However, be warned: there is also new research that suggests many parents end up regretting their choice of names. Baby website Channelmum, which carried out a member survey in 2019, found that one in seven parents regrets at least one part of their child's name. A staggering twenty-eight per cent of respondents admitted to telling their child they regret the choice, and more than one in ten said their child confessed that they hated their own name. Two of the most common reasons given were that the name suddenly became extremely popular, or that a celebrity chose the same one, and sadly nearly one in five members said they had felt pressured into using the name by a relative or other person. Which just underscores my most important rule about naming your own baby: you have to love it! Love it and you won't regret it; feel apathetic about it, and you'll almost certainly look back with remorse.

Controversial names adopted by real people

Adolf Hitler	Himmler	Mussolini
Beelzebub	Jezebel	Satan Stalin
Hannibal Lecter	Lucifer	Voldemort

One possible way to avoid potential regret or humiliation is to download the SSA's hard data on the most recent baby-name choices, and scour the names down at the bottom of the lists for inspiration. You are likely to find a wealth of unusual and currently unpopular names there, but it's comforting to know that your child won't be the only one in the world with that name. Suggestions from last year's data include Hurley, Luxley, Sayeda and Yanxi for girls; and Endrick, Jenner and Wylen for boys.

While avoiding any kind of possible connection to a fictional character is nigh on impossible, you can help make things easier for your child by educating them about their namesake and encouraging them to read more about them. Stay up to date with new cartoons and children's characters to prepare both yourself and your child for preschool and childhood. That way they can be proud of their name and have ammunition if things get rough in the schoolyard.

Masculine or feminine?

How do we define what makes a name masculine or feminine? Well, it may be to do with the sounds the letters create, either when written down or spoken aloud. Harder-sounding combinations (–ter, –it, –ld) tend to be found in masculine names, and softer-sounding combinations (–ie, –ay, –la) are more associated with feminine names. You therefore end up with Sophia, Joanie and Bella; or Harold, Walter, David and Oscar. If you're planning on choosing a feminine-sounding name, approach with caution: recent research suggests that girls who are given particularly 'girly' names—think Tiana, Kayla, or Isabella—are much more likely to misbehave when they reach school age. These 'feminine' girls were also far less likely to choose subjects at school such as math and science, while their sisters with more masculine names—such as Morgan, Alexis and Ashley—were encouraged to excel in these courses. Which is fascinating and scary in equal measure.

Nowadays, names are becoming more androgynous and loads of names appear in both boys' and girls' lists: Madison, Riley, Hayden and, of course, Alex—some form of which appears in the Top 100 for both boys and girls every year. Therefore, if you want a more gender-neutral name for your new arrival, you won't be alone. Interestingly, a study by the University of Illinois found that boys with androgynous names (the example given was Ashley) tend to act up and do worse in high school tests. The theory was that they get teased and compared to girls with the same name, so their academic progress stalls. Gah…teenagers can be jerks, can't they?

> A naming taboo in Imperial China prevented the masses from naming their babies after the reigning Emperor.

But what about your own gender? Does the fact you're a man or woman mean you're more likely to pick certain names for your child? Well, it looks like this isn't the case, but there might be an element of truth to it. Apparently, mothers are prone to picking names that are similar to, or exactly the same as, their maiden name, if they got rid of it when they got married. This system allows a mother to pass on a part of her own lineage, as well as the father's. A lot of celebrities do this, too, allowing a child to either use their middle name as an additional last name, or to ignore it altogether. Either way, it ensures the famous mom's name gets to stick around a bit longer!

Another study found that mothers tend to win the argument over who gets to pick the final name of a newborn, with four in ten moms ignoring the choices selected by dads, and one in ten dads just simply backing down. However, four in ten couples don't make the final decision until after the baby is born, and a third will argue about it before settling—but hey, at least they're talking about it! Now, I'm not saying that the person who grows the baby and goes through the process of removing said baby from her own body should get final say…but really that's exactly what I'm saying.

Nicknames

Nicknames are unavoidable. They can range from the common—Mike from Michael, Sam from Samantha—to the trendy, funny or downright insulting. Don't be put off if the name you love has an unfortunate nickname associated with it, though—if you don't encourage the use of nicknames, chances are they won't stick. Another way to avoid embarrassing nicknames is to select one for your child that you actually like so that others don't even get a mention. Call your daughter Elizabeth by the name Liz, Lizzie, or Libby if you don't like Betty or Beth, and no one will even consider the alternatives. You can pre-empt possible nicknames to some extent by saying the name you've chosen out loud and trying to find rhymes for it. This is a clever way to avoid children's chants and nursery rhyme-type insults, such as Dora the Explorer or Georgie Porgie. But don't be too concerned about schoolyard chants—most children are subjected to them at some point and emerge unscathed.

> Pronunciation matters: A Swedish couple was once banned from naming their child 'Brfxxccxxmnpccccllllmmnprxvclmnck-ssqlbb11116,' which they claimed was pronounced 'Albin'.

Your last name

Try to avoid first names that might lead to unfortunate phrases when combined with your surname, to prevent a lifetime of embarrassment for your child. The best way to work out if this might happen is to write down all the names you like alongside your child's surname and have someone else read them out loud. This second pair of eyes and ears might just spot something you didn't. The age of the internet has given parents a wonderful new weapon in their baby-naming arsenal: the search engine. Before you settle on anything final, try searching for any examples of the complete first, middle and last name of your new baby.

You may find out that your baby has an ax-murderer namesake—or, as with one of my colleagues, the same name as a well-known porn star.

> Use the Matador Network website to find out the most common last name in every country in the world. In the USA? Smith. Canada? Also Smith! And in the UK? You've guessed it…Smith.

Bizarre baby names from around the country

Boys	Girls
Aero	Ace
Burger	Kaixin
Donathan	Leeloo
Espn	Monalisa
Haven'T	Rogue
Kix	Sesame
Pawk	Thinn
Rysk	Yoga
Zaniel	Zealand

Initials

What last name will your baby have? Will it lend itself easily to amusing acronyms when coupled with certain first and middle names? My brother-in-law was going to be called Andrew Steven Schmitt before he was born, until his parents realized at the last minute what his initials would spell...

It's also worth taking the time to think about how credit cards display names or how your child's name would look written out on a form. Nobody should have to go through life known as S. Lugg because their parents didn't think that far ahead.

> One California family changed their daughter's name when she was three months old, from Ottilie to Margot. Their reason? Ottilie is a German name, and when it's pronounced in Europe it comes with hard T sounds (Ott-ti-lee). But due to the slacker T sounds of many regional accents in the USA, their poor daughter's name ended up sounding like Oddly...oddly enough.

And finally, consider the idea that a lot of people actually prefer to go by their initials rather than their given name. Think of all the JDs you know (hat-tip to *Scrubs* there, which we all revisited in 2020 thanks to the hugely successful rewatch podcast), or MJ from *Spider-Man*. There are millions of people walking around who are only known by initials, even with perfectly sensible first and middle names, simply because they prefer the way the moniker sounds. In fact, it might be a growing trend: 2020 data shows literally hundreds of babies being given formal names of just initials, such as DJ, KC and JC. My initials are ET though, so unless I want to go around with everyone telling me to 'phone home', I'm going to stick it out with just Eleanor. Thanks all the same.

Using family names

Some families have a strong tradition of using names for babies that come from the family tree. There are families where naming your son Augustine VIII is simply not an option—it's a rule. Another way families do this is to give children the name of their parent of the same sex and add 'Junior' (Jr.) to the end. This could only create a problem if that child then decides to carry on the tradition and name their child after themselves—after all, who wants to be known as Frederick Jr. Jr.?

> One expectant mom on Reddit sought out the advice of internet strangers in 2020 when she said her husband wanted to break her family's tradition of using the same name for firstborn sons. Her husband did not want to use the name for fear of his child being bullied in later life. The name in question? Gaylord, which wasn't given to a single baby last year.

There are pros and cons to using family names.

- **Pros:** Your child will feel part of a strong tradition, which will create a sense of security for them and help make them feel a complete member of the family. If you're having a problem selecting a name you and your partner both agree on, this is a very simple solution and will make your new child's family very happy.

- **Cons:** You might not actually like the name that's being passed down. Naming your child the twelfth Thumbelina in a row might not actually hold the same attraction for you as for the generation before. Another drawback could be if the cultural associations with a name have changed over time and it is no longer appropriate.

One way to include a family name is to compromise. You could use the name as a middle name, or refer to your baby by a nickname instead. Another possible solution is to use monikers—if your family is insisting your daughter be called Jade, maybe you could choose Giada instead. Or if your

"Text speak" spellings

Camron
Conna
Ema
Esta
Flicity
Jayk
Lora
Patryk
Samiul
Summa

partner is determined the next child be called Michael after himself, and it turns out to be a girl, choose Michaela in its place. In many Jewish families the tradition is to take the name of a deceased relative and give it to a new baby. If this thought fills you with dread, you could opt for a possible solution a lot of families adopt, which is to use the first initial instead. If you're not keen on Solomon, pick Samuel; if you don't like Ruth, choose Rebecca.

One couple changed their daughter's name in 2019 because other people couldn't pronounce it properly. Baby Lana, who has a Croatian mother and British father, was supposed to have a name to rhyme with Anna, but the spelling was officially changed to Lanna after months of correcting strangers and family members alike.

Spellings and pronunciation

Once you've finally agreed on a name, it's time to consider how you wish it to be spelled and pronounced. Some parents love experimenting with unusual variations of traditional names, while others prefer names to be instantly recognizable. Try to avoid making a common name too long or too unusual in its spelling as this will be the first thing your child has to learn how to write. They will also have to spell it out constantly during their lifetime, as other people misspell or mispronounce their name. Substituting the odd 'i' for a 'y' isn't too bad, but turning the name Jonathan into Jonnaythanne doesn't do anyone any favors.

A palindrome name is a name that is spelled the same backwards and forwards, as with Bob, Elle, Eve and Hannah.

According to the journal *Scientific American*, participants in one particular study were more likely to believe statements made by people with names they could pronounce, and distrust statements from those they could not. The study only used names from countries outside of the USA, to adjust for pre-existing prejudices, and found that the harder to pronounce the name, the less trustworthy the statement coming from the person seemed to be. Interesting stuff, and worth thinking about if you're debating whether to add that extra 'xyz' to your baby's name.

> A British man changed his name from Deano Wilson to Fire Exit in 2020. He claimed it was a comedy stunt so that he would always see his name up in lights.

Middle names

Giving your child a middle name is generally acknowledged to be standard practice these days. In fact, it has become fairly uncommon to name a child without a middle name, although the use of second and third names only became popular around the turn of the twentieth century. Before then, giving a child a middle name was seen as a status symbol; it was only really used when a man married a higher-class woman and they wanted to keep the woman's maiden name as a reminder of the child's heritage. Once the fashion caught on, it became popular to give more than one middle name to children of status, but it's only been since the 1900s that it has become standard for everyone.

Regardless of your status, a middle name can have just as much of an impact as a first name, so your choice for your own baby should be made as carefully as the decision about their first name.

> New Zealand has a law that baby names, including first, middle and last names, cannot exceed 100 characters, be offensive, be an official rank or title (such as King or Royal) or spelled with numbers or symbols.

Celebrities who go by their middle name

Antonio Banderas (José Antonio Domínguez Banderas)

Ashton Kutcher (Christopher Ashton Kutcher)

Bob Marley (Nesta Robert Marley)

Brad Pitt (William Bradley Pitt)

Kelsey Grammer (Allen Kelsey Grammer)

Reese Witherspoon (Laura Jeanne Reese Witherspoon)

Rihanna (Robyn Rihanna Fenty)

Will Ferrell (John William Ferrell)

Here are some common trends to help you choose.

- Opposite-length names. It has become popular to give a child either a long first name and short middle name (e.g. Jennifer Ruth, Nicholas John), or vice versa.

- Name from the family tree. Honoring your ancestors is another current trend. Parents are looking back to their own lineage for interesting, unusual or influential names.

- Unusual names. Parents who aren't brave enough to give their child an out-there name as a first name are using it as a middle name.

- Maiden name or other parent name. It is becoming increasingly common to use a parent's first name, or mother's maiden name, as a middle name for a baby.

You may have already decided what middle name to give your child due to tradition or culture, in which case the following advice may be moot. In some Hispanic cultures, for example, middle names are often the mother's last name or another name to promote the matriarchal lineage. Similarly, parents who have not taken each other's last names or are not married may choose to give their child one last name as a middle name and one as a last name so both parents are represented. Other traditions use an old family name, passed down to each firstborn son or daughter, to encourage a sense of family pride and history. A decision about what middle name to pass on may have therefore already been made for you, even before your own birth.

Many people actually choose to go by their middle name instead of their first name, so it could be seen as a safety net if you're worried your child won't like their name.

> Sweden has a pretty strict naming law, enacted in 1982, which says: 'First names shall not be approved if they can cause offense or can be supposed to cause discomfort for the one using it, or names which for some obvious reason are not suitable as a first name.' However, the Swedish government did recently approve the use of 'Google' as a middle name, so there's that.

Even the British royal family likes to give many middle names. Prince Charles's full name is Charles Philip Arthur George Mountbatten-Windsor and Prince William is William Arthur Philip Louis Mountbatten-Windsor. The newest direct-line heir to the throne is, of course, Prince Louis Arthur Charles, named after Lord Louis Mountbatten, his great-great-grandfather Albert Frederick Arthur George Windsor (King George VI), and of course his grandfather Prince Charles. Big sister Princess Charlotte Elizabeth Diana was named after the current queen and her late grandmother, Diana Spencer; and then there's her elder brother, Prince George Alexander Louis, also named after King George VI and Lord Louis Mountbatten. Deliciously, Prince Harry and Meghan Markle's son Archie, born in 2019, has only one middle name, Harrison – which actually means "son of Harry"! Isn't that fantastic?

Naming twins, triplets, and more

If you have discovered you are expecting multiples, congratulations! Naming multiples needn't be any different to naming a single child… unless you want it to be. You could stick to the same process everyone else does, by picking an individual name for each individual child. Even 'Octomom' Nadya Suleman chose eight different names for her octuplets, although they do all sound reasonably similar and biblical: Isaiah, Jeremiah, Jonah, Josiah, Maliyah, Makai, Nariyah and Noah. All eight children also share the middle name Angel.

> The official Guinness World Record for the most siblings baptized with the same initial is held by a Canadian family, who had ten sons and six daughters named with the letter E. However the unofficial challenger to this would be the Duggar family, whose nineteen children all have names starting with J.

Of course, when all's said and done you can just stick to giving each child a name unique to them. For triplets, quads and more, this is probably an easier choice than twisting your head around three names with the same meaning, or trying to create four anagrams you like for all of your babies. Some parents do like to use a theme, though, such as going down the alphabet (think Alastair, Benjamin, Christopher and David), or doing what the famous acting Phoenix clan did and giving each child a name to do with nature: River, Rain, Leaf (now Joaquin), Liberty and Summer.

Others choose matching initials (Cash and Cainen; Stella and Sophia), or names that mean the same. You could use two Roman deities, such as Jupiter and Juno, or monarchs of England, like Elizabeth and Victoria—or Henry and Arthur. Heck, choose your favorite characters from a children's book, like Roald Dahl's Matilda and Charlie, or even name your twins

Twin names with the same meaning

Bernard and Brian (strong)

Daphne and Laura (laurel)

Deborah and Melissa (bee)

Dorcas and Tabitha (gazelle)

Elijah and Joel (God)

Eve and Zoe (life)

Irene and Salome (peace)

Lucius and Uri (light)

Lucy and Helen (light)

Sarah and Almira (princess)

after a secret pregnancy craving. No, not Bacon and Cheeseburger, but maybe Olive and Rosemary or Basil and Brie.

The possibilities for triplets go even further. Think of the fun you could have! You could have a row of beautiful flowers, such as Daisy, Violet and Lily; or a collection of Shakespearean heroes: Beatrice, Helena and Antonio. Be bold with a set of House Stark kids from *Game of Thrones* (Brandon, Robb and Arya), or fabulous with some baby girls from *Clueless* (Cher, Tai and Dionne). As if! The point is, expecting multiples can be scary—make naming them stress-free and fun by getting really creative.

> When Jenny and Chris Marr became the proud parents of identical quads in 2020 (the odds of which are so small there are only seventy-two other cases ever documented), they named them Hudson, Harrison, Henry and Hardy.

Celebrity twin names of the past few years

Alexander and Ella (George and Amal Clooney)

Esther and Stella (Madonna)

Eva and Mateo (Cristiano Ronaldo and Georgina Rodriguez)

Hayes Taj and India Moss (Jonathan and Tara Tucker)

John and Gus (Julie Bowen and Scott Phillips)

Myla Rose and Charlene Riva, *and* Leo and Lenny (two sets for Roger and Mirka Federer!)

Poppy and Charlie (Anna Paquin and Stephen Moyer)

Rumi and Sir (Beyoncé and Jay Z)

Tristan and Sasha (Chris Hemsworth and Elsa Pataky)

Victoria and Ysabel (Michael Jordan and Yvette Jordan)

Vittoria Genghis and Lozen Orianna Judith (Hope Solo and Jerramy Stevens)

Names for triplets

Aidan, Diana and Nadia (anagrams)

Amber, Jade and Ruby (jewels)

Amy, May and Mya (anagrams)

Ava, Eva and Iva (similar)

Daisy, Lily and Rose (flowers)

Ginger, Saffron and Rosemary (herbs)

Jay, Raven and Robin (birds)

Olive, Violet and Sage (colors)

River, Rain and Summer (nature)

There are a few things to keep in mind when naming twins or multiples, but they are at least pretty simple ones.

- Don't use very long names. You will often find yourself needing to write both names down, so use shorter versions of the names you like, such as Max for Maximilian, or Eve for Evangeline.

- Don't get too complicated. Stick with traditional spellings if possible, like Cameron instead of Kammeryn and Elizabeth instead of Alyzybeth.

- Don't forget that your babies are still individuals. If you use names that sound so similar you often mix them up, your children may get frustrated as they get older and other people confuse them. Instead, keep those nearly identical names you love as middle names and explore more individual first names to match your babies' unique personalities.

Around the world in popular baby names

Country	Girls	Boys
England	Olivia, Amelia, Emily	Oliver, George, Harry
Wales	Olivia, Ava, Amelia	Oliver, Noah, Jacob
Scotland	Olivia, Emily, Isla	Jack, Oliver, James
Northern Ireland	Grace, Emily, Olivia	James, Noah, Jack
Republic of Ireland	Emily, Grace, Fiadh	Jack, James, Noah
Netherlands	Emma, Mila, Sophie	Noah, Daan, Lucas
Germany	Hannah, Emma, Mia	Noah, Ben, Paul
Sweden	Alice, Alicia, Astrid	Lucas, Liam, William
Norway	Gaïa, Emilia, Olivia	Matheo, Oliver, Jakob
Iceland	Hekla, Anna, Emilía	Aron, Kári, Brynjar
Portugal	Élea, Isabella, Emily	Matia, Matthéo, Einar
Spain	Chloe, Sophia, Mia	Eliyas, Matteo, Liam
New Zealand	Amelia, Charlotte, Isla	Oliver, Noah, Leo
Australia	Charlotte, Olivia, Amelia	Oliver, Jack, William
South Africa	Enzokuhle, Melokuhle, Amahle	Enzokuhle, Lethabo, Melokuhle

Part Two

Boys' names A–Z

Baby names vary widely in spelling and pronunciation. To simplify things, this book usually lists each name only once: under the most common initial and spelling. If a name has a common alternate spelling with a different initial, it may also be listed under that letter.

Boys' names

Aaron

Hebrew, meaning "mountain of strength." In the Bible, Aaron was the older brother of Moses and the first high priest of Israel.

Abasi

Egyptian Arabic, meaning "male"; Swahili, meaning "stern."

Abdiel

Hebrew, meaning "servant of God." Also the name of an important seraph in Milton's *Paradise Lost*.

Abdul
(alt. Abdullah)

Arabic, meaning "servant of God." Often followed with a suffix indicating who Abdul is the servant of (e.g. Abdul-Basit, servant of the creator).

Abel

Hebrew, meaning "breath" or "breathing spirit." The biblical son of Adam and Eve who was killed by his brother Cain.

Abelard

German, meaning "resolute."

Aberforth

Gaelic, meaning "mouth of the river Forth." Name of Dumbledore's brother in the *Harry Potter* series.

Abner

Hebrew, meaning "father of light." Abner was the commander of Saul's army in the Bible.

Abraham
(alt. Abram; abbrev. Abe)

Hebrew, meaning "exalted father." Famous Abrahams include President Abraham Lincoln and Abraham Van Helsing—the vampire hunter and doctor in Bram Stoker's *Dracula*.

Absalom
(alt. Absalon)

Hebrew, meaning "father/leader of peace." The name of King David's favorite son in the Bible, and one of Chaucer's curly-haired characters in *The Canterbury Tales*.

Acacio

Greek origin, meaning "thorny tree." Now widely used in Spain.

Ace

Latin, meaning "unit." Also used to mean "number one" or "the best."

Achebe

Yoruba, meaning "may the earth protect us."

Achilles

Greek, mythological hero of the Trojan War, whose heel was his only weak spot.

Achim

Hebrew, meaning "God will establish"; Polish, meaning "The Lord exalts." Also a shortened form of Joachim.

Ackerley

Old English, meaning "oak meadow."

Adam
(alt. Adome, Admon)

Hebrew, meaning "man" or "earth." The biblical creation story names Adam as the first man on Earth.

Adão

Portuguese variant of Adam, meaning "earth."

Addison

Old English, meaning "son of Adam." Also used as a female name.

Ade

Yoruba, meaning "peak" or "royal." A common name in Nigeria.

Adelard

French or German, meaning "brave" or "noble." Became popular in Canada during the 19th century.

Adin

Hebrew, meaning "slender" or "voluptuous"; Swahili, meaning "ornamental."

Aditya

Sanskrit, meaning "belonging to the sun." Refers to the offspring of Aditi—the mother of the gods.

Adlai

Hebrew, meaning "God is just," or sometimes "ornamental."

Adler

Old German, meaning "eagle."

Adley

English, meaning "son of Adam." Also used as a girls' name.

Adolf

(alt. Adolfo, Adolph)

Old German, meaning "noble majestic wolf." Popularity of the name plummeted after World War II, for obvious reasons.

Adonis

Phoenician, meaning "Lord." Adonis was the god of beauty and desire in ancient Greek mythology.

Adrian

(abbrev. Ade)

Latin origin, meaning "from Hadria," a town in northern Italy.

Adriel

Hebrew, meaning "of God's flock." Adriel was one of Saul's sons-in-law in the Bible.

Aeneas

Greek/Latin origin, meaning "to praise." Name of the hero who founded Rome in Virgil's *Aeneid*.

Aero

Greek, meaning "air."

Aeson

Greek, after the father of Jason in ancient Greek mythology.

Afonso

Portuguese, meaning "eager noble warrior." King Afonso of Portugal was nicknamed "The Conqueror" during the Middle Ages.

Agamemnon

Greek, meaning "leader of the assembly." Figure in mythology who commanded the Greeks at the siege of Troy.

Agathon

Greek, meaning "good" or "superior." The name of a tragic poet in ancient Greece.

Agustin

Latin/Spanish, meaning "venerated."

Ahab

Hebrew, meaning "father's brother." Name of the obsessed captain in Herman Melville's *Moby-Dick*.

Ahijah

Hebrew, meaning "brother of God" or "friend of God." Common name in the Bible.

Ahmed

Arabic/Turkish, meaning "worthy of praise." Also one of the prophet Muhammad's many given names.

Aidan

(alt. Aden, Aiden)

Gaelic, meaning "little fire." Derives from Aodh, the name of a Celtic sun god.

Aidric

Old English, meaning "oaken."

Airyck

Old Norse, from Eric, meaning "eternal ruler."

Ajani

Yoruba, meaning "he fights for what he is"; Sanskrit, meaning "of noble birth."

Ajax

Greek, meaning "mourner of the Earth." A Greek hero from the siege of Troy.

Ajay

Hindi, meaning "unconquerable." One of the most popular names in India.

Ajit

Sanskrit, meaning "invincible." Another name for Shiva or Vishnu in Hindu mythology.

Akeem

Arabic, meaning "wise or insightful." Popular name in Nigeria.

Akio

Japanese, meaning "bright man." Akio Morita was one of the founders of Sony.

Akira

Japanese, meaning "intelligent." Also the name of one of the most successful Japanese anime films of all time.

Akiva

Hebrew, meaning "to protect" or "to shelter." Rabbi Akiva is an important figure in the Jewish faith.

Akon

American English, meaning "flower." Made popular after rapper Akon.

Aksel

Hebrew/Danish, meaning "father of peace."

Aladdin

Arabic, meaning "servant of Allah." Character in *The Arabian Nights*, made popular by Disney.

Alan

(alt. Allan, Allen, Allyn, Alun)

Gaelic or Old French, meaning "rock." One of the oldest names still widely used in Western countries, dating back to the 11th century.

Alaric

Old German, meaning "noble regal ruler." Also the name of a king who helped bring about the fall of the Roman Empire.

Alastair

(alt. Alasdair, Alastor, Allister; abbrev. Al, Ali)

Greek/Gaelic, meaning "defending men." Also the name of a demon in the horror series *Supernatural*.

Alban

Latin, meaning "from Alba"; Welsh and Scottish Gaelic for "Scotland."

Alberic

Germanic, meaning "Elfin king."

Albert

(alt. Adalberto, Adelbert, Alberto, Elbert)

Old German, meaning "noble, bright, famous." Prince Albert was the husband of Queen Victoria.

Albus

(alt. Albin)

Latin, meaning "white." Albus Dumbledore is headmaster of Hogwarts School in the *Harry Potter* series.

Alcaeus

Greek, meaning "strength." The name of an ancient Greek poet.

Alden

Old English, meaning "old friend."

Aldis

Latvian, meaning "from the old house."

Aldo

Latin, meaning "the tall one." Also the name of the main gorilla character in *Planet of the Apes*.

Aldric

English, meaning "old king."

Aled

Welsh, meaning "child" or "offspring."

Aleph

Hebrew, meaning "first letter of the alphabet," or "leader." The aleph is the first character of many Middle Eastern alphabets.

Alessio

Italian, meaning "defender."

Alexander

(alt. Alexandro, Alessandro, Alejandro; abbrev. Al, Alec, Alek, Alex, Alexei, Sandro, Sandy, Xander, Zander)

Greek, meaning "defending men." Alexander the Great was an undefeated fourth-century king whose empire stretched from Greece to modern Pakistan. The abbreviation Alexei is enduringly popular in Russia.

Alfonso

Germanic/Spanish, meaning "noble and prompt, ready to struggle." Alfonso Cuarón is the director of the film *Gravity* and *Roma*, among others. Actor Alfonso Ribeiro is known for *Fresh Prince of Bel Air* and *America's Funniest Home Videos*.

Alford
Old English, meaning "old river/ ford."

Alfred
(alt. Alfredo; abbrev. Alf, Alfi, Alfie)
English, meaning "elf" or "magical counsel." Name of legendary English king Alfred the Great.

Algernon
(abbrev. Algie)
French, meaning "with a moustache." A popular name for the nobility in 18th- and 19th-century England. Flowers for Algernon is a novel by Daniel Keyes.

Ali
(alt. Allie)
Arabic, meaning "noble, sublime."

Alijah
Hebrew, meaning "the Lord is my God."

Alois
German, meaning "famous warrior." Also the name of Adolf Hitler's father.

Alok
Sanskrit, meaning "cry of triumph."

Alon
Hebrew, meaning "oak tree." A popular name in Jewish communities.

Alonso
(alt. Alonzo)
Germanic, meaning "noble and ready."

Aloysius
Italian saint's name, meaning "fame and war."

Alpha
First letter of the Greek alphabet and synonymous with "beginning."

Alphaeus
Hebrew, meaning "changing." Father of two of the Apostles in the Bible.

Alpin
Gaelic, meaning "related to the Alps." The House of Alpin was a dynasty of Scottish kings.

Altair
Arabic, meaning "flying" or "bird." Altair is one of the brightest stars seen in the night sky.

Alter
Yiddish, meaning "old man."

Alton
Old English, meaning "old town."

Alvin
(alt. Alvie)
English, meaning "friend of elves." Often associated with Alvin and the Chipmunks.

Alwyn
(alt. Alwen)
Welsh, meaning "wise friend."

Amachi
African, meaning "who knows what God has brought us through this child."

Amadeus
Latin, meaning "God's love." One of composer Wolfgang Amadeus Mozart's many given names.

Amadi
Igbo, meaning "appeared destined to die at birth." Often given to babies who survive against the odds.

Amado
Spanish, meaning "God's love."

Amador
Spanish, meaning "one who loves." Two towns in California were named after rancher José María Amador.

Amari
Hebrew, meaning "given by God." Used for both boys and girls.

Amarion
(alt. Omarion)
Arabic, meaning "populous, flushing." Made popular after R&B singer Omarion.

Amasa
Hebrew, meaning "burden." Found in the Bible.

Ambrose
Greek, meaning "undying, immortal." St. Ambrose of Milan was one of the four original doctors of the Church.

Americo
Germanic, meaning "ever powerful in battle."

Amias
Latin, meaning "loved."

Amir
(alt. Emir)
Arabic, meaning "chieftain" or "commander." Amir or Emir is a title for a high-ranking sheikh in many Muslim communities.

Amit
Hindi, meaning "infinite." One of the many name of the Hindu god Shri Ganesha.

Ammon
Hebrew, meaning "the hidden one." The Ammonites were an ancient group of people named in the Bible.

Amory
German/English, meaning "work" and "power."

Amos

Hebrew, meaning "encumbered" or "burdened."

Anacletus

Latin, meaning "called back" or "invoked." Also the name of the third Pope.

Anakin

American English, meaning "warrior." Made famous by Anakin Skywalker in the *Star Wars* films.

Ananias

Greek/Italian, meaning "answered by the Lord." Ananias Dare was the first baby born to English parents in the New World, making him the first ever "modern" American.

Anastasius
(alt. Anastasios)

Greek, meaning "resurrection." A very popular name for popes, emperors, and saints.

Anatole

French, meaning "sunrise."

Anders

Greek, meaning "lion man." A very popular name in Sweden.

Anderson

English, meaning "male." Anderson Cooper is a TV host.

Andrew
(alt. Andreas, Andre; abbrev. Andy)

Greek, meaning "man" or "warrior." Andrew Lincoln is known for his role in *The Walking Dead*.

Androcles

Greek, meaning "glory of a warrior." *Androcles and the Lion* was a well-known folktale in the second century, and influenced Aesop's *Fables*.

Angel

Greek, meaning "messenger." A very popular name in Hispanic communities. Used for both boys and girls.

Angelo

Italian, meaning "angel."

Angus
(abbrev. Gus)

Scottish, meaning "one choice." Name of Merida's horse in *Brave*.

Anil

Sanskrit, meaning "air" or "wind."

Anselm

German, meaning "helmet of God." St. Anselm was an influential figure in the formation of Christianity.

Anson

English, meaning "son of Agnes." Anson Jones was the last independent President of Texas, before it became incorporated into the USA.

Anthony
(alt. Antony; abbrev. Ant, Tony)
English, from the old Roman family name. *Antony and Cleopatra* is a Shakespearean play about the romance between Roman general Mark Antony and Cleopatra of Egypt.

Antipas
Hebrew, meaning "for all or against all." Herod Antipas is acknowledged as being responsible for the executions of John the Baptist and Jesus Christ in the Bible.

Antwan
(alt. Antoine)
Old English, meaning "flower."

Apollo
Greek, meaning "to destroy." Greek god of poetry, music, and the sun.

Apostolos
Greek, meaning "apostle." The Apostolos is a text believed to have been written by one of the Apostles.

Ara
Armenian, from the legendary king of the same name.

Aragorn
Literary, used by Tolkien in *The Lord of the Rings* trilogy.

Aram
Hebrew, meaning "Royal Highness." Also the name of an ancient region in modern-day Syria.

Aramis
Latin, meaning "swordsman." One of the three musketeers in Alexandre Dumas's novel.

Arcadio
Greek/Spanish, meaning "paradise."

Archibald
(alt. Archie, Archy)
Old German, meaning "genuine/bold/brave." Archie is the son of Prince Harry and Meghan Markle.

Ardell
Latin, meaning "eager, burning with enthusiasm."

Arden
Celtic, meaning "high."

Ares
Greek, meaning "ruin." Son of Zeus and Hera, and the Greek god of war.

Ari
Hebrew, meaning "lion" or "eagle." Also used to refer to an important man in Hebrew.

Arias
Germanic, meaning "lion."

Ariel

Hebrew, meaning "lion of God." One of the archangels, the angel of healing and new beginnings.

Arild

Old Norse, meaning "battle commander."

Aris

Greek, meaning "best figure." Popular name in Greece.

Ariston

Greek, meaning "the best." Also the name of Plato's father.

Aristotle

Greek, meaning "best." Also an ancient Greek philosopher.

Arjun

Sanskrit, meaning "bright and shining." Taken from Arjuna, an ancient and legendary archer.

Arkady

Greek, region of central Greece. Popular throughout Eastern Europe.

Arlan

Gaelic, meaning "pledge" or "oath."

Arlie

Old English place name, meaning "eagle wood."

Arliss

(alt. Arlis)

Hebrew, meaning "pledge." A 1990s sitcom.

Arlo

Spanish, meaning "barberry tree."

Armani

(alt. Armand)

Old German, meaning "soldier." A well-known Italian fashion house.

Arnaldo

Spanish, meaning "eagle power."

Arnav

Indian, meaning "the sea."

Arnold

(abbrev. Arnie)

Old German, meaning "eagle ruler." Arnold Schwarzenegger is an actor, former bodybuilder, and former governor of California.

Arrow

English, from the common word denoting weaponry.

Art

Irish, from the name of a warrior in Irish mythology, Art Oenfer (Art the Lonely). Also used as a shortened form of Arthur.

Artemis

Greek/Spanish, meaning 'perfect'. Artemis Fowl is the anti-hero of Eoin Cowlfer's YA novels.

Arthur

(abbrev. Art, Artie, Artis)

Celtic, probably from "artos," meaning "bear." Made famous by the tales of King Arthur and the Knights of the Round Table.

Arturo

Celtic or Italian, meaning "strong as a bear."

Arvel

From the Welsh "Arwel," meaning "wept over." Arvel Crynyd appears in *Star Wars*.

Arvid

English, meaning "eagle in the woods." Popular name in Scandinavia.

Arvind

Sanskrit, meaning "red lotus." Also derived from the word for "white lotus," upon which the Hindu goddess Lakshmi sits.

Arvo

Finnish, meaning "value" or "worth."

Asa

Hebrew, meaning "doctor" or "healer." Popular with Puritans in the 17th century.

Asante

African, meaning "thank you." Also the language of the Ashanti people.

Asher

Hebrew, meaning "fortunate" or "lucky." One of the 12 sons of Jacob in the Bible.

Ashley

Old English, meaning "ash meadow." Used for both boys and girls.

Ashok

Sanskrit, meaning "not causing sorrow." Popular in India and Sri Lanka.

Ashton

English, meaning "settlement in the ash-tree grove." The middle but chosen name of actor Ashton Kutcher.

Aslan

Turkish, meaning "lion." The name of the lion from C. S. Lewis's *The Lion, The Witch and The Wardrobe*.

Asriel

(alt. Azriel)

Hebrew, meaning "God is my help." Lord Asriel is an important character in the *His Dark Materials* trilogy. Azriel is the name of the angel of death in Christianity and Judaism.

Astrophel

Latin, meaning "star lover."

Athanasios

Greek, meaning "eternal life." Extremely popular in ancient and modern Greece.

Atílio
Portuguese, meaning "father."

Atlas
Greek, meaning "to carry." In ancient Greek mythology Atlas was a Titan forced to carry the weight of the heavens.

Atlee
Hebrew, meaning "God is just."

Atticus
Latin, meaning "from Athens." Atticus Finch is a central character in Harper Lee's *To Kill A Mockingbird*.

Auberon
(alt. Oberon)

Old German, meaning "royal bear." Oberon is the Fairy King in Shakespeare's *A Midsummer Night's Dream*.

Aubrey
Old German, meaning "power." Used for both boys and girls.

Auden
Old English, meaning "old friend." W. H. Auden is considered one of the most influential 20th-century poets.

Audie
Old English, meaning "noble strength." Audie L. Murphy was one of the most decorated US soldiers during World War II.

August
Latin, meaning "magnificent."

Augustus
(alt. Augustas; abbrev. Gus)

Latin, meaning "venerated." Also the name of a spoiled child in *Charlie and the Chocolate Factory*.

Aurelien
French, meaning "golden." An ancient Roman emperor.

Austin
Latin, meaning "venerated." Also the city in Texas.

Avi
Hebrew, meaning "father of a multitude of nations."

Awnan
Irish, meaning "little Adam."

Axel
(alt. Aksel, Axl)

Hebrew, meaning "father is peace." Made famous by Guns 'n' Roses frontman Axl Rose.

Azarel
(alt. Azaryah)

Hebrew, meaning "helped by God." Also an evil spirit in the Bible.

Azuko
African, meaning "past glory." Popular in Japan.

B

Boys' names

Babe

American English, meaning "baby." George Herman "Babe" Ruth was a legendary baseball player.

Baden

German, meaning "battle." Also the name of a city in Switzerland known for its hot springs.

Bailey

English, meaning "bailiff." Baileys is a popular Irish crème liqueur.

Baird

Scottish, meaning "poet" or "one who sings ballads."

Bakari

Swahili, meaning "hope" or "promise."

Baker

English, from the word "baker."

Baldwin

Old French, meaning "bold, brave friend."

Balin

Old English, meaning "powerful and strong." Balin was one of the Knights of the Round Table.

Balthazar

Babylonian, meaning "protect the king." Also the name of one of the Three Wise Men in the Nativity story.

Balwinder
(alt. Balvinder)

Hindi, meaning "merciful, compassionate."

Bannon

Irish, meaning "descendant of O'Banain."

Barack

African, meaning "blessed." Made popular by the 44th President of the United States Barack Obama.

Barclay

Old English, meaning "birch tree meadow"; Persian, meaning "messenger."

Barker

Old English, meaning "shepherd."

Barnaby
(abbrev. Barney)

Greek, meaning "son of consolation." *Barnaby Rudge* is one of Charles Dickens's less well-known novels.

Barnard

English, meaning "strong as a bear."

Baron

Old English, meaning "young warrior." A title given to certain men of nobility in Europe. The name of Donald and Melania Trump's son.

Barrett

English, meaning "strong as a bear."

Barron

Old German, meaning "old clearing."

Barry
(abbrev. Baz)

Irish Gaelic, meaning "fair haired." *Great Gatsby* film director Baz Luhrman's real name is Mark.

Bartholomew
(abbrev. Bart, Barty)

Hebrew, meaning "son of the farmer." Bartholomew "Bart" Simpson appears in *The Simpsons*.

Barton

Old English, meaning "barley settlement." The name of several towns in the UK.

Baruch

Hebrew, meaning "blessed." Also the name of a Jewish blessing ceremony.

Bascom

Old English, meaning "from Bascombe."

Bashir

Arabic, meaning "well educated" and "wise." British journalist Martin Bashir is known for his infamous interviews with Diana, Princess of Wales, and Michael Jackson.

Basil

Greek, meaning "royal, kingly." Also the name of the herb.

Basim

Arabic, meaning "smile."

Bastien

Greek, meaning "revered."

Baxter

Old English, meaning "baker." One of the most popular names for towns across the USA.

Bayard

French, meaning "auburn haired." Bayard Rustin was one of Martin Luther King Jr.'s mentors and advisors during the Civil Rights Movement.

Bayo

Yoruba, meaning "to find joy."

Beau

French, meaning "handsome." Actor Beau Bridges' real name is Lloyd Vernet Bridges.

Beck

Old Norse, meaning "stream." Singer Beck Hansen is usually known as just "Beck."

Beckett

Old English, meaning "beehive" or "bee cottage."

Beckham

English, meaning "homestead by the stream." Finding popularity as a given name due to English soccer star David Beckham.

Belarius

Shakespearean, meaning "a banished lord"; from the play *Cymbeline*.

Benedict

Latin, meaning "blessed." Made popular by British actor Benedict Cumberbatch.

Benjamin
(abbrev. Ben, Benny)

Hebrew, meaning "son of the south." Benjamin Franklin was one of the Founding Fathers of the USA.

Bennett

French/Latin vernacular form of Benedict, meaning "blessed."

Benoit

French form of Benedict, meaning "blessed."

Benson

English, meaning "son of Ben."

Bentley

Old English, meaning "bent grass meadow." Popularity has increased since the shows *16 and Pregnant* and *Teen Mom* first aired.

Benton

Old English, meaning "town in the bent grass."

Beriah

Hebrew, meaning "in fellowship" or "in envy." The son of Asher in the Bible.

Bernard
(abbrev. Bernie)

Germanic, meaning "strong, brave bear."

Berry

Old English, meaning "berry." Also used as a shortened form of Bernard.

Berton

Old English, meaning "bright settlement." Berton Averre is the guitarist from The Knack.

Bertrand
(alt. Bertram; abbrev. Bert, Bertie)

Old English, meaning "illustrious." The name of a *Sesame Street* muppet. Bertram (Bertie) Wooster was one of P. G. Wodehouse's most beloved characters. Bert is also a shortened form of Albert.

Bevan

Welsh, meaning "son of Evan."

Bicknell

Old English, meaning "from Bicknell."

Bilal

Arabic, meaning "wetting, refreshing." Popular in many Muslim communities.

Birch

Old English, meaning "bright" or "shining." Also a type of tree.

Birger

Norwegian, meaning "rescue."

Bishop

Old English, meaning "bishop." Bishops are members of the Church who oversee several parishes and jurisdictions.

Bjorn

Old Norse, meaning "bear." Bjorn Ulvaeus was one of the founding members of ABBA.

Bladen

Hebrew, meaning "hero."

Blaine
(alt. Blayne)

Irish Gaelic, meaning "yellow." Has risen in profile due to entertainer David Blaine, known for his magic, illusions, and extreme stunts.

Blair

English, meaning "plain."

Blaise

French, meaning "lisp" or "stutter."

Blake

Old English, meaning "dark, black."

Blaze
(alt. Blas)

German, meaning "firebrand." Also the name of a mountain in the Alps.

Bo

Scandinavian, from Robert, meaning "bright fame." Also the name of the Obamas' pet dog.

Boaz

Hebrew, meaning "swiftness" or "strength." Found in the Bible.

Boden
(alt. Bodie)

Scandinavian, meaning "shelter" or "messenger."

Bogumil

Slavic, meaning "God's favor."

Bond

Old English, meaning "peasant farmer." Often associated with the fictional character James Bond.

Boris

Slavic, meaning "battle glory." Boris Yeltsin was the president of Russia during the 1990s. Boris Johnson is a British politician.

Boston
(alt. Bosten)

English, meaning "town by the woods."

Bowen

Welsh, meaning "son of Owen." The Bowen knot is a common sight in heraldic symbolism.

Boyd

Scottish Gaelic, meaning "yellow."

Bradley
(abbrev. Brad)

Old English, meaning "broad" or "wide." Actor Brad Pitt's full name is William Bradley Pitt.

Brady

Irish, meaning "large-chested." Made famous by *The Brady Bunch*.

Bradyn
(alt. Braden, Bradan)

Gaelic, meaning "descendant of Bradan."

Bram

Gaelic, meaning "raven." Bram Stoker was the author of *Dracula*.

Brando

Old Norse, meaning "sword" or "flaming torch." Name of the movie star Marlon Brando.

Brandon
(abbrev. Bran)

Old English, meaning "gorse." Bran Stark is a main character in *Game of Thrones*.

Brandt

Old English, meaning "beacon."

Brannon

Gaelic, meaning "raven."

Branson
English, meaning "son of Brand."

Brant
Old English, meaning "hill."

Braulio
Greek, meaning "shining."

Braxton
English, meaning "Brock's town." Associated with Braxton Hicks contractions during pregnancy.

Brayden
Irish, meaning "broad meadow."

Brendan
Gaelic, meaning "prince." Actor Brendan Fraser is known for his role in *The Mummy* film series.

Brennan
Gaelic, meaning "teardrop."

Brent
English, meaning "hill." Ice hockey star Brent Seabrook currently plays for the Chicago Blackhawks.

Brenton
English, meaning "hill town."

Brett
(alt. Bret)
English, meaning "a Breton." Made popular by Poison lead vocalist Bret Michaels.

Brian
(alt. Bryan, Bryant)
Gaelic, meaning "high" or "noble." Singer songwriter Brian Wilson was a founding member of The Beach Boys. Actor Bryan Cranston is best known for *Breaking Bad*.

Brice
Latin, meaning "speckled."

Brier
French, meaning "heather." Also the name of a type of thorny plant.

Brock
Old English, meaning "badger." One of the more popular characters in the Pokémon franchise.

Broderick
English, meaning "ruler."

Brody
Gaelic, meaning both "ditch" and "brother." Brody Jenner is known for being part of the Jenner/Kardashian clan.

Brogan
Irish, meaning "sturdy shoe."

Bronwyn
(alt. Bronwen)
Welsh, meaning "fair breast." The spelling of Bronwyn is more common for boys, and Bronwen for girls.

Brooklyn

American English, from the New York City borough of the same name. Brooklyn Beckham is the eldest son of David and Victoria Beckham.

Bruce

Scottish, meaning "high" or "noble." The former name of Olympian decathlete and Jenner/Kardashian clan member Caitlyn Jenner.

Bruno

Germanic, meaning "brown." Bruno Tonioli is a judge on *Dancing With The Stars*.

Bryce

Scottish, meaning "of Britain."

Bryden

Irish, meaning "strong one."

Bryson
(alt. Brycen)

Welsh, meaning "descendant of Brice." Bryson was the name of an ancient Greek philosopher and also a mathematician from the same time.

Bubba

American English, meaning "boy." The restaurant chain Bubba Gump Shrimp Co. takes its name from the characters of Benjamin Buford "Bubba" Blue and Forrest Gump in the movie *Forrest Gump*.

Buck

American English, meaning "goat" or "deer," specifically a male deer.

Buddy
(alt. Bud)

American English, meaning "friend." Buddy has been used as a stage name by a number of musicians including Buddy Holly and Buddy Guy.

Burdett

Middle English, meaning "bird."

Burke

French, meaning "fortified settlement."

Burl

French, meaning "knotty wood."

Buzz

American English, from Busby, meaning "village in the thicket." Buzz Aldrin was the second man on the moon and Buzz Lightyear appears in Disney's *Toy Story* film series.

Byron

Old English, meaning "barn." Famous Byrons include the Romantic poet Lord Byron.

C Boys' names

Cabot
Old English, meaning "to sail."

Cade
(alt. Caden, Caiden, Kayden)
English, meaning "round, lumpy."
A character in the novel *Gone With The Wind*.

Cadence
Latin, meaning "with rhythm."
Poetry, music, and marching all have some type of cadence.

Cadogan
Welsh, meaning "battle glory and honor." Sir Cadogan is a knight in a painting in the *Harry Potter* series.

Caedmon
Celtic, meaning "wise warrior." An early English poet.

Caelan
Gaelic, meaning "slender."

Caerwyn
(alt. Carwyn, Gerwyn)
Welsh, meaning "white fort" or "settlement."

Caesar
(alt. Cesar)
Latin, meaning "head of hair." Made famous by the first Roman emperor, Julius Caesar.

Caetano
Portuguese, meaning "from Gaeta, Italy."

Caillou
French, meaning "pebble." Name of a children's cartoon character.

Cain
Hebrew, meaning "full of beauty." Brother of Abel in the Bible.

Cainan

Hebrew, meaning "possessor" or "purchaser."

Cairo

Egyptian city near Giza. Also home of the Great Pyramids.

Calder

Scottish, meaning "rough waters."

Caleb
(alt. Cal, Calen)

Hebrew, meaning "dog." Found in the Bible.

Calix

Greek, meaning "very handsome."

Callahan

Irish, meaning "contention" or "strife."

Callum
(alt. Calum)

Gaelic, meaning "dove." Very popular name in Ireland.

Calvin
(alt. Kalvin)

French, meaning "little bald one." Associated with the comic strip *Calvin and Hobbes* and fashion line Calvin Klein.

Camden
(alt. Kamden)

Gaelic, meaning "winding valley." A district in north London, UK, known for its market.

Cameron

Scottish Gaelic, meaning "crooked nose." Used for boys and girls.

Camillo

Latin, meaning "free born" or "noble."

Campbell

Scottish Gaelic, meaning "crooked mouth." The name of a famous brand of soup.

Canaan

Hebrew, meaning "to be humbled." A region heavily referenced in the Bible.

Candido

Latin, meaning "candid" or "honest." Candido Jacuzzi was the inventor of the Jacuzzi tub.

Canon
(alt. Cannon)

French, meaning "of the church." Originally given to members of a certain order in the Church.

Canton

French, meaning "dweller of corner." Also the name given to provinces of Switzerland.

Cappy

Italian, meaning "lucky." Can also be a nickname for Captain.

Carden

Old English, meaning "wool carder"—which refers to someone who would "card" wool to remove impurities from it.

Carey

Gaelic, meaning "love." Used for both boys and girls.

Carl

(alt. Carlo, Carlos, Karl)

Old Norse, meaning "free man." Carl Jung was a famous psychologist.

Carlton

Old English, meaning "free peasant settlement." Carlton is a character in the sitcom *The Fresh Prince of Bel Air*.

Carmelo

Latin, meaning "garden" or "orchard."

Carmen

Latin/Spanish, meaning "song." The title of an opera by French composer Georges Bizet. Used for boys and girls.

Carmine

Latin, meaning "song." Also the name of a bright-red pigment used in the production of red fruit juices.

Carnell

English, meaning "defender of the castle."

Carson

(alt. Carsten)

Scottish, meaning "marshdwellers." Carson Daly is a late night TV host.

Carter

Old English, meaning "transporter of goods." Jimmy Carter was the 39th President of the United States and Carter Camper is an American professional ice hockey player.

Cary

Celtic, meaning "love." Old Celtic river name. Cary Elwes is a current actor and Cary Grant was the stage name of the dashing English-American actor of the 1930s–1950s.

Case

(alt. Casey, Kace, Kacey, Kasey)

Irish Gaelic, meaning "alert" or "watchful."

Cash

Latin, shortened form of Cassius, meaning "empty, hollow." Associated with musician Johnny Cash.

Casimer

Slavic, meaning "famous destroyer of peace."

Cason

Latin, from Cassius, meaning "empty, hollow."

Casper
(alt. Caspar, Kaspar, Kasper)
Persian, meaning "treasurer." The ghost character in *Casper the Friendly Ghost*.

Caspian
English, meaning "of the Caspy people." Taken from the children's novel *Prince Caspian*.

Cassidy
Gaelic, meaning "curly haired." Originated from the last name Caiside.

Cassius
(alt. Cassio)
Latin, meaning "empty, hollow." Legendary boxer Muhammad Ali's birth name was Cassius Clay.

Cathal
Celtic, meaning "battle rule." Variation of Charles.

Cato
Latin, meaning "all-knowing." Also the name of a character in *The Hunger Games*.

Cecil
Latin, meaning "blind." Cecil B. DeMille was a legendary film director.

Cedar
English, name of an evergreen tree.

Cedric
Welsh, meaning "spectacular bounty." Taken from Sir Walter Scott's novel *Ivanhoe*.

Celestino
Spanish/Italian meaning "heavenly."

Chad
(alt. Chadrick)
Old English, meaning "warlike, warrior." Also the name of an African country.

Chaim
(alt. Chayyim)
Hebrew, meaning "life."

Champion
English, from the word "warrior."

Chance
English, meaning "good fortune."

Chandler
Old English, meaning "candle maker and seller." Made famous by Chandler Bing from 1990s sitcom *Friends*.

Charles
(alt. Charley, Charlie; abbrev. Chas)
Old German, meaning "free man." Charles, Prince of Wales, is heir to the British throne.

Chase
(alt. Chace)

Old French, meaning "huntermen." Actor Chace Crawford is known for his role on TV series *Gossip Girl*.

Chaska

Native American name usually given to first son.

Che

Spanish, shortened form of José. Made famous by Che Guevara.

Chesley

Old English, meaning "camp on the meadow."

Chesney

English, meaning "place to camp." Also used as a girls' name.

Chester

Latin, meaning "camp of soldiers." Chester Arthur was the 21st President of the United States and Chester Bennington was the lead singer of rock band Linkin Park.

Chima

Old English, meaning "hilly land."

Christian
(abbrev. Chris)

English, from the word "Christian." Actor Christian Slater is known for his roles in *Heathers* and *Breaking In*.

Christopher
(alt. Christophe, Kristopher; abbrev. Chris, Kris)

Greek, meaning "bearing Christ inside." Christopher Columbus is credited with discovering America.

Cian

Irish, meaning "ancient." Father of Lug in Gaelic mythology.

Ciaran

Irish, meaning "black." Actor Ciaran Hinds is known for, among others, *Justice League* and his voice work as Gree in *Rio 2*, and the Troll King in *Frozen*.

Cicero

Latin, meaning "chickpea." Also the Roman philosopher and orator.

Cimarron

City in western Kansas.

Ciprian

Latin, meaning "from Cyprus." Popular in ancient Rome.

Ciro

Spanish, meaning "sun." Also the title of a 17th-century opera.

Clancy

Old Irish, meaning "red warrior." Clancy has been a popular name for US actors, writers and sports stars. Also a character in *The Simpsons*.

Clarence

Latin, meaning "one who lives near the river Clare." Clarence Thomas is one of the current Associate Justices of the Supreme Court.

Clark

Latin, meaning "clerk." Superman's human name is Clark Kent.

Claude
(alt. Claudie, Claudio, Claudius)

Latin, meaning "lame."

Claus

Variant of Nicholas, meaning "people of victory." Associated with Santa Claus.

Clay

English, from the word "clay." Singer Clay Aiken is known for his appearances on *American Idol*.

Clement
(alt. Clem)

Latin, meaning "merciful." Also the taken name for 14 different popes.

Cletus

Greek, meaning "illustrious." Cletus Spuckler is a hillbilly character in *The Simpsons*.

Clifford
(alt. Clifton; abbrev. Cliff)

English, meaning "ford by a cliff." Associated with children's character Clifford the Big Red Dog.

Clinton
(alt. Clint)

Old English, meaning "fenced settlement." Actor Clint Eastwood is known for dozens of movie roles, both as an actor and as a director.

Clive

Old English, meaning "cliff" or "slope." Clive Owen is an actor and Clive Davis is a record producer and record label executive.

Clyde

Scottish, from the river that passes through Glasgow. Also the name of one half of the bank robber duo Bonnie and Clyde.

Coby
(alt. Koby, Kobe)

Diminutive of Jacob, meaning "he who supplants." Also used as a girls' name.

Colden

Old English, meaning "dark valley."

Cole
(alt. Coley)

Old French, meaning "coal black." Composer Cole Porter is known for dozens of popular songs and musicals.

Colin

Gaelic, meaning "young creature." Actor Colin Firth is known for his roles in *Pride and Prejudice* and *Kingsman*. Colin Powell was a US secretary of state and is a retired army general.

Colson

Old English, meaning "coal black."

Colton

English, meaning "swarthy." Actor Colton Haynes is known for his role in *Arrow*.

Columbus

Latin, meaning "dove."

Colwyn

Welsh, from the river in Wales.

Conan

Gaelic, meaning "wolf." Comedian Conan O'Brien is known for his work as a late-night TV host.

Conley

Gaelic, meaning "sensible."

Connell

(alt. Connolly)

Irish, meaning "high" or "mighty."

Connor

(alt. Conrad, Conroy)

Irish, meaning "lover of hounds." Very popular name in Ireland.

Constant

(alt. Constantine)

English, from the word "constant." Popular with Puritans during the 17th century.

Cooper

Old English, meaning "barrel maker."

Corban

(alt. Corbin, Corby)

Hebrew, meaning "dedicated and belonging to God."

Corbett

(alt. Corby)

Norman French, meaning "young crow."

Cordell

Old English, meaning "cord maker." An old term for people who made or sold cords.

Corey

Gaelic, meaning "hill hollow." Corey Hart is a Canadian singer who rose to fame in the 1980s.

Corin

Latin, meaning "spear."

Cormac

Gaelic, meaning "impure son." American writer Cormac McCarthy is the author of modern classics *No Country for Old Men* and *The Road*.

Cornelius

(alt. Cornell)

Latin, meaning "horn." Cornelius Fudge is the Minister for Magic in the *Harry Potter* series.

Cortez

Spanish, meaning "courteous."

Corwin

Old English, meaning "heart's friend" or "companion."

Cosimo

(alt. Cosme, Cosmo)

Italian, meaning "order" or "beauty." Masculine form of Cosima.

Coty

French, meaning "riverbank." Refers to people who live on the French coast.

Coulter

(alt. Colt)

English, meaning "young horse."

Courtney

Old English, meaning "domain of Curtis." Used for both boys and girls.

Covey

English, meaning "flock of birds."

Cowan

Gaelic, meaning "hollow in the hill."

Craig

Welsh, meaning "rock." Comedian Craig Ferguson is known for his work as a late night TV host.

Crispin

Latin, meaning "curly haired." A patron saint of shoemakers.

Croix

French, meaning "cross."

Cruz

Spanish, meaning "cross." Made famous after David and Victoria Beckham chose it for their third son.

Curran

Gaelic, meaning "dagger" or "hero."

Curtis

(alt. Curt)

Old French, meaning "courteous." Curtis Mayfield was a soul and R&B singer and Curtis LeMay was a general in the US Air Force during World War II.

Cutler

Old English, meaning "knife maker."

Cyprian

English, meaning "from Cyprus." Also the name of an early Christian bishop and writer.

Cyril

Greek, meaning "master" or "Lord." Associated with St. Cyril.

Cyrus

Persian, meaning "Lord." Cyrus the Great was a ruler of Persia in ancient times.

Boys' names

Dai

Welsh, meaning "darling."
Sometimes used as a girls' name.

Daichi

Japanese, meaning "great wisdom."

Daisuke

Japanese, meaning "lionhearted."

Dakari

African, meaning "happy."

Dakota

Native American, meaning "friend" or "ally." Both North and South Dakota take their names from the Native American tribe of the same name.

Dale

Old English, meaning "valley." Dale Earnhardt Jr. is one of the best-known NASCAR drivers.

Dallin

English, meaning "dweller in the valley."

Dalton

English, meaning "town in the valley."

Daly

Gaelic, meaning "assembly."

Damarion

Greek, meaning "gentle."

Damian
(alt. Damon)

Greek, meaning "to tame, subdue." Actor Damian Lewis is known for his role in *Homeland*.

Dane

Old English, meaning "from Denmark." Dane Cook is known for his stand-up comedy.

Daniel

(abbrev. Dan, Danny)

Hebrew, meaning "God is my judge." Found in the Bible.

Dante

Latin, meaning "lasting." Name of the Italian 13th-century poet Dante Alighieri.

Darby

Irish, meaning "without envy."

Darcy

(alt. Darcey)

Gaelic, meaning "dark." Mr. Darcy is a main character in Jane Austen's *Pride and Prejudice*.

Dario

(alt. Darius)

Greek, meaning "kingly." Dario Argento is an Italian film director known for his horror fims.

Darnell

Old English, meaning "the hidden spot."

Darragh

Irish, meaning "dark oak."

Darren

(alt. Darrian)

Gaelic, meaning "great." Darren Aronofsky is a film director and producer.

Darrick

Old German, meaning "power of the tribe."

Darryl

(alt. Darrell, Daryl)

Old English, meaning "open." Comedian Darrell Hammond was known for his roles on *Saturday Night Live*. The spelling Daryl is more commonly used as a girls' name.

Darshan

Hindi, meaning "vision."

Darwin

Old English, meaning "dear friend." Often associated with naturalist and author Charles Darwin.

Dash

(alt. Dashawn)

American English, meaning "enlightened one." Dash is a character in Disney Pixar's *The Incredibles*.

Dashiell

French, meaning "page boy." Author Dashiell Hammett was known for his detective novels.

David

(alt. Daffyd, Davian; abbrev. Dave, Davey, Davie)

Hebrew, meaning "beloved." David was a king of Israel who killed the giant Goliath in the Bible.

Davis

Old English, meaning "son of David."

Dawson

Old English, meaning "son of David." Associated with 1990s teen drama *Dawson's Creek*.

Dax
(alt. Daxton)

French, from the town in southwestern France. Actor Dax Shepard is known for his role in *Parenthood*.

Dayal

Indian, meaning "kind."

Dayton

Old English, meaning "David's place." Also the name of a city in Ohio.

Dean
(alt. Dino)

Old English, meaning "valley." Actor and reality TV star Dean McDermott is married to Tori Spelling.

Declan

Irish, meaning "full of goodness." Declan Porter was a character on the soap opera *Revenge*.

Dedric

Old English, meaning "gifted ruler."

Deegan
(alt. Deagon, Daegan)

Irish, meaning "black-haired."

Deepak
(alt. Deepan)

Indian, meaning "illumination." Deepak Chopra is known for his work as a doctor and author.

Del
(alt. Delano, Delbert, Dell)

Old English, meaning "bright shining one."

Demetrius

Greek, meaning "harvest lover." One of the star-crossed lovers in Shakespeare's *A Midsummer Night's Dream*.

Dempsey

Irish, meaning "proud."

Denham
(alt. Denholm)

Old English, meaning "valley settlement."

Dennis
(alt. Denny, Denton)

English, meaning "follower of Dionysius." The main character in comic strip *Dennis the Menace*.

Denver

Old English, meaning "green valley." City in Colorado.

Denzel
(alt. Denzil)

English, meaning "fort." Actor Denzel Washington is known for his roles in *Malcolm X* and *Philadelphia*.

Deon

Greek, meaning "of Zeus." The male version of Dionne.

Derek

English, meaning "power of the tribe." Dancer and choreographer Derek Hough is known for his work on *Dancing With The Stars*.

Dermot

Irish, meaning "free man." Actor Dermot Mulroney is known for his roles in *My Best Friend's Wedding* and *New Girl*.

Desmond
(abbrev. Des)

Irish, meaning "from south Munster." Former Archbishop Desmond Tutu is a high-profile South African social activist.

Destin

French, meaning "destiny."

Devyn
(alt. Devin, Devon)

Irish, meaning "poet."

Long names

Alexander	Bartholomew
Christopher	Demetrius
Giovanni	Maximillian
Montgomery	Nathaniel
Sebastian	Zachariah

Dewey
(alt. Dewi)

Welsh, meaning "beloved." One of Donald Duck's three nephews.

Dexter
(alt. Dex)

Latin, meaning "right-handed." Became more popular since the massive success of TV drama *Dexter*.

Didier

French, meaning "much desired."

Diego

Spanish, meaning "supplanter." A character in children's cartoon *Dora the Explorer*.

Dietrich

Old German, meaning "power of the tribe."

Diggory

English, meaning "dyke." Cedric Diggory is a character in the *Harry Potter* series.

Dilbert

English, meaning "day-bright." Main character in the comic strip of the same name.

Dimitri

(alt. Dimitrios, Dimitris)

Greek, meaning "prince." Popular name for boys in Russia.

Dion

Greek, short form of Dionysius.

Dirk

Variant of Derek, meaning "power of the tribe." Famous Dirks include actors Dirk Bogarde and Dirk Benedict.

Dominic

Latin, meaning "Lord." Actor Dominic Monaghan is known for his roles in *Lost* and *The Lord of the Rings*.

Donald

(alt. Donal, Donaldo; abbrev. Don, Donnie)

Gaelic, meaning "great chief." Famous Donalds include the 45th US President Donald Trump, actor Donald Sutherland, and Donald Duck.

Donato

Italian, meaning "gift." Given name of the Italian sculptor Donatello.

Short names

Al	Ben
Dai	Ed
Jay	Jon
Max	Rio
Sam	Ty

Donnell

(alt. Donnie, Donny)

Gaelic, meaning "world fighter."

Donovan

Gaelic, meaning "dark-haired chief."

Doran

Gaelic, meaning "exile."

Dorian

Greek, meaning "descendant of Doris." The title character of Oscar Wilde's *The Picture of Dorian Gray*.

Douglas

(alt. Dougal, Dougie)

Scottish, meaning "black river." Author Douglas Adams wrote *The Hitchhiker's Guide to the Galaxy*.

Draco

Latin, meaning "dragon." Draco Malfoy is a main character in the *Harry Potter* series.

Drake

Greek, meaning "dragon." Canadian rapper and actor Drake's full name is Aubrey Drake Bell.

Drew

Greek, from Andrew, meaning "man" or "warrior." Drew Carey is known for his work in comedy and as a TV host.

Dudley

Old English, meaning "people's field." The name of Harry's cousin in the *Harry Potter* series.

Duff

Gaelic, meaning "swarthy."

Duke

Latin, meaning "leader." Became popular as a first name after the birth of Giuliana and Bill Rancic's son Duke.

Duncan

Scottish, meaning "dark warrior." King Duncan is a character in Shakespeare's *Macbeth*.

Dustin
(alt. Dusty)

French, meaning "brave warrior." Actor Dustin Hoffman is known for his roles in *Rain Man* and *Tootsie*.

Dwayne

Irish Gaelic, meaning "swarthy." Actor Dwayne Johnson was known as "The Rock" during his professional wrestling career.

Dwight

Flemish, meaning "blond." Dwight D. Eisenhower was the 34th President of the United States.

Dwyer

Gaelic, meaning "dark wise one."

Dylan
(alt. Delyn, Dillon)

Welsh, meaning "son of the sea." Dylan Thomas was a famous Welsh poet.

Boys' names

Eamon
(alt. Eames, Eamonn)

Irish, meaning "wealthy protector." Eamonn Walker is known for his role in TV series *Oz*.

Earl
(alt. Earle, Errol)

English, meaning "nobleman, warrior." Became popular after the sitcom *My Name is Earl*.

Ebenezer
(abbrev. Ebb)

Hebrew, meaning "stone of help." The main character in Charles Dickens's *A Christmas Carol* is Ebenezer Scrooge.

Edgar
(alt. Elgar)

Old English, meaning "wealthy spear." Gothic author Edgar Allen Poe wrote "The Raven," among other poems.

Edison

English, meaning "son of Edward." Thomas Edison was one of the most influential American inventors.

Edmund

English, meaning "wealthy protector." Sir Edmund Hillary became the first Westerner to reach the summit of Mount Everest, in 1953.

Edric

Old English, meaning "rich and powerful."

Edsel

Old German, meaning "noble." Car pioneer Henry Ford named his son Edsel.

Edward
(alt. Eduard; abbrev. Ed, Eddie, Eddy, Ned, Ted)

Old English, meaning "wealthy guard." A character in the *Twilight* series.

Edwin
English, meaning "wealthy friend."

Efrain
Hebrew, meaning "fruitful."

Egan
Irish, meaning "fire."

Einar
Old Norse, meaning "battle leader."
A popular name for boys in Iceland.

Eladio
Greek, meaning "Greek."

Elam
Hebrew, meaning "eternal." The son
of Shem and of Noah in the Bible.

Eldon
Old English, meaning "Ella's hill."

Eldred
(alt. Eldridge)
Old English, meaning "old venerable
counsel."

Elgin
Old English, meaning "high minded."
Also the name of a town in Scotland.

Eli
(alt. Eliah)
Hebrew, meaning "high." Eli
Whitney is credited with inventing
the cotton gin.

Elijah
(alt. Elias, Elio, Ellis; abbrev. Eli)
Hebrew, meaning "the Lord is my
God." Elias is the Greek form of
the same name, Elio is the Spanish
version and Ellis the Welsh version.
Actor Elijah Wood played Frodo in
The Lord of the Rings.

Ellery
Old English, meaning "elder tree."

Elliott
Variant of Elio, meaning "the Lord is
my God." Elliot was the little boy in
the classic film E.T.

Ellison
English, meaning "son of Ellis."

Elmer
(alt. Elmo)
Old English, meaning "noble";
Arabic, meaning "aristocratic."
Associated with the children's
characters Elmer the Elephant and
Elmo from Sesame Street.

Elon
Hebrew, meaning "oak tree."

Elroy
French, meaning "king." A cartoon
character in The Jetsons.

Elton
Old English, meaning "Ella's town."
Sir Elton John is one of the most
successful recording artists of all time.

Elvin

English, meaning "elf-like." Elvin Bale was a huge circus performer known for cannonball stunts.

Elvis

Figure in Norse mythology. Made famous by the singer Elvis Presley.

Emanuel
(alt. Immanuel, Imanol)

Hebrew, meaning "God is with us."

Emeric

German, meaning "work rule." St. Emeric was known for living a pure and pious life.

Emile
(alt. Emiliano, Emilio)

Latin, meaning "eager." Emile is Remy the rat's older brother in Disney's *Ratatouille*.

Emlyn

Welsh, from the UK town of Newcastle Emlyn.

Emmett

English, meaning "universal." Emmett Kelly was known for his role as Weary Willie, the Depression-era clown.

Emrys

Welsh, meaning "immortal." Said to be the birth name of the magician Merlin.

Enoch

Hebrew, meaning "dedicated." Enoch is an ancestor of Noah in the Bible.

Enrico
(alt. Enrique)

Italian form of Henry, meaning "home ruler."

Enzo

Italian, short for Lorenzo, meaning "laurel." Enzo Ferrari was the founder of the Ferrari car company.

Ephron
(alt. Effron, Efron)

Hebrew, meaning "dust."

Erasmo
(alt. Erasmus)

Greek, meaning "to love."

Eric

Old Norse, meaning "ruler." Famous Erics include legendary guitarist Eric Clapton.

Ernest
(alt. Ernesto, Ernie, Ernst)

Old German, meaning "serious." Author Ernest Hemingway wrote the novel *The Old Man and the Sea*, among others.

Erskine

Scottish, meaning "high cliff."

Erwin

Old English, meaning "boar friend."

Ethan

(alt. Etienne)

Hebrew, meaning "long lived." Ethan Hawke is an actor. Ethan Coen and his brother Joel are award-winning film producers and directors.

Eugene

Greek, meaning "well born." Eugene Allen was a butler at the White House for 34 years and the inspiration for the film *The Butler*.

Evan

Welsh, meaning "God is good." Evan Williams founded Twitter.

Everard

Old English, meaning "strong boar."

Everett

English, meaning "strong boar."

Ewan

(alt. Ewald, Ewell)

Old English, from Owen, meaning "well born" or "noble." Actor Ewan McGregor is known for his roles in *Moulin Rouge* and the *Star Wars* series.

Exton

English, meaning "on the river Exe."

Ezra

Hebrew, meaning "helper." Name of the poet Ezra Pound.

Boys' names

Fabian
(alt. Fabien, Fabio)
Latin, meaning "one who grows beans."

Fabrice
(alt. Fabrizio)
Latin, meaning "works with his hands."

Faisal
(alt. Faison)
Arabic, meaning "resolute."

Faron
Spanish, meaning "pharaoh," and Gaelic for "thunder."

Farrell
Gaelic, meaning "hero."

Faulkner
Latin, from "falcon."

Faustino
Latin, meaning "fortunate."

Felipe
(alt. Filippo)
Spanish, meaning "lover of horses."

Felix
(alt. Felice)
Italian/Latin, meaning "happy." Felix the Cat was first developed as a cartoon during the silent movie era.

Fennel
Latin, name of a herb.

Ferdinand
(alt. Fernando)
Old German, meaning "bold voyager." Ferdinand was a popular name for Roman emperors and kings of Spain.

Fergus
(alt. Ferguson)

Gaelic, meaning "supreme man."
King Fergus is Merida's father in
Disney's *Brave*.

Ferris

Gaelic, meaning "rock." The lead
character from 1980s cult film *Ferris
Bueller's Day Off*.

Fidel

Latin, meaning "faithful." Fidel Castro
was president of Cuba from 1976 to
2008.

Finbarr

Gaelic, meaning "fair head."

Finian

Gaelic, meaning "fair." St. Finnian is
an important Irish saint.

Finlay
(alt. Finley)

Gaelic, meaning "fair-haired
courageous one." Actor Finlay
Robertson is known for his role in TV
series *Doctor Who*.

Finn
(alt. Fynn)

Irish Gaelic, meaning "fair."
Associated with the novel
Huckleberry Finn and the *Star Wars*
series.

Finnegan

Gaelic, meaning "fair." *Finnegans
Wake* is a work by James Joyce.

Fintan

Gaelic, meaning "little fair one."
Fintan supposedly saved one of
Noah's granddaughters from the
flood.

Flavio

Latin, meaning "yellow hair." *Flavio*
is the name of an opera by Handel.

Florencio
(alt. Florentino)

Latin, meaning "from Florence."

Florian
(alt. Florin)

Slavic/Latin, meaning "flower,"
though it is a masculine name.
Popular in Germany and Switzerland
and the name of the patron saint of
Poland.

Floyd

Welsh, meaning "gray haired."
Floyd is the given name of two
title-winning American professional
boxers.

Flynn

Gaelic, meaning "with a ruddy
complexion." Flynn Rider is
Rapunzel's unlikely love interest in
Disney's *Tangled*.

Fortunato

Italian, meaning "lucky."

Forrest

(alt. Forest)

Old French, meaning "woodsman." Made popular by the movie Forrest Gump.

Foster

Old English, meaning "woodsman."

Fotini

(alt. Fotis)

Greek, meaning "light."

Famous male guitarists

Brian (May)

Carlos (Santana)

Chuck (Berry)

Eddie (Van Halen)

Eric (Clapton)

Frank (Zappa)

Jeff (Beck)

Jimi/Jimmy (Hendrix/Page)

Joe (Satriani)

Keith (Richards)

Prince (Rogers Nelson)

Francesco

(alt. Francis, Francisco, Franco, François)

Latin, meaning "from France." After the election of Pope Francis, Francesco has become the most popular name for baby boys in Italy.

Frank

(alt. Frankie, Franklin, Franz)

Middle English, meaning "free landholder." Famous Franks include singers Frank Sinatra and Frank Zappa, and 32nd US President Franklin D. Roosevelt.

Fraser

(alt. Frasier)

Scottish, meaning "of the forest men." Frasier was a 1990s sitcom revolving around main character, Dr. Frasier Crane.

Frederick

(alt. Fred, Freddie, Freddy)

Old German, meaning "peaceful ruler." There is a spelling or pronunciation variation of Frederick in virtually every Western language.

Furman

Old German, meaning "ferryman."

G

Boys' names

Gabino
Latin, meaning "God is my strength."

Gabriel
(alt. Gale)
Hebrew, meaning "hero of God."
An archangel of God.

Gael
(alt. Gale)
English, old reference to the Celts.
Gale has increased in popularity since
The Hunger Games series.

Gage
(alt. Gaige)
Old French, meaning "pledge."

Galen
Greek, meaning "healer." Name of
an ancient Roman philosopher.

Galileo
Italian, meaning "from Galilee."
Galileo Galilei was an important
physicist during the Scientific
Revolution.

Ganesh
Hindi, meaning "Lord of the
throngs." One of the Hindu deities.

Gannon
Irish, meaning "fair skinned."

Gareth
(alt. Garth)
Welsh, meaning "gentle." Also the
name of one of the Knights of the
Round Table.

Garfield
Old English, meaning "spear field."
Also the name of the cartoon cat.

Garland

English, as in "garland of flowers."

Garrett

(alt. Garet, Gared, Garratt, Garrod)

Derived in the Middle Ages from Gerald or Gerard. Garret the Great was a political powerhouse in 15th-century Ireland.

Gary

(alt. Garry, Geary)

Germanic, meaning "spear." The name peaked in popularity in the 1950s, when actor Gary Cooper won an Oscar. Modern Garys include actor Gary Oldman.

Gaspar

(alt. Gaspard)

Persian, meaning "treasurer." A children's cartoon character from *Gaspar and Lisa*.

Gaston

From the region in the south of France.

Gavin

(alt. Gawain)

Scottish/Welsh, meaning "little falcon." Gavin DeGraw and Gavin Christopher are both singers.

Gene

Greek, shortened form of Eugene, meaning "well born." Made popular by actor and dancer Gene Kelly.

Gennaro

Italian, meaning "of Janus."

Geoffrey

(abbrev. Geoff)

Old German, meaning "peace." Actor Geoffrey Rush appeared in *Shine* and the *Pirates of the Caribbean* series.

George

(alt. Giorgio)

Greek, meaning "farmer." Queen Elizabeth's great-grandson Prince George is third in line to the British throne.

Gerald

(alt. Geraldo, Gerard, Gerardo, Gerhard)

Old German, meaning "spear ruler." Former President of the United States Gerald Ford is the only person to have served as both president and vice president without being elected to either position, thanks to two infamous resignations before him.

Geronimo

Italian, meaning "sacred name." Geronimo led the Apache Indians against the Spanish in the 19th century.

Gerry

English, meaning "independent." Famous Gerrys include singer Gerry Rafferty.

Gert

Old German, meaning "strong spear."

Gervase

Old German, meaning "with honor." Gervase Peterson is a long-time *Survivor* contestant.

Giacomo

Italian, meaning "God's son." Legendary womanizer Casanova's full name was actually Giacomo Girolame Casanova.

Gibson

English, meaning "son of Gilbert." The name of a legendary guitar company.

Gideon

Hebrew, meaning "tree cutter." Found in the Bible.

Gilbert
(alt. Gilberto)

French, meaning "bright promise." One half of the famous comedy opera duo Gilbert and Sullivan.

Giles

Greek, meaning "small goat."

Gino

Italian, meaning "well born."

Giovanni

Italian form of John, meaning "God is gracious." Actor Giovanni Ribisi is known for his roles in *Friends* and *Avatar*.

Giulio

Italian, meaning "youthful."

Giuseppe

Italian form of Joseph, meaning "Jehovah increases."

Glen
(alt. Glenn, Glyn)

English, from the word "glen." Glenn Miller was a world-renowned big band director and composer.

Godfrey

German, meaning "peace of God." Now associated woith the comedian Godfrey.

Gordon

Gaelic, meaning "large fortification." Gordon Ramsay is a chef and reality TV star.

Gottlieb

German, meaning "good love." Also one of composer Mozart's birth names.

Graeme
(alt. Graham)

English, meaning "gravelled area."

Grant

English, from the word "grant."

Granville

English, meaning "gravelly town." Granville Woods was the first African-American electrical engineer after the Civil War.

Gray
(alt. Grey)

English, from the word "gray."

Grayson

English, meaning "son of gray."

Green

English, from the word "green." The Green Lantern is a superhero from DC Comics.

Gregory
(alt. Gregorio, Grieg; abbrev. Greg)

English, meaning "watcher." Actor Gregory Peck was known for his role in *To Kill A Mockingbird*.

Griffin

English, from the word "griffin." A mythological creature.

Guido

Italian, meaning "guide." Popularized after the show *Jersey Shore*.

Guillaume

French form of William, meaning "strong protector."

Gulliver

English, meaning "glutton." Made popular after the publication of *Gulliver's Travels* by Jonathan Swift.

Gunther

German, meaning "warrior." Gunther von Hagans is the *Body Works* artist.

Gurpreet

Indian, meaning "love of the teacher."

Gustave
(abbrev. Gus)

Scandinavian, meaning "royal staff."

Guy

Englishform of Guido, meaning "guide." Chef Guy Fieri regularly appears on the Food Network.

H

Boys' names

Habib
Arabic, meaning "beloved one."

Haden
(alt. Haiden, Hayden, Haydn)
English, meaning "hedged valley."

Hades
Greek, meaning "sightless." Name of the underworld in Greek mythology.

Hadrian
From Hadria, a north Italian city. The name of an influential Roman emperor.

Hadwin
Old English, meaning "friend in war."

Hakeem
Arabic, meaning "wise and insightful." Actor Hakeem Kae-Kazim is known for his role in *Hotel Rwanda*.

Hamid
Arabic, meaning "praiseworthy." Hamid Karzai was the president of Afghanistan 2004–14.

Hamilton
Old English, meaning "flat-topped hill." Alexander Hamilton was one of the nation's Founding Fathers.

Hamish
Scottish form of James, meaning "he who supplants."

Hampus
Swedish form of Homer, meaning "pledge." Hampus Lindholm currently plays for the Anaheim Ducks.

Hamza
Arabic, meaning "lamb." Also a letter in the Arabic alphabet.

Han

(alt. Hannes, Hans)

Scandinavian, meaning "the Lord is gracious." Han Solo is a central character in the *Star Wars* films.

Hank

German, form of Henry, meaning "home ruler." Singer Hank Williams was a country superstar.

Hansel

German, meaning "the Lord is gracious." *Hansel and Gretel* is a children's fairy tale by the Brothers Grimm.

Hardy

English, meaning "tough."

Harlan

English, meaning "dweller by the boundary wood."

Harland

Old English, meaning "army land." KFC was founded by Colonel Harland David Sanders.

Harley

Old English, meaning "hare meadow." Associated with the Harley Davidson motorcycle company.

Harmon

Old German, meaning "soldier."

Harold

Scandinavian, meaning "army ruler." Actor Harold Ramis was known for his roles in *Ghostbusters* and *Stripes*.

Harrison

(alt. Harison)

Old English, meaning "son of Harry." Famous Harrisons include actor Harrison Ford, and it is the middle name of the son of Prince Harry and Megan Markle.

Harry

Old German, form of Henry, meaning "home ruler." Famous Harrys include fictional character Harry Potter and singer Harry Styles.

Hart

Old English, meaning "stag."

Harvey

Old English, meaning "strong and worthy." The title character of the film *Harvey*, starring James Stewart.

Haskell

Hebrew, meaning "intellect."

Hassan

Arabic, meaning "handsome." Hassan Rouhani is the current president of Iran.

Heart

English, from the word "heart."

Heath

English, meaning "heath" or "moor." Actor Heath Ledger was known for his roles in *Brokeback Mountain* and *The Dark Knight*.

Heathcliff

English, meaning "cliff near a heath." Also the main male character in Emily Bronte's novel *Wuthering Heights*.

Heber

Hebrew, meaning "partner."

Hector

Greek, meaning "steadfast."

Henry

(alt. Hal, Hale, Henri, Hendrik, Hendrix)

Old German, meaning "home ruler." Eight kings of England were called Henry. Harry is often used as a name by boys given the name Henry, as with Prince Harry, who is officially Prince Henry of Wales.

Henson

English, meaning "son of Henry."

Herbert

(alt., Herb, Heriberto; abbrev. Bert, Herbie)

Old German, meaning "illustrious warrior." Herbert Hoover was the 31st President of the United States.

Herman

(alt. Herminio, Hermon)

Old German, meaning "soldier." Herman Melville was the author of *Moby-Dick*.

Hermes

Greek, meaning "messenger." Hermes was the messenger of the gods in Greek mythology.

Herschel

Yiddish, meaning "deer."

Hezekiah

Hebrew, meaning "God gives strength."

Hideki

Japanese, meaning "excellent trees." The prime minister of Japan during World War II was Hideki Tojo.

Hideo

Japanese, meaning "excellent name."

Hilario

Latin, meaning "cheerful, happy."

Hilary

(alt. Hillary)

English, meaning "cheerful." Sir Edmund Hillary became the first Westerner to reach the summit of Mount Everest, in 1953.

Hillel

Hebrew, meaning "greatly praised."

Hilliard

Old German, meaning "battle guard."

Hilton

Old English, meaning "hill settlement." The name of a large hotel chain.

Hiram
(alt. Hyrum)

Hebrew, meaning "exalted brother."

Hiro

Spanish, meaning "sacred name." Hiro is a character on *Heroes*.

Hiroshi

Japanese, meaning "generous."

Hirsch

Yiddish, meaning "deer."

Hobart

English, meaning "bright and shining intellect."

Hodge

English, meaning "son of Roger."

Hogan

Gaelic, meaning "youth." Became well known after the success of sitcom *Hogan's Heroes* in the 1960s. Also made famous by wrestler Hulk Hogan.

Holden

English, meaning "deep valley." Holden Caulfield is the teenage protagonist of *The Catcher in the Rye*.

Hollis

Old English, meaning "holly tree."

Homer

Greek, meaning "pledge." Famous Homers include the ancient Greek poet, and Homer Simpson from *The Simpsons*.

Honorius

Latin, meaning "honorable."

Horace

Latin, common name of the Roman poet Quintus Horatius Flaccus.

Houston

Old English, meaning "Hugh's town."

Howard

Old English, meaning "noble watchman." Famous Howards include Howard Carter, who discovered the tomb of King Tut, and Howard Hughes, the aviator and movie maker.

Howell

Welsh, meaning "eminent and remarkable."

Hoyt

Norse, meaning "spirit" or "soul," or Old English meaning "hill inhabitant." Hoyt Fortenberry is a character in *True Blood*.

Hristo

From Christo, meaning "follower of Christ."

Hubert

German, meaning "bright and shining intellect." Givenchy's founder was Count Hubert de Givenchy.

Hudson

Old English, meaning "son of Hugh." Associated with the Hudson River.

Hugh
(alt. Hugo, Huw, Ugo)

Old German, meaning "soul, mind, and intellect." Famous Hughs include actors Hugh Jackman, Hugh Laurie, and Hugh Grant.

Humbert

Old German, meaning "famous giant." Became well known due to the paedophile protagonist of Vladimir Nabokov's *Lolita*.

Humphrey

Old German, meaning "peaceful warrior." Actor Humphrey Bogart is best known for his role in *Casablanca*.

Hunter

English, from the word "hunter." Name of singer Hunter Hayes.

Hurley

Gaelic, meaning "sea tide."

Huxley

Old English, meaning "Hugh's meadow."

I

Boys' names

Iago
Spanish, meaning "he who supplants." Also the name of the villain in Shakespeare's *Othello*.

Ian
(alt. Iain, Ion)
Gaelic, variant of John, meaning "God is gracious." Novelist Ian Fleming wrote the "James Bond" novels.

Ianto
Welsh, meaning "gift of God."

Ibrahim
Arabic, meaning "father of many." An Arabic name for the father of Islam, Abraham.

Ichabod
Hebrew, meaning "glory is good." Also the name of the protagonist in *The Legend of Sleepy Hollow*.

Ichiro
Japanese, meaning "firstborn son."

Idris
Welsh, meaning "fiery leader." Actor Idris Elba is known for his roles in *Luther* and *Mandela: Long Walk to Freedom*.

Ifan
Welsh variant of John, meaning "God is gracious."

Ignacio
Latin, meaning "ardent" or "burning."

Ignatz
German, meaning "fiery."

Igor
Russian, meaning "Ing's soldier."

Ikaika
Hawaiian, meaning "strong."

Ike
Hebrew, short for Isaac, meaning "laughter." Famous Ikes include singer Ike Turner and former US President Dwight D. Eisenhower (known as Ike).

Ilan
Hebrew, meaning "tree."

Ilias
Greek variant of Elijah, Hebrew, meaning "the Lord is my God."

Indiana
Latin, meaning "from India." Also the name of a US state.

Indigo
English, describing a deep blue color derived from a plant.

Indio
Spanish, meaning "indigenous people."

Ingo
Danish, meaning "meadow."

Inigo
Spanish, meaning "fiery." Inigo Montoya is a character in *The Princess Bride*.

Ioannis
Greek, meaning "the Lord is gracious."

Ira
Hebrew, meaning "full grown and watchful."

Irvin
(alt. Irving, Irwin)
Gaelic, meaning "green and fresh water." Composer Irving Berlin is known for songs such as "White Christmas."

Isaac
(alt. Isaak)
Hebrew, meaning "laughter." Isaac was the son of Abraham and Sarah in the Bible and the Qur'an.

Isadore
(alt. Isidore, Isidro)
Greek, meaning "gift of Isis."

Isai
(alt. Isaiah, Isaias, Izaiah)
Arabic, meaning "protection and security."

Iser
Yiddish, meaning "God wrestler."

Ishmael
(alt. Ismael)
Hebrew, meaning "God listens." The narrator and protagonist of *Moby-Dick*, by Herman Melville.

Israel

Hebrew, meaning "God perseveres."
Also the name of the country.

Istvan

Hungarian variant of Stephen,
meaning "crowned."

Itai

Hebrew, meaning "the Lord is with
me."

Ivan

A Slavic version of John, meaning
"God is gracious." Several Russian
tsars bore the name, including the
infamous Ivan the Terrible. Ivan
Rodriguez was a Major League
Baseball player for many years.

Ivanhoe

Russian, meaning "God is gracious."
Also title of the novel by Walter
Scott.

Ivey

English, variant of Ivy.

Ivo

French, from the word "yves,"
meaning "yew tree."

Ivor

Scandinavian, meaning "yew."
Associated with the Ivor Novello
songwriting awards.

Ivory

English, from the word "ivory."

Boys' names

Jabari
Swahili, meaning "valiant."

Jabez
Hebrew, meaning "borne in pain."

Jace
(alt. Jaece, Jase, Jayce)
Hebrew, meaning "healer."

Jacek
(alt. Jacirto)
Polish, meaning "hyacinth." Derived from the Greek name Hyakinthos, which comes from a myth about a beautiful boy.

Jack
(alt. Jackie, Jacky, Jacques, Jaquez)
From the Hebrew John, meaning "God is gracious." Famous Jacks include actors Jack Black, Jack Nicholson, and Jack Lemmon.

Jackson
(alt. Jaxon)
English, meaning "son of Jack." Artist Jackson Pollock is known for his large, paint-splashed paintings.

Jacob
(alt. Jaco, Jacobo, Jago)
Hebrew, meaning "he who supplants." A main character in the *Twilight* series.

Jaden
(alt. Jadyn, Jaeden, Jaiden, Jaidyn, Jayden, Jaydin)
Hebrew, meaning "Jehovah has heard." Will Smith and Jada Pinkett Smith's son is Jaden.

Jafar
Arabic, meaning "stream." The villain in Disney's *Aladdin*.

Jagger

Old English, meaning "one who cuts." Made famous by Rolling Stones singer Mick Jagger.

Jaheem
(alt. Jaheim)

Hebrew, meaning "raised up."

Jahir

Hindi, meaning "jewel."

Jaime
(alt. Jamie))

Variant for James, meaning "he who supplants." "J'aime" is also French for "I love."

Jair
(alt. Jairo)

Hebrew, meaning "God enlightens."

Jake

Shortened form of Jacob, meaning "he who supplants." Famous Jakes include actor Jake Gyllenhaal and pitcher Jake Peavy.

Jalen

American English, meaning "healer" or "tranquil." Derives from the Greek Galen.

Jali

Gujarati, meaning "latticed screen."

Jalon

Greek, meaning "healer" or "tranquil."

Jamaal
(alt. Jamal, Jamar, Jamarcus, Jamari, Jamarion, Jamir)

Arabic, meaning "handsome." Jamar is a modern variant of the name.

James
(abbrev. Jamie, Jaimie, Jim, Jimmy)

English, meaning "he who supplants." Famous Jameses include actors James Franco, James Coburn, and Jim Carey, and fictional characters James Bond and James T. Kirk.

Jameson
(alt. Jamison)

English, meaning "son of James." Associated with Jameson Irish Whiskey.

Jamil

Arabic, meaning "handsome."

Jamin

Hebrew, meaning "son of the right hand."

Jan
(alt. Janko, János)

Slavic, from John, meaning "the Lord is gracious." Also a term of endearment in Arabic, meaning "dear."

Janus

Latin, meaning "gateway." Roman god of doors, beginnings and endings.

Japheth
(alt. Japhet)

Hebrew, meaning "comely." One of the sons of Noah.

Jared
(alt. Jarem, Jaren, Jaret, Jarod, Jarrod)

Hebrew, meaning "descending." Actor Jared Leto appeared in *Dallas Buyers' Club*.

Jarlath

Gaelic, from Iarlaith, from St. Iarlaithe mac Loga.

Jarom

Greek, meaning "to raise and exalt." One of the prophets in the Book of Mormon.

Jarrell

Variant of Gerald, meaning "spear ruler."

Jarrett

Old English, meaning "spearbrave."

Jarvis

Old German, meaning "with honor."

Jason
(alt. Jayce)

Greek, meaning "healer." Famous Jasons include actors Jason Sudeikis and Jason Bateman, and singer Jason Derulo.

Jasper

Greek, meaning "treasure holder" or "speckled stone." Jasper as a stone has been used for jewelry for thousands of years.

Javen

Arabic, meaning "youth." One of Noah's grandsons in the Bible.

Javier

Spanish, meaning "bright." Actor Javier Bardem appeared in *Skyfall*.

Jay

Latin, meaning "jaybird." Associated with rapper Jay-Z.

Jaylan
(alt. Jaylen, Jalon)

Greek, meaning "healer."

Jeevan

Indian, meaning "life."

Jefferson

English, meaning "son of Jeffrey." Thomas Jefferson was the third president of the United States.

Jeffrey
(abbrev. Jeff)

Old German, meaning "peace." Famous Jeffs include actors Jeff Bridges and Jeff Daniels.

Jensen
(alt. Jenson)

Scandinavian, meaning "son of Jan." Famous Jensens include actor Jensen Ackles and Formula 1 driver Jenson Button.

Jeremy
(alt. Jem)

Hebrew, meaning "the Lord exalts." Famous Jeremys include Jeremy Renner and Jeremy Irons.

Jeriah

Hebrew, meaning "Jehovah has seen."

Jericho

Arabic, meaning "city of the moon." Site of the epic biblical Battle of Jericho.

Jermaine

Latin, meaning "brotherly." Jermaine Jackson was one of the original members of the Jackson Five.

Jerome

Greek, meaning "sacred name."

Jerry

English, from Gerald, meaning "spear ruler." Famous Jerrys include presenter Jerry Singer, comedian Jerry Seinfeld, and the film *Jerry Maguire*.

Jesse

Hebrew, meaning "the Lord exists." Famous Jesses include outlaw Jesse James.

Jesus

Hebrew, meaning "the Lord is Salvation" and the Son of God.

Jet
(alt. Jett)

English, meaning "black gemstone."

Jethro

Hebrew, meaning "eminent." Famous Jethros include the band Jethro Tull, and the father-in-law of Moses in the Bible.

Jiri
(alt. Jiro)

Czech, meaning "farmer."

Joachim

Hebrew, meaning "established by God." The name of the Virgin Mary's father in the Bible.

Joah
(alt. João)

Hebrew, meaning "God is gracious."

Joaquin
Hebrew, meaning "established by God." Academy Award-winner Joaquin Phoenix changed his name to "Leaf" as a child to match his siblings River and Rain.

Joel
Hebrew, meaning "Jehovah is the Lord." Famous Joels include comedian Joel McHale and singer Joel Madden.

John
(alt. Jon, Johnny)
Hebrew, meaning "God is gracious." Famous Johns include musicians John Lennon and John Legend, and comedian Jon Stewart. Actor Johnny Depp and singer Johnny Cash are both also Johns by birth.

Jolyon
English, meaning "young."

Jonah
(alt. Jonas)
Hebrew, meaning "dove." A figure in the Bible who was swallowed by a whale.

Jonathan
(alt. Johnathan, Johnathon, Jonathon; abbrev. Jon, Johnny, Jonny, Jonty)
Hebrew, meaning "God is gracious." Famous Jonathans include actors Jonathan Taylor Thomas and Jonathan Rhys Meyers, and author Jonathan Swift.

Jordan
(alt. Jory, Judd)
Hebrew, meaning "downflowing." Michael Jordan is a legendary basketball player.

Jorge
From George, meaning "farmer." Actor Jorge Garcia is known for his role as Hurley in Lost.

José
Spanish variant of Joseph, meaning "God increases." Associated with Jose Cuervo tequila.

Joseph
(abbrev. Joe, Joey, Joss)
Hebrew, meaning "Jehovah increases." Famous Josephs include actor Joseph Gordon-Levitt and baseball legend Joe DiMaggio.

Joshua
(alt. Joshué; abbrev. Josh)
Hebrew, meaning "Jehovah is salvation." The leader of the Israelites after Moses' death in the Bible. Actor Josh Hutcherson is known for his role in The Hunger Games trilogy.

Josiah
Hebrew, meaning "God helps." One of the kings of Judah in the Bible.

Jovan
Latin, meaning "the supreme God."

Joweese

Native American, meaning "chirping bird." More commonly used for girls originally, it has now become a boys' name.

Joyce

Latin, meaning "joy." Used for boys and girls.

Juan

Spanish variant of John, meaning "God is gracious." Juan Pablo Galavis was a notorious contestant on the TV show *The Bachelor*.

Jubal

Hebrew, meaning "ram's horn."

Jude

Hebrew, meaning "praise" or "thanks." Associated with the Beatles' song "Hey Jude."

Judson

Variant of Jude, meaning "praise" or "thanks."

Julian

(alt. Julien, Julio; abbrev. Jules)

Greek, meaning "belonging to Julius." The original calendar in the Roman Empire was the Julian calendar.

Julius

Latin, meaning "youthful." Julius Caesar was a Roman emperor.

Junior

Latin, meaning "the younger one." Can also be used as a suffix to names to denote a name that has been passed down generations—for example James Earl Carter, Sr. was the father of US President James Earl Carter, Jr.

Junius

Latin, meaning "young."

Jupiter

Latin, meaning "the supreme God." Jupiter was king of the Roman gods and the god of thunder.

Juraj

Hebrew, meaning "God is my judge."

Jurgen

German form of George, meaning "farmer."

Justice

English, from the word "justice," meaning a set of moral values, ethics, and law.

Justin

(alt. Justus)

Latin, meaning "just and upright." Famous Justins include singers Justin Timberlake and Justin Bieber.

Juwan

Hebrew, meaning "the Lord is gracious."

Boys' names

Kabelo

African, meaning "gift."

Kade

Scottish, meaning "from the wetlands."

Kadeem

Arabic, meaning "one who serves." Actor Kadeem Hardison is known for his role in *A Different World*.

Kaden

(alt. Kadin, Kaeden, Kaedin, Kaiden)
Arabic, meaning "companion."

Kadir

Arabic, meaning "capable and competent."

Kafka

Czech, meaning "bird-like." Name of the influential author Franz Kafka.

Kahekili

Hawaiian, meaning "the thunder." Also the name of several kings of Maui.

Kai

Greek, meaning "keeper of the keys." Kai also means "dog" in Cornish, "ocean water" in Hawaiian, and "food" in Maori.

Kaito

Japanese, meaning "ocean and sake dipper." One of the most popular names for boys in Japan.

Kalani

Hawaiian, meaning "sky."

Kale

German, meaning "free man."

Kaleb

Hebrew, meaning "dog" or "aggressive." Also an alternate spelling for Caleb.

Kalen
(alt. *Kaelen, Kalan*)

Gaelic, meaning "uncertain."

Kaleo
Hawaiian, meaning "the voice." Kaleo Kanahele is a silver medal-winning paralympian in volleyball.

Kamari
Indian, meaning "the enemy of desire."

Kamil
Arabic, meaning "perfection"; Polish/Slovakian, meaning "religious service attender."

Kane
Gaelic, meaning "little battler." The title character of the film *Citizen Kane*.

Kani
Hawaiian, meaning "sound."

Kanye
Town in Botswana. Made popular by rapper Kanye West.

Kareem
(alt. *Karim*)

Arabic, meaning "generous." Kareem Abdul-Jabur is a legendary basketball player.

Karl
(alt. *Karlson*)

Old German, meaning "free man." Actor Karl Urban is known for his roles in *The Lord of the Rings* and *Star Trek*.

Kavon
Gaelic, meaning "handsome."

Kayden
Arabic, meaning "companion."

Kazimierz
Polish, meaning "declares peace."

Kazuki
Japanese, meaning "radiant hope."

Kazuo
Japanese, meaning "harmonious man." Depending on the characters/spellings used, Kazuo can also mean "first son" or "first in leadership."

Keagan
(alt. *Keegan, Kegan*)

Gaelic, meaning "small flame."

Keane
Gaelic, meaning "fighter."

Keanu
Hawaiian, meaning "breeze." Actor Keanu Reeves is known for his roles in *Speed* and *The Matrix* trilogy.

Keary
Gaelic, meaning "black-haired."

Keaton
English, meaning "place of hawks."

Keeler
Gaelic, meaning "beautiful and graceful."

Keenan
(alt. Kenan, Keenen)
Gaelic, meaning "little ancient one." Keenen Ivory Wayans is one of the Wayans comedy brothers.

Keiji
Japanese, meaning "govern with discretion."

Keir
Gaelic, meaning "dark-haired" or "dark-skinned."

Keith
Gaelic, meaning "woodland." Keith Richards is one of the legendary members of the Rolling Stones.

Kekoa
(alt. Koa)
Hawaiian, meaning "brave one" or "soldier."

Kelby
Old English, meaning "farmhouse near the stream."

Kell
(alt. Kellan, Kellen, Kelley, Kelly, Kiel)
Norse, meaning "spring." Associated with the ancient Book of Kells.

Kelsey
Old English, meaning "victorious ship." Actor Kelsey Grammer is known for his roles in *Cheers* and *Frasier*.

Kelton
Old English, meaning "town of the keels."

Kelvin
Old English, meaning "friend of ships." A kelvin is a unit of temperature measurement.

Kendal
Old English, meaning "the Kent river valley."

Kendon
Old English, meaning "brave guard."

Kendrick
Gaelic, meaning "royal ruler."

Kenelm
Old English, meaning "bold."

Kenji
Japanese, meaning "intelligent second son." Also the name of a period in Japanese history in the 13th century.

Kennedy

Gaelic, meaning "helmet head."
The Kennedy family is a prominent
American Catholic dynasty, whose
members included the 35th
President of the United States, John
F. Kennedy.

Kenneth

(alt. Kenne; abbrev. Ken)

Gaelic, meaning "born of fire." Sir
Kenneth Branagh is an acclaimed
actor of stage and screen.

Kennison

English, meaning "son of Kenneth."

Kent

English, meaning "rim or border."
Associated with Clark Kent, aka
Superman.

Kenton

English, meaning "town of Ken."

Kenya

(alt. Kenyatta, Kenyon)

From the country and mountain in
Africa.

Kenzo

Japanese, meaning "wise." Kenzo is
the name of a fashion brand.

Keola

Hawaiian, meaning "life."

Keon

(alt. Keoni)

Persian, meaning "King of Kings."
In Hawaiian, the name also means
"God is gracious."

Kepler

German, meaning "hat maker."

Kermit

(alt. Kerwin)

Gaelic, meaning "without envy."
Associated with Kermit the Frog.

Kerr

English, meaning "wetland." Kerr
Smith is an American actor.

Keshav

Indian, meaning "beautiful haired."
One of the names for Vishnu in the
Hindu religion.

Kevin

Gaelic, meaning "handsome
beloved." Famous Kevins include
actors Kevin Bacon and Kevin Kline.

Khalid

(alt. Khalif)

Arabic, meaning "immortal." Actor
Khalid Abdalla is known for his roles
in *United 93* and *The Kite Runner*.

Khalil

Arabic, meaning "friend." Khalil
Gibran is an influential poet, writer,
and philosopher.

Kian
(alt. Keyon, Kyan)

Persian, meaning "king or realm." In Ireland, the same spelling also means "ancient."

Kiefer

German, meaning "barrel maker." *24* star Kiefer Sutherland's full name is Kiefer William Frederick Dempsey George Rufus Sutherland.

Kieran
(alt. Kieron, Kyron)

Gaelic, meaning "black." Actor Kieran Culkin is known for his role in *Scott Pilgrim vs. the World*.

Kijana

Swahili, meaning "youth."

Kilby

English, from the town of the same name.

Kilian

Irish, meaning "bright-headed."

Kimani

African, meaning "beautiful and sweet."

King

English, meaning "male ruler of state."

Kingsley

English, meaning "the king's meadow." Kingsley Shacklebolt is a character in the *Harry Potter* series.

Kirby

German, meaning "settlement by a church." Also the name of a small, pink, bubble-like video game character.

Kirk

Old German, meaning "church." Famous Kirks include Kirk Douglas and Captain James T. Kirk from *Star Trek*.

Klaus

German, meaning "victorious."

Kobe
(alt. Koda, Kody)

Japanese, meaning "a Japanese city." Basketball legend Kobe Bryant passed away unexpectedly in 2020.

Kofi

Ghanaian, meaning "born on Friday." Kofi Annan was the secretary general of the UN until 2006.

Kohana

Japanese, meaning "little flower."

Kojo

Ghanaian, meaning "Monday."

Korben
(alt. Korbin)

Gaelic, meaning "a steep hill." Korben Dallas is a character in *The Fifth Element*.

Kramer

German, meaning "shopkeeper." Kramer is a character from *Seinfeld*.

Kurt

German, meaning "courageous advice." Famous Kurts include *Glee* character Kurt, actor Kurt Russell, and the late Nirvana singer Kurt Cobain.

Kurtis

French, meaning "courtier."

Names of poets

Alfred (Lord Tennyson)

Allen (Ginsberg)

Dylan (Thomas)

Geoffrey (Chaucer)

Langston (Hughes)

Ralph (Waldo Emerson)

Robert (Burns)

Seamus (Heaney)

Walt (Whitman)

William (Wordsworth)

Kwame

Ghanaian, meaning "born on Saturday."

Kyden

English, meaning "narrow little fire."

Kyle
(alt. Kylan, Kyleb, Kyler)

Gaelic, meaning "narrow and straight." Actor Kyle Massey is known for his roles on The Disney Channel.

Kyllion

Irish, meaning "war."

Kylo
(alt. Kyloh)

American English, from the Latin word for "sky." Kylo Ren is a main character in the modern *Star Wars* films.

Kyree

From Cree, a Canadian tribe.

Kyros

Greek, meaning "legitimate power."

L

Boys' names

Laban
Hebrew, meaning "white." Laban is the brother of Rebekah in the Bible.

Lachlan
Gaelic, meaning "from the land of lakes."

Lacy
Old French, after the place in France. Masculine form of Lacey.

Lalit
Hindi, meaning "beautiful."

Lamar
(alt. Lemar)
Old German, meaning "water." Lamar Odom is known for his marriage to Khloe Kardashian and his skills as a basketball player.

Lambert
Scandinavian, meaning "land brilliant."

Lambros
Greek, meaning "brilliant and radiant."

Lamont
Old Norse, meaning "law man."

Lance
French, meaning "land." Lance Armstrong is a disgraced former racing cyclist.

Lancelot
Variant of Lance, meaning "land." The name of one of the Knights of the Round Table.

Landen
(alt. Lando, Landon, Landyn, Langdon)
English, meaning "long hill."

Lane
(alt. Layne)
English, from the word "lane."

Lannie
(alt. Lanny)

German, meaning "precious." Also a nickname for Roland or Orlando.

Larkin

Gaelic, meaning "rough" or "fierce." Philip Larkin was a famous poet.

Laron

French, meaning "thief."

Lasse

Finnish, meaning "girl." (Still, ironically, a boy's name.) Lasse Holstrom is a film director and Lasse Viren one of the all-time great long distance runners.

Laszlo

Hungarian, meaning "glorious rule."

Lathyn

Latin, meaning "fighter."

Latif

Arabic, meaning "gentle."

Laurel

Latin, meaning "bay." One of the founders of Jamaican ska music was Laurel Aitken. More commonly a girls' name.

Laurent

French, from Laurence, meaning "man from Laurentum." The founder of fashion line YSL was Yves Saint Laurent.

Lawrence
(alt. Lars, Lawrence; abbrev. Larry)

Latin, meaning "man from Laurentum." Actor Laurence Olivier was a stage legend also known for his roles in dozens of Hollywood movies. Larry King is a longstanding live TV presenter.

Lawson

Old English, meaning "son of Lawrence."

Lazarus

Hebrew, meaning "God is my help."

Leandro

Latin, meaning "lion man."

Lear

German, meaning "of the meadow." The title character in Shakespeare's play *King Lear*.

Lee
(alt. Leigh)

Old English, meaning "meadow" or "valley." Famous Lees include actor Lee Marvin and JFK assassin Lee Harvey Oswald.

Leib

Yiddish, meaning "lion."

Leif
(alt. Leiv, Lief, Liev)

Scandinavian, meaning "heir." Actor Liev Schreiber is known for his roles in *X-Men Origins: Wolverine*, and the *Scream* trilogy.

Leith
From the Scottish town of the same name.

Lennox
(alt. Lenny)

Gaelic, meaning "with many elm trees." Famous Lennoxes include boxer Lennox Lewis.

Leo
Latin, meaning "lion." Also the name of the star sign.

Leon
Latin, meaning "lion." Associated with the band Kings of Leon.

Leonard
Old German, meaning "lion strength." Actor Leonard Nimoy was known for his role in *Star Trek*.

Leonardo
Italian, meaning "bold lion." Artist Leonardo da Vinci painted the *Mona Lisa*.

Leopold
German, meaning "brave people."

Leroy
French, meaning "king." The title character of the song "Bad Bad Leroy Brown."

Lesley
(alt. Leslie; abbrev. Les)

Scottish, meaning "holly garden." Used for boys and girls.

Lester
English, meaning "from Leicester."

Lewis
French, meaning "renowned fighter." Famous Lewises include comedian Lewis Black and author Lewis Carroll.

Lexar
(alt. Lex, Lexer)

Shortened form of Alexander, meaning "man's defender."

Liam
German, meaning "helmet." Famous Liams include actor Liam Neeson and One Direction member Liam Payne.

Lincoln
English, meaning "lake colony." Abraham Lincoln was the 16th President of the United States.

Lindsay
(alt. Lindsey)

Scottish, meaning "linden tree." Singer Lindsey Buckingham is a founding member of Fleetwood Mac. Used for boys and girls.

Linus
Latin, meaning "lion." A character in the *Peanuts* cartoon.

Lionel

English, meaning "lion." Famous Lionels include singer Lionel Richie, and composer Lionel Bart.

Llewellyn

Welsh, meaning "like a lion."

Lloyd

Welsh, meaning "gray-haired and sacred." Andrew Lloyd Webber is the composer of *Cats* and other musicals.

Logan

Gaelic, meaning "hollow." Increased in popularity after 2017's *Logan* Wolverine film.

Lonnie

English, meaning "lion strength."

Lorcan

Gaelic, meaning "little fierce one."

Louis

(alt. Lou, Louie, Luigi, Luis)

French, meaning "famous warrior." Famous Louises include fifth in line to the British throne Prince Louis and designer Louis Vuitton.

Lucas

(alt. Lukas, Luca)

English, meaning "man from Luciana." George Lucas is the legendary *Star Wars* producer.

Lucian

(alt. Lucio)

Latin, meaning "light."

Ludwig

German, meaning "famous fighter." Ludwig van Beethoven was a hugely influential composer.

Luke

(alt. Luc, Luka)

Latin, meaning "from Lucanus" (in southern Italy). Famous Lukes include the Gospel of Luke from the Bible, *Star Wars* character Luke Skywalker, and actor Luke Perry.

Lupe

Latin, meaning "wolf." Lupe Fiasco is a rapper.

Luther

German, meaning "soldier of the people." Superman's arch-enemy is supervillain Lex Luther.

Lyle

French, meaning "the island." Lyle Lovett is a country singer-songwriter and actor.

Lyn

(alt. Lyndon)

Spanish, meaning "pretty." Used for both boys and girls.

M Boys' names

Mac
(alt. Mack, Mackie)
Scottish, meaning "son of."

Macaulay
Scottish, meaning "son of the phantom." Actor Macaulay Culkin starred in the *Home Alone* films.

Mace
English, meaning "heavy staff" or "club." Also a shortened form of Mason.

Mackenzie
Scottish, meaning "the fair one." Actor Mackenzie Crook is known for his roles in *Pirates of the Caribbean* and *Game of Thrones*.

Mackland
Scottish, meaning "land of Mac."

Macon
French, from the name of towns in France and Georgia.

Macsen
Scottish, meaning "son of Mac."

Madden
(alt. Mads)
Irish, meaning "descendant of the hound." Associated with the Madden NFL gaming series.

Maddox
(alt. Maddux)
English, meaning "good" or "generous." Derived from Madoc, who was a legendary Welsh prince. Name chosen by Angelina Jolie for her first adopted child, now Maddox Jolie-Pitt.

Madison
(alt. Madsen)

Irish, meaning "son of Madden." James Madison was the fourth President of the United States.

Magnus
(alt. Manus)

Latin, meaning "great." Popular name in Scandinavia.

Maguire

Gaelic, meaning "son of the beige one." The title character of the movie *Jerry Maguire*.

Mahesh

Hindi, meaning "great ruler." One of the names for Lord Shiva in the Hindu faith.

Mahir

Arabic, meaning "skillful."

Mahlon

Hebrew, meaning "sickness."

Mahmoud

Arabic, meaning "praiseworthy." Mahmoud Ahmadinejad was the president of Iran until 2013.

Mahoney

Irish, meaning "bear."

Major

English, from the word "major."

Makal

From Michael, meaning "close to God."

Makani

Hawaiian, meaning "wind."

Makis

Hebrew, meaning "gift from God."

Mako

Hebrew, meaning "God is with us."

Malachi
(alt. Malachy)

Irish, meaning "messenger of God." The name of a Jewish prophet in the Bible.

Malcolm

English, meaning "Columba's servant." Well-known Malcolms include activist Malcolm X, and sitcom *Malcolm in the Middle*.

Mali

Arabic, meaning "full and rich." Also the name of a West African republic.

Manfred

Old German, meaning "man of peace." Associated with the band Manfred Mann.

Manish
(alt. Manesh)

English, meaning "manly."

Manley

English, meaning "manly and brave."

Mannix

Gaelic, meaning "little monk."
Associated with the show *Mannix*.

Manoi
(alt. Manos)

Japanese, meaning "love springing
from intellect."

Manuel

Hebrew, meaning "God is with us."

Manus

Gaelic, meaning "great." Popular
during the Viking period.

Manzi

Italian, meaning "steer."

Marcel
(alt. Marcelino, Marcello)

French, meaning "little warrior."
Marcel Marceau was perhaps the
most famous mime of all time.

Mariano

Latin, meaning "from the god Mars."
Also a tribute to the Virgin Mary.

Mario
(alt. Marius)

Latin, meaning "manly." Famous
Marios include presenter Mario
Lopez, and Nintendo character
Mario.

Mark
*(alt. Marc, Marco, Marcus, Marek,
Markus)*

English, meaning "from the god
Mars." Famous Marks include
the Gospel of Mark in the Bible,
and actors Mark Hamill and Mark
Wahlberg.

Marley
(alt. Marlin, Marlow)

Old English, meaning "meadow near
the lake." Famous Marleys include
singer Bob Marley, and the infamous
Labrador dog Marley.

Marlon

English origin, meaning "little hawk."
Actor Marlon Brando is a famous
bearer of this name.

Marshall

Old French, meaning "caretaker of
horses."

Martin
(alt. Marty)

Latin, meaning "dedicated to Mars."
Famous Martins include actors
Martin Freeman and Martin Sheen,
and director Martin Scorsese.

Marvel

English, from the word "marvel."
Associated with Marvel comic books.

Marvin

Welsh, meaning "sea friend."
Famous Marvins include singer
Marvin Gaye, composer Marvin
Hamlish, and character Marvin
the Martian.

Mason

English, from the word for someone
who works with either stone or brick.

Mathias

(alt. Matthias)

Hebrew, meaning "gift of God."
Matthias was the apostle chosen to
replace Judas in the Bible.

Matthew

(alt. Mathieu; abbrev. Matt)

Hebrew, meaning "gift of the Lord."
Famous Matthews include the Gospel
of Matthew from the Bible, and
actors Matthew McConaughey and
Matthew Perry.

Maurice

(alt. Mauricio)

Latin, meaning "dark skinned" or
"Moorish." Famous Maurices
include children's author Maurice
Sendak.

Maverick

American English, meaning
"nonconformist leader." Made
popular by the movie *Top Gun*.

Maximillian

(alt. Max, Maxie, Maxim, Maximilian)

Latin, meaning "greatest." Also the
name of several Roman emperors.
More common now in the
abbreviated form Max, as with actor
Max Greenfield.

Maximino

Latin, meaning "little Max."

Maxwell

Latin, meaning "Maccus' stream."
Actor Maxwell Caulfield is known for
his role in *Dynasty*.

Maynard

Old German, meaning "brave." A
character from *Desperate Housewives*.

McArthur

Scottish, meaning "son of Arthur."
Associated with General Douglas
MacArthur.

McCoy

Scottish, meaning "son of Coy."

Mckenna

(alt. Mackenna)

Irish Gaelic, meaning "son of the
handsome one." Also used as a girl's
name.

Mearl

English, meaning "my earl."

Mederic

French, meaning "doctor."

Mekhi

African, meaning "who is God?"
Actor Mekhi Phifer is known for his
roles in *ER* and *8 Mile*.

Mel

Gaelic, meaning "smooth brow."
Famous Mels include actor Mel
Gibson. Also an abbreviation for
Melvin.

Melbourne

From the city in Victoria, Australia.

Melchior

Persian, meaning "king of the city."
The name of one of the Three Kings
in the Bible.

Melton

English, meaning "town of Mel."

Melva

Hawaiian, meaning "plumeria."

Melville

Scottish, meaning "town of Mel."
Author Herman Melville wrote
Moby-Dick.

Melvin

(alt. Melvyn; abbrev. Mel)

English, meaning "smooth brow."
Actor Melvyn Douglas was known for
his roles in *Hud* and *Being There*.

Memphis

Greek, meaning "established and
beautiful." Also the name of the
Tennessee city.

Mercer

English, from the word "mercer."

Merl

French, meaning "blackbird."

Merlin

Welsh, meaning "sea fortress." Merlin
is perhaps the most famous wizard
of all, appearing in stories from the
medieval era.

Merrick

Welsh, meaning "Moorish."

Merrill

Gaelic, meaning "shining sea."

Merritt

English, from the word "merit."

Merton

Old English, meaning "town by the
lake."

Meyer

Hebrew, meaning "bright farmer."

Michael

*(alt. Michel, Michele, Miguel; abbrev.
Mick, Mickey, Mike, Mikey)*

Hebrew, meaning "resembles
God." Famous Michaels include the
archangel, singers Michael Jackson
and Michael Bublé, and legendary
basketball player Michael Jordan.

Michalis
(alt. Miklos)

Greek form of Michael, meaning "resembles God."

Michelangelo

Italian, meaning "Michael's angel." Name of the famous Italian artist who painted the Sistine Chapel.

Milan

From the name of the Italian city. Also the name of Shakira's oldest son.

Miles
(alt. Milo, Milos, Myles)

English, from the word "miles." Famous Mileses include trumpeter Miles Davies, singer Miles Kane, and *Star Trek: Next Generation* character Miles O'Brien.

Milton

English, meaning "miller's town." Poet John Milton was the author of *Paradise Lost*.

Miro

Slavic, meaning "peace."

Misha

Russian, meaning "who is like God."

Mitchell
(abbrev. Mitch)

English, meaning "who is like God."

Modesto

Italian, meaning "modest." Also the name of a Californian town.

Moe

Hebrew, meaning "God's helmet." Moe is a character from *The Simpsons*.

Mohamed
(alt. Mohammad, Mohamet, Mohammed, Muhammad)

Arabic, meaning "praiseworthy." Acknowledged as the prophet and founder of Islam.

Monroe

Gaelic, meaning "mouth of the river Rotha."

Monserrate

Latin, meaning "jagged mountain."

Montague
(abbrev. Monty)

French, meaning "pointed hill."

Montana

Latin, meaning "mountain." Also the name of the state.

Monte

Italian, meaning "mountain."

Montgomery
(abbrev. Monty)

Variant of Montague, meaning "pointed hill." Actor Montgomery Clift was known for his roles in *From Here to Eternity* and *A Place in the Sun*.

Moody

English, from the word "moody."

Mordecai

Hebrew, meaning "little man."

Morgan

Welsh, meaning "circling sea." Famous Morgans include actor Morgan Freeman and filmmaker Morgan Spurlock. Can be both a boys' and girls' name.

Moritz

Latin, meaning "dark skinned and Moorish." Also a German variation of Maurice.

Moroccan

Arabic, meaning "from Morocco." Popularized by Mariah Carey's choice for her son.

Morpheus

Greek, meaning "shape." The Roman god of dreams in the epic poem *Metamorphoses*.

Morris

Welsh, meaning "dark-skinned and Moorish."

Morrison

English, meaning "son of Morris." Associated with singer and guitarist Jim Morrison.

Mortimer

French, meaning "dead sea."

Morton

Old English, meaning "moor town."

Moses
(alt. Moshe, Moshon)

Hebrew, meaning "savior." A key figure in the Bible.

Moss

English, from the word "moss."

Mungo

Gaelic, meaning "most dear." Lake Mungo is in Australia.

Murphy

Irish, meaning "sea warrior." Murphy's Law states if something can go wrong, it will.

Murray

Gaelic, meaning "lord and master."

Mustafa

Arabic, meaning "chosen." Also a name for the prophet Muhammad in Islam.

Myron

Greek, meaning "myrrh."

Boys' names

Najee

Arabic, meaning "dear companion." Also the name of an influential jazz musician.

Nakia

Arabic, meaning "pure."

Nakul

Indian, meaning "mongoose." Choreographer Nakul Dev Mahajan has made a name for himself as a mainstream Bollywood choreographer.

Nana
(alt. Nanna)

Ghanaiian, meaning "Your Royal Highness."

Naphtali

Hebrew, meaning "wrestling." One of Joseph's brothers in the Bible.

Napoleon

Italian origin, meaning "man from Naples." Name of the French general who became Emperor of France.

Narciso

Latin, from the myth of Narcissus, who drowned after gazing at his own reflection.

Nash

English, meaning "at the ash tree." Singer-songwriter Graham Nash is known for his involvement with Crosby, Stills & Nash.

Nasir

Arabic, meaning "helper."

Nathan
(alt. Nathaniel; abbrev. Nate)

Hebrew, meaning "God has given." Found in the Bible.

Naveen

Indian, meaning "new." Actor Naveen Andrews is known for his roles in *Lost* and *The English Patient*.

Ned

Originally a nickname for Edward, meaning "wealthy guard." Ned Stark is a character from *Game of Thrones*.

Neftali

Hebrew, meaning "struggling."

Nehemiah

Hebrew, meaning "comforter."

Neil

(alt. Neal, Niall)

Irish, meaning "champion." Famous Neils include astrophysicist Neil deGrasse Tyson, actor Neil Patrick Harris, and singer Neil Young.

Neilson

Irish, meaning "son of Neil."

Nelson

Variant of Neil, meaning "champion." Famous Nelsons include Nelson Mandela and Lord Horatio Nelson.

Nemo

Latin, meaning "nobody." Made popular after the Disney/Pixar film *Finding Nemo*.

Neo

Latin, meaning "new." Neo is a character in "The Matrix" trilogy.

Nephi

Greek, meaning "cloud."

Nessim

Arabic, meaning "breeze."

Nestor

Greek, meaning "traveler." Also the name of a king in ancient Greek mythology.

Neville

Old French, meaning "new village." Neville Longbottom is a character in the *Harry Potter* series.

Newton

English, meaning "new town." Scientist Sir Isaac Newton is celebrated as the discoverer of gravity.

Nicholas

(alt. Nicklas, Nicolas, Niklas, Nikola; abbrev. Nick, Nicky, Nicoi)

Greek, meaning "victorious." Famous Nicholases include St. Nicholas (the original Santa Claus), actor Nicolas Cage, and alchemist Nicholas Flamel.

Nigel

Gaelic, meaning "champion."
Producer Nigel Lythgoe is known for his work on *So You Think You Can Dance.*

Nikhil

Sanskrit, meaning "whole" or "entire."

Nikita

Greek, meaning "unconquered."
Used for both boys and girls.

Nimrod

Hebrew, meaning "we will rebel."
Found in the Bible.

Nissim

Hebrew, meaning "wonderful things."

Noah

Hebrew, meaning "peaceful." Found in the Bible.

Noel

French, meaning "Christmas."
Famous Noels include comedian and actor Noel Coward.

Nolan

Gaelic, meaning "champion."

Norbert

Old German, meaning "northern brightness."

Norman

(abbrev. Norm)

Old German, meaning "northerner."
The Norman people of the Middle Ages originated from Normandy in France.

Normand

French, meaning "from Normandy."

Norris

Old French, meaning "northerner."

Norton

English, meaning "northern town."

Norval

French, meaning "northern town."

Norwood

English, meaning "northern forest."

Nova

Latin, meaning "new." Also the name of a vast nuclear explosion in a white dwarf star.

Nuno

Latin, meaning "ninth."

Nunzio

Italian, meaning "messenger."

Boys' names

Oakley

English, meaning "from the oak meadow." The name of a brand of clothing.

Obadiah

Hebrew, meaning "God's worker." Used throughout the Bible to indicate a servant of God.

Obama

African, meaning "crooked." Surname of the 44th President of the United States.

Obed

Hebrew, meaning "servant of God."

Oberon
(abbrev. Obi, Obie)

Old German, meaning "royal bear." The Fairy King in Shakespeare's *A Midsummer Night's Dream*.

Octave
(alt. Octavian, Octavio)

Latin, meaning "eight." An octave is a series of eight notes in a musical scale.

Oda
(alt. Odell, Odie, Odis)

Hebrew, meaning "praise God."

Ogden

Old English, meaning "oak valley."

Oisin

Celtic, meaning "fawn." From an ancient Irish poet.

Ola

Norse, meaning "precious." Ola Nordmann is a personification of Norway, in the same way Uncle Sam represents the USA.

Olaf
(alt. Olan)

Old Norse, meaning "ancestor." The name of the animated snowman in Disney's *Frozen*.

Oleander

Hawaiian, meaning "joyous."

Oleg
(alt. Olen)

Russian, meaning "holy."

Olin

Russian, meaning "rock."

Oliver
(alt. Olivier; abbrev. Ollie, Olly)

Latin, meaning "olive tree." Associated with the musical *Oliver!* and Disney's *Oliver and Company*.

Omar
(alt. Omari, Omarion)

Arabic, meaning "speaker." Actor Omar Epps is known for his roles in TV shows *House* and *Resurrection*.

Ora

Latin, meaning "hour."

Oran
(alt. Oren, Orrin)

Gaelic, meaning "light and pale."

Orange

English, from the the fruit and the color.

Orion

Greek, from the Ancient Greek legend of a massive hunter.

Orlando
(alt. Orlo)

Old German, meaning "old land." Famous Orlandos include actor Orlando Bloom, the Shakespearean character Orlando from *As You Like It*, and the city of Orlando in Florida.

Orpheus

Greek, meaning "beautiful voice." A legendary ancient Greek musician, poet, and prophet.

Orson

Latin, meaning "bear." Film director Orson Welles was known for the movies *Citizen Kane* and *Touch of Evil*.

Orville

Old French, meaning "gold town." Associated with popcorn brand Orville Redenbacher.

Osaka

From the Japanese city.

Osborne
(alt. Osbourne)

Norse, meaning "bear god." Associated with Sharon and Ozzy Osbourne's family.

Oscar

Old English, meaning "spear of the gods." The Oscars is the nickname for the Academy Awards.

Oswald

German, meaning "God's power." Oswald the Lucky Rabbit was Walt Disney's first creation.

Otha
(alt. Otho)

German, meaning "wealth."

Othello

Old German, meaning "wealth." From the Shakespearean character and play.

Otis

German, meaning "wealth." Otis Redding was a legendary singer and several US sports stars share the same given name.

Otten

German, meaning "son of Otto."

Otto

German, meaning "wealthy." Anne Frank's father was called Otto Frank.

Owain

Welsh, meaning "youth."

Owen
(alt. Eoghan, Eoin)

Welsh, meaning "well born and noble" or "little warrior." Famous Owens include actor Owen Wilson. Eoghan and Eoin are the Irish variants.

Oz

Hebrew, meaning "strength." Associated with *The Wizard of Oz*.

P

Boys' names

Pablo

Spanish, meaning "little." Famous Pablos include artist Pablo Picasso.

Paco

Native American, meaning "eagle." Paco Rabanne is a Spanish fashion designer and brand name. His real first name is Francisco.

Padma

Sanskrit, meaning "lotus."

Padraig
(alt. Podrick)

Irish, meaning "noble." Podrick Payne is a character in *Game of Thrones*.

Panos

Greek, meaning "all holy."

Paolo

Italian, meaning "little."

Paresh

Sanskrit, meaning "supreme standard."

Parker

Old English, meaning "park keeper."

Pascal

Latin, meaning "Easter child." The feminine form is Pascale.

Patrick
(alt. Patrice; abbrev. Paddy, Pat)

Irish, meaning "noble." St. Patrick is the patron saint of Ireland.

Patten
(alt. Patton)

English, meaning "noble." Patton Oswalt is a comedian.

Paul

Hebrew, meaning "small." Paul was one of Jesus's main disciples.

Pavel
Latin, meaning "small."

Pax
Latin, meaning "peace."

Paxton
English, meaning "town of peace."

Payne
Latin, meaning "peasant."

Payton
Latin, meaning "peasant's town."

Pedro
Spanish form of Peter, meaning "rock."

Penn
English, meaning "hill." Penn Jillette is a magician and one half of Penn and Teller.

Percival
(alt. Percy)
French, meaning "pierce the valley." The name of one of the Knights of the Round Table.

Perez
Hebrew, meaning "breach." Famous Perezes include Perez Morton, the lawyer and revolutionary Boston patriot, and professional gossiper Perez Hilton.

Pericles
Greek, meaning "far-famed." Pericles was an influential ancient Greek general and statesman.

Perrin
Greek, meaning "rock."

Perry
English, meaning "rock." Associated with the series *Perry Mason*.

Pervis
English, meaning "purveyor."

Peter
(alt. Pedro, Petros, Pierre, Piers; abbrev. Pete)
Greek, meaning "rock." St. Peter was one of Jesus's disciples in the Bible.

Peyton
Old English, meaning "fighting man's estate." Peyton Manning recently retired from professional football.

Philip
(alt. Phillip; abbrev. Phil, Pip)
Greek, meaning "lover of horses." Famous Philips include husband of Queen Elizabeth II, Prince Philip, Philip the Apostle, and author Philip Pullman.

Philo
Greek, meaning "love."

Phineas
(alt. Pinchas)

Hebrew, meaning "oracle." A character in the cartoon *Phineas and Ferb*.

Phoenix

Greek, meaning "dark red." In ancient Greek mythology, a phoenix is a bird that has the power to regenerate itself from its ashes.

Pierce
(alt. Pierson)

Meaning "son of Piers."

Placido

Latin, meaning "placid." Placido Domingo is a famous tenor opera singer.

Pradeep

Hindi, meaning "light."

Pranav

Sanskrit, meaning "spiritual leader."

Presley

Old English, meaning "priest's meadow." Made famous by legendary singer Elvis Presley.

Preston

Old English, meaning "priest's town." Preston Burke is a character from *Grey's Anatomy*.

Primo

Italian, meaning "first." Also a slang term for "excellent."

Primus

Latin, meaning "first." Often used as a name for villains in Marvel comic books.

Prince

English, from the word "prince." Associated with singer and guitarist Prince.

Prospero

Latin, meaning "prosperous." Prospero is the protagonist in Shakespeare's play *The Tempest*.

Pryce
(alt. Prize)

Old French, meaning "prize."

Pryor

English, meaning "first." Famous Pryors include legendary comedian Richard Pryor.

Psalm

Old English, meaning "hymn." The name of Kim Kardashian-West's fourth child.

Ptolemy

Greek, meaning "aggressive" or "warlike."

Boys' names

Qabil
(alt. Quabil, Quadim)
Arabic, meaning "able."

Quadir
Arabic, meaning "powerful."

Quaid
Irish, meaning "fourth."

Quemby
Norse, meaning "from the woman's estate."

Quentin
(alt. Quinten, Quintin, Quinton, Quintus)
Latin, meaning "fifth." Director Quentin Tarantino has been behind numerous successful movies, including *Kill Bill* and *Django Unchained*.

Quillan
Gaelic, meaning "sword."

Quillon
Gaelic, meaning "club."

Quincy
Old French, meaning "estate of the fifth son." Quincy Jones is a music mogul.

Quinlan
Gaelic, meaning "fit, shapely, and strong."

Quinn
Gaelic, meaning "counsel." Quinn is a character from *Glee*.

R Boys' names

Radames

Slavic, meaning "famous joy." A character in the Verdi opera *Aida*.

Raekwon

Hebrew, meaning "God has healed." Associated with Raekwon of Wu-Tang Clan.

Rafael

(alt. Rafe, Rafer, Raffi, Raphael)

Hebrew, meaning "God has healed." One of the archangels in the Bible.

Ragnar

Old Norse, meaning "judgment warrior." Ragnar Lodbrok was a legendary Norse ruler from the Viking era.

Raheem

(alt. Rahim)

Arabic, meaning "merciful and kind."

Rahm

Hebrew, meaning "mercy."

Rahul

(alt. Raoul, Raul)

Indian, meaning "efficient." Rahul was the Buddha's son.

Raiden

(alt. Rainen)

From the Japanese god of thunder.

Rainer

Old German, meaning "deciding warrior."

Raj

Sanskrit, meaning "kingdom," and Polish, meaning "heaven."

Rajesh

(alt. Ramesh)

Indian, meaning "ruler of kings."

Raleigh

Old English, meaning "deer's meadow." Made famous by the explorer Sir Walter Raleigh.

Ralph

Old English, meaning "wolf." Famous Ralphs include actor Ralph Fiennes, fashion brand Ralph Lauren, and character Ralph from *The Simpsons*.

Ram

English, from the word for a male sheep.

Ramiro

Germanic, meaning "powerful in battle." Popular name for baby boys in Argentina.

Ramsey
(alt. Ramsay)

Old English, meaning "wild garlic island." Gordon Ramsay is a celebrity chef.

Randall
(alt. Randal, Randolph, Randy)

Old German, meaning "wolf shield." Can be traced back to the poem "Lord Randall" in 1882.

Raniel

English, meaning "God is my happiness."

Ranjit

Indian, meaning "influenced by charm."

Rannoch

Gaelic, meaning "fern." Also the name of an area in the Scottish Highlands.

Rashad

Arabic, meaning "good judgment."

Rashid
(alt. Rasheed)

Indian, meaning "rightly guided." Ar-Rashid, meaning "The Guide," is one of Allah's names in the Islamic tradition.

Rasmus

Greek, meaning "beloved."

Raven

English, from the word for the large, black bird.

Ravi

Hindi, meaning "sun."

Ray

English, from the word "ray." Famous Rays include singer Ray Charles. Other well-known Rays were actually given the name Raymond.

Raymond
(alt. Rayner; abbrev. Ray)

English, meaning "advisor." Title character of the sitcom *Everybody Loves Raymond*. Actors Ray Winstone and Ray Liotta are both Raymonds.

Raz

Israeli, meaning "secret" or "mystery."

Reagan

(abbrev. Reggie)

Irish, meaning "little king." Ronald Reagan was the 40th President of the United States.

Reginald

(abbrev. Reg, Reggie)

Latin, meaning "regal." Singer Sir Elton John's birth name is Reginald Kenneth Dwight.

Regis

Latin, meaning "of the king."

Reid

Old English, meaning "by the reeds."

Reilly

(alt. Riley)

Irish, meaning "courageous."

Remus

Latin, meaning "swift." Famous Remuses include Romulus and Remus of the ancient Roman myth, and the *Harry Potter* character Remus Lupin.

Rémy

French, meaning "from Rheims."

Renatus

(alt. Renat, Renate, Renato, Rene)

Latin, meaning "rebirth."

Reno

Latin, meaning "renewed." Also the name of the city in Nevada.

Reuben

Spanish, meaning "a son." The name of a sandwich containing corned beef, Swiss cheese, and sauerkraut.

Reuel

Hebrew, meaning "friend of God."

Rex

Latin, meaning "king." The kings of ancient Rome were called Rex, before it became a republic.

Rey

Spanish, meaning "king"; Telugu, meaning "friend."

Reynold

Latin, meaning "king's advisor."

Rhodes

German, meaning "where the roses grow." Also the name of the Greek island.

Rhodri

Welsh, meaning "ruler of the circle."

Rhys

(alt. Reece, Riece)

Welsh, meaning "enthusiasm." Famous Rhyses include actors Jonathan Rhys Meyers and Rhys Ifans.

Richard

(alt. Ricardo, Rikardo; abbrev. Dick, Dickie, Richie, Rick, Ricki, Ricky, Ritchie)

Old German, meaning "powerful leader." Famous Richards include 37th President of the United States Richard Nixon, and actor Richard Gere.

Ridley

English, meaning "cleared wood." Director Sir Ridley Scott is known for the films *Gladiator* and *Thelma & Louise*.

Rigby

English, from the place in Lancashire. Often associated with the Beatles' song "Eleanor Rigby."

Riky

Irish Gaelic, meaning "courageous."

Ringo

English, meaning "ring." Ringo Starr was the drummer with the Beatles.

Rio

Spanish, meaning "river." *Rio* is a song by Duran Duran and associated with the Brazilian city Rio de Janeiro.

Riordan

Gaelic, meaning "bard."

Rishi

Sanskrit, meaning "scribe."

Roald

Scandinavian, meaning "ruler." Roald Dahl is the author of *Charlie and the Chocolate Factory* and many other children's books.

Robert

(alt. Roberto; abbrev. Bob, Bobby, Dobby, Rob, Robbie)

Old German, meaning "bright fame." Famous Roberts include actors Robert de Niro and Robert Pattinson, and legendary singers Bob Dylan and Bob Marley.

Robin

English, from the word for the small, flame-breasted bird. Famous Robins include comedian Robin Williams, singer Robin Thicke, and outlaw legend Robin Hood.

Robinson

English, meaning "son of Robin." The eponymous hero of the novel *Robinson Crusoe*.

Rocco

(alt. Rocky)

Italian, meaning "rest." Also the name of Madonna's son.

Roderick

(abbrev. Rod, Roddy)

German, meaning "famous power." A character from the TV series *The Following*.

Rodney
(abbrev. Rod, Roddy)
Old German, meaning "island near the clearing."

Rodrigo
Spanish form of Roderick, meaning "famous power." Famous Rodrigos include Spanish composer Joaquin Rodrigo.

Roger
Old German, meaning "spear man." Famous Rogers include athlete Sir Roger Bannister, The Who singer Roger Daltrey, and tennis pro Roger Federer.

Roland
(alt. Rowland)
Old German, meaning "renowned land."

Rolf
Old German, meaning "wolf."

Rollie
(alt. Rollo)
Old German, meaning "renowned land."

Roman
Latin, meaning "from Rome." Associated with the Roman people.

Romeo
Latin, meaning "pilgrim to Rome." Made famous by Shakespeare's play *Romeo and Juliet*. Also the name of David and Victoria Beckham's second son.

Ronald
(alt. Ron, Ronnie)
Norse, meaning "mountain of strength." Ron Weasley is a character in the *Harry Potter* series.

Ronan
Gaelic, meaning "little seal."

Rory
English, meaning "red king." Rory Calhoun was an actor. Golfer Rory McIlroy has won the US Open.

Ross
(alt. Russ)
Scottish, meaning "cape."

Rowan
(alt. Roan, Rohan)
Gaelic, meaning "little red one." Rowan Atkinson is a comedian and comic actor, and also the voice of Zazu in *The Lion King*.

Roy
Gaelic, meaning "red." Famous Roys include singer Roy Orbison.

Ruben
Hebrew, meaning "son."

Rudolph
(alt. Rudy)

Old German, meaning "famous wolf." The name of Santa's legendary reindeer.

Rufus

Latin, meaning "red-haired." Actor Rufus Sewell is known for his role in *A Knight's Tale*.

Rupert

Variant of Robert, meaning "bright fame." Actor Rupert Grint is known for his role in the *Harry Potter* series.

Russell

Old French, meaning "little red one." Comedian Russell Brand is known for his role in *Arthur*.

Rusty

English, meaning "ruddy."

Ryan

Gaelic, meaning "little king." Famous Ryans include actors Ryan Gosling and Ryan Reynolds, and comedian Ryan Stiles.

Ryder

English, meaning "horseman."

Rye

English, from the word "rye."

Ryker

From Richard, meaning "powerful leader." *Ryker's Island* is a fictional prison facility in Marvel Comics stories.

Rylan

English, meaning "land where rye is grown."

Ryley

Old English, meaning "rye clearing."

Boys' names

Saber
(alt. *Sabre*)
French, meaning "sword."

Sagar
African, meaning "ruler of the water."

Sage
English, meaning "wise." Can also refer to the herb.

Sakari
Native American, meaning "sweet."

Salim
(alt. *Saleem*)
Arabic, meaning "secure." The Salim Khan family are a Bollywood dynasty.

Salvador
Spanish, meaning "savior." Famous Salvadors include artist Salvador Dali.

Salvatore
Italian, meaning "savior." There have been dozens of the Italian, Sicilian, or New York mafia called Salvatore.

Samir
Arabic, meaning "pleasant companion."

Samson
Hebrew, meaning "son of Sam." The biblical Samson had extraordinary strength.

Samuel
(alt. *Sam, Sama, Sammie, Sammy*)
Hebrew, meaning "God is heard." Famous Samuels include a prophet from the Bible, actor Samuel L. Jackson, and author Samuel Langhorne Clemens (known as Mark Twain).

Sandeep
(alt. Sundeep)
Hindi, meaning "lighting the way."

Sanjay
Hindi, meaning "victory." Sanjay Gupta is a well-known TV doctor.

Santana
Spanish, meaning "saint." Associated with guitarist Carlos Santana.

Santiago
Spanish, meaning "Saint James." Also the name of the capital city of Chile.

Santino
Spanish, meaning "little Saint James."

Santo
(alt. Santos)
Latin, meaning "saint."

Old name, new fashion

Augustus	Norris
Bertrand	Percival
Edgar	Reginald
Felix	Sebastian
Gilbert	Theodore
Hector	Winston
Jasper	

Sasha
(alt. Sacha, Sascha)
Russian, derived from Alexander, meaning "defending men." Sasha can be used for boys or girls.

Sawyer
English, meaning "one who saws wood." Associated with the novel *Tom Sawyer*.

Scott
(alt. Scottie)
English, meaning "from Scotland." Scott Dixon is an IndyCar champion, and cartoonist Scott Adams created *Dilbert*.

Seamus
Irish variant of James, meaning "he who supplants." Seamus Heaney is a Nobel Prize-winning poet.

Sean
(alt. Shaun, Shawn)
Variant of John, meaning "God is gracious." Famous Seans include actors Sean Penn and Sean Connery.

Sebastian
(alt. Sébastien; abbrev. Basti, Seb)
Greek, meaning "revered." The name of the crab character in Disney's *The Little Mermaid*.

Sergio
(alt. Serge)
Latin, meaning "servant."

Seth

Hebrew, meaning "appointed." Famous Seths include actors Seth MacFarlane and Seth Greene.

Severus

Latin, meaning "severe." Severus Snape is a character in the *Harry Potter* series.

Seymour

English, from the place name in northern France. Famous Seymours include Principal Seymour Skinner of *The Simpsons*, and the late actor Philip Seymour Hoffman.

Shane

Variant of Sean, meaning "God is gracious." Famous Shanes include actors Shane West and Shane Harper.

Sharif

Arabic, meaning "honored." Also a name for descendants of one of Muhammad's grandchildren.

Shea

Gaelic, meaning "admirable."

Shelby

Norse, meaning "willow." Associated with the Mustang car.

Sherlock

English, meaning "fair-haired." The name of the lead character in Sir Arthur Conan Doyle's "Sherlock Holmes" novels.

Sherman

Old English, meaning "shear man."

Shmuel

Hebrew, meaning "his name is God."

Shola

Arabic, meaning "energetic."

Sidney
(alt. Sid, Sydney)

English, meaning "wide meadow." Actor Sidney Poitier is known for his roles in *Guess Who's Coming to Dinner* and *In The Heat of the Night*.

Sigmund

Old German, meaning "victorious hand." Associated with neurologist Sigmund Freud.

Silvanus
(alt. Silvio)

Latin, meaning "woods." An Ancient Roman deity of woods and fields.

Simba
(alt. Sim)

Swahili, meaning "lion." Associated with the character from Disney's *The Lion King*.

Simon
(alt. Simeon)

Hebrew, meaning "to hear." Famous Simons include music producer Simon Cowell and actor Simon Pegg.

Sinbad

Persian, meaning "Lord of Sages." Fictional merchant adventurer.

Sindri

Norse, meaning "dwarf."

Sipho

African, meaning "the unknown one."

Sire

English, from the word used to address reigning kings or nobility.

Sirius

Hebrew, meaning "brightest star." Sirius Black is a character from the *Harry Potter* series.

Skipper

English, meaning "ship captain."

Skyler

Dutch, meaning "guarded" or "scholar."

Solomon

Hebrew, meaning "peace." One of the most important kings in the Bible and the Torah.

Sonny

American English, meaning "son." Singer Sonny Bono was half of Sonny and Cher.

Soren

Scandinavian, meaning "brightest star."

Spencer

English, meaning "guardian." Famous Spencers include actor Spencer Tracy and reality TV star Spencer Pratt.

Spike

English, from the word "spike." Director Spike Lee is known for *Do the Right Thing* and *4 Little Girls*.

Stanford

English, meaning "stone ford." Made famous by Stanford University.

Stanley
(alt. Stan)

English, meaning "stony meadow." Famous Stanleys include director Stanley Kubrick, actor Stanley Tucci, and comic book writer Stan Lee.

Stavros

Greek, meaning "cross."

Stellan

Latin, meaning "starred."

Steno

German, meaning "stone."

Stephen
(alt. Stefan, Stefano, Steffan, Steven; abbrev. Steve, Stevie)

English, meaning "crowned." Famous Stephens include author Stephen King, physicist Stephen Hawking, and actor Stephen Fry.

Stewart
(alt. Stuart)

English, meaning "steward." Stewart Copeland was the American drummer in The Police.

Stoney
English, meaning "stone like."

Storm
English, from the word "storm."

Sven
Norse, meaning "boy." The name of the reindeer in Disney's *Frozen*.

Syed
(alt. Sayyid)

Arabic, meaning "lucky." Associated with the character from *Lost*.

Sylvester
Latin, meaning "wooded." The name of the cartoon cat.

T

Boys' names

Tacitus
Latin, meaning "silent, calm." Also the name of an ancient Roman historian.

Tad
English, from the word "tadpole."

Taj
Indian, meaning "crown." Made famous by the Indian palace the Taj Mahal.

Takashi
Japanese, meaning "praiseworthy."

Takoda
Sioux, meaning "friend to everyone."

Talbot
(alt. Tal)
English, meaning "command of the valley." Aristocratic name.

Tamir
Arabic, meaning "tall and wealthy."

Tanner
Old English, meaning "leather-maker."

Taras
(alt. Tarez)
Scottish, meaning "crag." Taras was the son of Poseidon in ancient Greek mythology.

Tarek
(alt. Tarik)
Arabic, meaning "to strike."

Tarian
Welsh, meaning "shield."

Tariq
Arabic, meaning "morning star."

Tarquin
Latin, from the Roman clan name. Tarquin Hall is a poet.

Tarun

Hindi, meaning "young."

Tatanka

Hebrew, meaning "bull." Legendary Native American leader Sitting Bull's Western name was Tatanka Lyotake.

Tate

English, meaning "cheerful." Actor Tate Donovan is known for his role in the TV series *Damages*.

Taurean

English, meaning "bull-like." Also used to describe people born under the Taurus star sign.

Tavares

English, meaning "descendant of the hermit."

Tave
(alt. Tavian, Tavis, Tavish)

French, from Gustave, meaning "royal staff"; in Nordic cultures it can mean "guarantor."

Taylor
(alt. Tay)

English, meaning "tailor." Famous Taylors include actor Taylor Lautner and singer Taylor Hanson.

Tennessee

Native American, meaning "river town." Also the name of the state.

Terence
(alt. Terrill, Terry)

English, meaning "tender." Actor Terence Stamp is known for his roles in *Billy Budd* and *The Collector*.

Tex

English, meaning "Texan."

Thane
(alt. Thayer)

Scottish, meaning "landholder." Actor Thane Bettany is the father of actor Paul Bettany.

Thatcher
(alt. Thaxter)

Old English, meaning "roof thatcher."

Thelonious

Latin, meaning "ruler of the people." Thelonious Monk was an influential jazz pianist and composer.

Theodore
(abbrev. Ted, Teddy, Theo)

Greek, meaning "God's gift." Theodore Roosevelt was the 26th President of the United States.

Theophile

Latin, meaning "beloved of God," also "one who loves God."

Theron

Greek, meaning "hunter."

Thierry

French variant of Terence, meaning "tender." Made famous by soccer star Thierry Henry.

Thomas
(alt. Thom, Tom, Tomlin, Tommy)

Aramaic, meaning "twin." Famous Thomases include inventor Thomas Edison and children's character Thomas the Tank Engine.

Thomson
(alt. Thomsen)

English, meaning "son of Thomas." "Thomsen" means "twin" in Aramaic.

Thor

Norse, meaning "thunder." Thor was a hammer-wielding deity in Norse mythology.

Tiago

From Santiago, meaning "Saint James." Also used as a shortened form of Santiago.

Tiberius

English, meaning "from the river Tiber."

Tibor

Latin, from the river Tiber; Hungarian, meaning "a short meeting."

Tieman
(alt. Tiemann)

Gaelic, meaning "lord."

Tilden
(alt. Till)

English, meaning "fertile valley."

Timothy
(alt. Tim, Timmie, Timmy, Timon)

Greek, meaning "God's honor." Famous Timothys include actors Timothy Dalton, Timothy Spall, and Christopher Timothy.

Tito
(alt. Titus, Tizian)

Latin, meaning "defender." Associated with singer Tito Jackson, from the Jackson Five.

Tobias
(alt. Toby)

Hebrew, meaning "God is good."

Todd
(alt. Tod)

English, meaning "fox." Famous Tods include Todd Flanders in *The Simpsons* and Todd Alquist in *Fargo*.

Tonneau

French, meaning "barrel."

Torey

Norse, meaning "Thor."

Torin

Gaelic, meaning "chief."

Torquil

Gaelic, meaning "helmet";
Scandinavian, from Thor the god of
thunder and lightning.

Toshi

Japanese, meaning "reflection."

Travis

French, meaning "crossover." Famous
Travises include actor Travis Fimmel
and drummer Travis Barker.

Trevor
(alt. Tvevin)

Welsh origin, meaning "great
settlement." Comedian Trevor Noah
currently hosts *The Daily Show*.

Trey
(alt. Tyree)

French, meaning "three." Sometimes
used as a nickname for a third-born
child.

Tristan
(alt. Tristram)

Celtic from the romantic hero in the
tale of Tristan and Isolde. Also one of
the Knights of the Round Table.

Troy

Gaelic, meaning "descended from
the soldier." Troy was a legendary
city in ancient Greece.

Tudor

Variant of Theodore, meaning "God's
gift." Also the name of the British
dynasty which included Henry VIII
and Elizabeth I.

Tyler

English, meaning "tile maker."

Tyrell

French, meaning "puller." Associated
with House Tyrell from *Game of
Thrones*.

Tyrone

Gaelic, meaning "Owen's county."

Tyson

English, meaning "son of Tyrone."
Mike Tyson is widely regarded as one
of the best heavyweight boxers of all
time, as well as the most ferocious
and controversial.

U

Boys' names

Uberto
(alt. Umberto)
Italian, variant of Hubert, meaning "bright or shining intellect."

Udo
German, meaning "power of the wolf."

Ulf
German, meaning "wolf." Also the name of a Danish Viking chief.

Ulrich
German, meaning "noble ruler."

Ultan
Irish, meaning "from Ulster."

Ulysses
Greek, meaning "wrathful." Made famous by the mythological voyager from ancient Greece.

Upton
English, meaning "high town."

Urho
Finnish, meaning "brave."

Uri
(alt. Uriah, Urias)
Hebrew, meaning "my light." Famous Uris include magician Uri Geller.

Uriel
Hebrew, meaning "angel of light." One of the archangels in the Bible.

Usher
English, from the word "usher." Associated with the R&B star Usher.

Uzi
Hebrew, meaning "my strength." A type of submachine gun.

Uzzi
(alt. Uzziah)
Hebrew, meaning "the Lord is my strength." Found in the Bible.

Boys' names

Vadim

Russian, meaning "scandal maker."
Vadim the Bold was a legendary
warrior in Eastern Europe during the
ninth century.

Valdemar

German, meaning "renowned leader."

Valente

Latin, meaning "valiant."

Valentine

(alt. Valentin, Valentino; abbrev. Val)
English, from the word "valentine."
St. Valentine's Day is named after
Valentinus, who was said to have
healed the broken heart of his jailer's
daughter.

Valerio

Italian, meaning "to be strong."

Van

Dutch, meaning "son of." Famous
Vans include the band Van Halen,
singer Van Morrison, and the brand
of shoe.

Vance

English, meaning "marshland."
Vance Astrovik is the real name of
the comic book hero Justice.

Vangelis

Greek, meaning "good news."
Vangelis is a modern Greek
composer.

Varro

Latin, meaning "strong."

Varun

Hindi, meaning "water god."
Shortened form of Varuna, who is
the Hindu god of all water.

Vasilis
(alt. Vasilly)
Greek, meaning "kingly."

Vaughan
Welsh, meaning "little."

Vernell
French, meaning "green and flourishing."

Verner
German, meaning "army defender." The German form of Werner, although Verner is a more common spelling in Europe.

Vernon
(alt. Vernie)
French, meaning "alder grove." Vernon Dursley is a character in the *Harry Potter* series.

Versilius
Latin, meaning "flier."

Vester
Latin, meaning "wooded." Associated with the guitar maker.

Victor
(alt. Vic, Viktor)
Latin, meaning "champion." Author Victor Hugo wrote *Les Miserables*.

Vidal
(alt. Vidar)
Spanish, meaning "life-giving." Vidal Sassoon is famed as a hairstylist.

Vijay
Hindi, meaning "conquering."

Vikram
Hindi, meaning "sun."

Ville
French, meaning "town."

Vincent
(abbrev. Vin, Vince, Vinnie)
English, meaning "victorious." Famous Vincents include actor Vince Vaughn, artist Vincent van Gogh, and soccer player turned actor Vinnie Jones.

Virgil
Latin, meaning "staff bearer." From the ancient Roman poet of the same name.

Vito
Spanish, meaning "life." Vito Corleone is a character from *The Godfather*.

Vittorio
Italian, meaning "victory."

Vitus
Latin, meaning "life." Associated with St. Vitus, or the medcial condition Saint Vitus Dance.

Vivian

(alt. Vyvian; abbrev. Viv)

Latin, meaning "lively." Used as a name for boys and girls.

Vladimir

Slavic, meaning "prince." Famous Vladimirs include Russian President Vladimir Putin, and legendary warrior Vladimir the Impaler—also known as Dracula.

Volker

German, meaning "defender of the people."

"Bad boy" names

Ace	Conan
Arnie	Guy
Axel	Rhett
Bruce	Spike
Buzz	Tyson

Von

Norse, meaning "hope." In Germany, "von" also means "of" or "from," and is used to denote origin, such as Ulrich von Liechtenstein.

Boys' names

Wade

English, meaning "to move forward" or "to go." Wade Robson is a contemporary dance choreographer.

Waldemar

German, meaning "famous ruler."

Walden

English, meaning "valley of the Britons." Famed as the title of the book by Henry Thoreau.

Waldo

Old German, meaning "rule." "Where's Waldo" is a popular children's book character.

Walker

English, meaning "a fuller."

Wallace

English, meaning "foreigner" or "stranger." One of the cartoon duo *Wallace and Gromit*.

Wally

German, meaning "ruler of the army."

Walter
(alt. Walt)

German, meaning "ruler of the army." Famous Walters include *Breaking Bad*'s Walter White, and the movie *The Secret Life of Walter Mitty*.

Ward

English, meaning "guardian."

Wardell

Old English, meaning "watchman's hill."

Warner

German, meaning "army guard." Made famous as the name of the movie studio Warner Brothers.

Warren

German, meaning "guard" or "the game park." Warren Buffett is a business tycoon and philanthropist.

Warwick

Old English, meaning "buildings near the weir." Associated with actor Warwick Davis.

Washington

English, meaning "clever" or "clever man's settlement." George Washington was the first President of the United States.

Wassily
(alt. Vasily))

Greek, meaning "royal" or "kingly." Wassily Kandinsky was an abstract artist.

Watson

English, meaning "son" or "son of Walter." Dr. Watson is a character from the "Sherlock Holmes" stories.

Waverley
(alt. Waverly)

English, meaning "quaking aspen."

Waylon

English, meaning "land by the road." Associated with country singer Waylon Jennings.

Wayne

English, meaning "a cartwright." Famous Waynes include comedian Wayne Brady and rapper Lil Wayne.

Webster

English, meaning "weaver."

Weldon

English, meaning "from the hill of well" or "hill with a well."

Wells

English, meaning "from the hill of well" or "hill with a well."

Wendell
(alt. Wendel)

German, meaning "spring."

Werner

German, meaning "army guard." Werner Heisenberg was a Nobel prize winner and inspiration for the alter ego of Walter White in *Breaking Bad*.

Weston

English, meaning "from the west town."

Wheeler

English, meaning "wheel maker."

Whitley

English, meaning "white wood."

Whitman

Old English, meaning "white man." Made famous by author and poet Walt Whitman.

Whitney

Old English, meaning "white island."

Wilber
(alt. Wilbur)

Old German, meaning "bright will." Wilbur Wright helped invent the first powered airplanes.

Wilder

English, meaning "wild and uncontrolled".

Wiley

Old English, meaning "beguiling" or "enchanting."

Wilford

Old English, meaning "the ford by the willows." Associated with actor Wilford Brimley.

Wilfred
(alt. Wilfredo, Wilfrid; abbrev. Wilf)

English, meaning "to will peace."

Wilhelm
(alt. Willem)

German, meaning "strong willed warrior." The "Wilhelm Scream" is a movie sound effect used in hundreds of movies.

Wilkes
(alt. Wilkie)

Old English, meaning "strong willed protector" or "strong and resolute protector." John Wilkes Booth was the assassin of President Lincoln.

William
(abbrev. Bill, Billy, Will, Willie, Willy)

English (Teutonic), meaning "strong protector" or "strong willed warrior." Famous Williams include William Shakespeare, Prince William, and rapper Will.i.am.

Willis

English, meaning "server of William." Actor Bruce Willis is known for his roles in *Die Hard* and *The Fifth Element*.

Willoughby

Old Norse and Old English, meaning "from the farm by the trees."

Wilmer

English (Teutonic), meaning "famously resolute." Actor Wilmer Valderrama is known for his role in *That 70's Show*.

Wilmot

English, meaning "resolute mind."

Wilson

English, meaning "son of William." Famous Wilsons include legendary R&B singer Wilson Pickett.

Wilton

Old Norse and English, meaning "from the farm by the brook/ streams."

Windell
(alt. Wendell)

German, meaning "wanderer" or "seeker." Actor Windell Middlebrooks was known for his role in the TV series *Scrubs*.

Windsor

Old English, meaning "river bank" or "landing place." The British Royal family is known as the House of Windsor.

Winfield

English, meaning "from the field of Wina."

Winslow

Old English, meaning "victory on the hill." Associated with the sitcom *Family Matters*.

Winston

English, meaning "from Wine's town." Sir Winston Chruchill was prime Minister of Great Britain during World War II.

Winter

Old English, meaning "to be born in the winter."

Winthrop

Old English, meaning "village of friends."

Winton

Old English, meaning "a friend's farm."

Wirrin

Aboriginal, meaning "a tea tree."

Wistan

Old English, meaning "battle stone" or "mark of the battle."

Wittan

Old English, meaning "farm in the woods" or "farm by the woods."

Wolf
(alt. Wolfe)

English, meaning "strong as a wolf." A wild animal in the dog family.

Wolfgang

Teutonic, meaning "the path of wolves." The composer Mozart's chosen name was Wolfgang Amadeus Mozart.

Wolfrom

Teutonic, meaning "raven wolf."

Wolter

Dutch, a form of Walter meaning "ruler of the army."

Woodburn

Old English, meaning "a stream in the woods."

Woodrow

English, meaning "from the row of houses by the wood." Woodrow Wilson was the 28th President of the United States.

Woodward

English, meaning "guardian of the forest."

Woody

American English, meaning "path in the woods." Famous Woodys include filmmaker Woody Allen and the character of Woody from the *Toy Story* series.

Worcester

Old English, meaning "from a Roman site." A tangy sauce of the same name.

Worth

American English, meaning "worth much" or "wealthy place" or "wealth and riches."

Wren

Old English, meaning "tiny bird."

Wright

Old English, meaning "to be a craftsman" or "from a carpenter." Wilbur and Orville Wright were the inventors of powered aircraft.

Wyatt

Teutonic, meaning "from wood" or "from the wide water." Famous Wyatts include director Rupert Wyatt, Wild West sheriff Wyatt Earp, and comedian Wyatt Cenac.

Wynn

(alt. Wyn)

Welsh, meaning "very blessed" or "the fair blessed one"; Old English, meaning "friend."

Boys' names

Xadrian
American English, a combination of X and Adrian, meaning "from Hadria."

Xanthus
Greek, meaning "golden haired."

Xavier
Latin, meaning "to the new house."

Xenon
Greek, meaning "the guest." One of the noble gases.

Xerxes
Persian, meaning "ruler of the people" or "respected king." Name of a king who attempted to invade the Greek mainland, but failed.

Xylander
Greek, meaning "man of the forest."

X

Y

Boys' names

Yaal

Hebrew, meaning "ascending" or "one to ascend."

Yadid

Hebrew, meaning "the beloved one."

Yadon

Hebrew, meaning "against judgment." Associated with the Pokémon character.

Yahir

Spanish, meaning "handsome one."

Yair

Hebrew, meaning "the enlightening one" or "illuminating." The spelling Jair appears in the Bible.

Yakiya

Hebrew, meaning "pure" or "bright."

Yanis
(alt. Yannis)

Greek, a form of John meaning "gift of God."

Yarden

Hebrew, meaning "to flow downward."

Ye

Chinese, meaning "bright one" or "light."

Yehuda

Hebrew, meaning "to praise and exalt." Often translated as Judah, who was a son of Jacob in the Bible.

Yered

Hebrew, a form of Jared, meaning "descending."

Yerik

Russian, meaning "God-appointed one."

Yervant

Armenian, meaning "king of people."

Yitzak
(alt. Yitzaak)

Hebrew, meaning "laughter" or "one who laughs."

Ynyr

Welsh, meaning "to honor."

Yobachi

African, meaning "one who prays to God" or "prayed to God."

Yogi

Japanese, meaning "one who practices yoga" or "from yoga." Made famous by the cartoon character Yogi Bear.

Yona

Native American, meaning "bear"; Hebrew, meaning "dove." A name used to refer to ancient people who spoke Greek.

York

Celtic, meaning "yew tree" or "from the farm of the yew tree." Also an historic city in the UK.

Yosef

Hebrew, meaning "added by God" or "God shall add." Hebrew form of Joseph.

Yuri

Aboriginal, meaning "to hear"; Japanese, meaning "one to listen"; Russian, a form of George meaning "farmer."

Yves

French, meaning "miniature archer" or "small archer." Fashion brand YSL was founded by Yves Saint Laurent.

Boys' names

Zachariah
(alt. Zac, Zach, Zachary)

Hebrew, meaning "remembered by the Lord" or "God has remembered." Famous Zachs include actors Zach Braff and Zach Galifianakis.

Zad

Persian, meaning "my son."

Zadok

Hebrew, meaning "righteous one." "Zadok the Priest" is a well-known coronation anthem and has been sung at every crowning of a king or queen in the UK since 1727.

Zador

Hungarian, meaning "violent demeanor." Zador was the priest who anointed Solomon in the Bible.

Zafar

Arabic, meaning "triumphant."

Zaid

African, meaning "increase the growth" or "growth."

Zaide

Yiddish, meaning "the elder ones." Also the name of an unfinished opera by Mozart.

Zain
(alt. Zane)

Arabic, meaning "the handsome son." Actor Billy Zane is known for his roles in *Titanic* and *The Phantom*.

Zaire

African, meaning "river from Zaire." Zaire is the old name for Democratic Republic of the Congo.

Zarek

Persian, meaning "God protect our king." Associated with the Marvel comic book character.

Zayn
Arabic, meaning "masculine beauty."
Made famous by singer Zayn Malik.

Zuma
Arabic, meaning "peace."

A name for all seasons

Spring	Summer	Fall	Winter
Alvern	Augustus	Aki	Aquilo
Attwell	Balder	Akiko	Caldwell
Avir	Cain	Demitrius	Colden
Bradwell	Dax	Dionysus	Crispin
Jarek	Leo	Forrest	Darke
Kell	Sky	George	Eirwen
Marcus	Somers	Goren	Gennaio
Rain	Sunny	Hunter	Jack
Tamiko	Theros	Red	Mistral

Part Three

Girls' names
A–Z

Baby names vary widely in spelling and pronunciation. To simplify things, this book usually lists each name only once: under the most common initial and spelling. If a name has a common alternate spelling with a different initial, it may also be listed under that letter.

Girls' names

A'mari

Variation of the Swahili or Muslim name Amira, meaning "princess."

Aanya

Sanskrit, meaning "the inexhaustible." Also variation of the Russian name Anya.

Aaryanna

Derivative of the Latin and Greek name Ariadne, meaning "the very holy one."

Abigail

(alt. Abagail, Abbigail, Abigale, Abigayle; abbrev. Abbey, Abbie, Abby, Abi)

Hebrew, meaning "my father's joy." Found in the Bible. The biblical Greek version of the name is Abigaia. Also the name of several Hawaiian princesses.

Abilene

(alt. Abelena, Abilee)

Latin and Spanish, meaning "hazelnut."

Abra

Female variation of Abraham. Also Sanskrit, meaning "clouds."

Abril

Spanish for the month of April; Latin, meaning "open."

Acacia

Greek, meaning "point" or "thorn." Also a species of flowering trees and shrubs.

Acadia

Greek, meaning "paradise." Originally, a French colony in Canada.

Ada
(alt. Adair, Adia)

Hebrew, meaning "adornment." Ada Lovelace is widely credited for being the world's first computer programmer, in the 19th century.

Adalee

German, meaning "noble." Also a contraction of Ada and Lee.

Adalia

Hebrew, meaning "God is my refuge." A genus of ladybug.

Addison
(alt. Addisyn, Addyson; abbrev. Addie, Addy, Adi)

English, meaning "son of Adam." Can be used for girls or boys.

Adelaide
(alt. Adalyn, Adalynn, Adelaida, Adeline, Adelina, Adelyn; abbrev. Addie, Addy, Adi)

Old German, meaning "noble kind." Popular after the rule of William IV and Queen Adelaide of England in the 19th century. Adeline Whitney was a children's author in that period.

Adele
(alt. Adela, Adelia, Adell, Adella, Adelle)

German, meaning "noble" or "nobility." Made famous by the singer Adele.

Aden
(alt. Addien)

Hebrew, meaning "decoration."

Aderyn

Welsh, meaning "bird." Also the name of several places in Wales.

Adesina

Yoruba, meaning "she paves the way." Usually given to a first-born daughter.

Adina
(alt. Adena)

Hebrew, meaning "high hopes" or "precious." Found in the Bible.

Adira

Hebrew, meaning "noble" or "powerful." Also the north Italian city.

Adley

English, meaning "son of Adam." Can be used for girls or boys.

Adrienne
(alt. Adriane, Adriana, Adrianna, Adrianne)

Greek, meaning "from the city of Hadria," or Latin meaning "dark." A feminine form of Adrian.

Aegle

Greek, meaning "brightness" or "splendor." The name of several characters in ancient Greek mythology.

Aerin

Variant of Erin, meaning "peace-making." Taken from J. R. R. Tolkien's novels.

Aerith

Modern American, from the video game *Final Fantasy VII*.

Aero
(alt. Aeron)

Greek, meaning "flight."

Aerolynn

Combination of the Greek Aero, meaning "water," and the English Lynn, meaning "waterfall."

Africa

Celtic, meaning "pleasant," as well as the name of the continent.

Afsaneh

Iranian, meaning "a fairy tale."

Afsha

Persian, meaning "one who sprinkles light."

Afton

Originally a name of a river in Scotland.

Agatha
(abbrev. Aggie)

From St. Agatha, the patron saint of bells, meaning "good." Made famous by mystery novelist Agatha Christie.

Aglaia

Greek, meaning "brilliance." One of the three ancient Greek graces.

Agnes

Greek, meaning "virginal" or "pure." St. Agnes of Rome is the patron saint of girls.

Agrippina

Latin, meaning "born feet first." The name of several influential women of ancient Rome.

Aida

Arabic, meaning "reward" or "present." The title of an opera by Giuseppe Verdi.

Aidanne
(alt. Aidan, Aidenn)

Gaelic, meaning "fire."

Ailbhe

Irish, meaning "noble" or "bright."

Aileen
(alt. Aelinn, Aleen, Aline, Alline)

Gaelic variant of Helen, meaning "light."

Ailith
(alt. Ailish)

Old English, meaning "seasoned warrior."

Ailsa

Scottish, meaning "pledge from God." Also the name of a Scottish island.

Aina

Scandinavian, meaning "forever."

Aine
(alt. Aino)

Celtic, meaning "happiness." The Celtic goddess of summer.

Ainsley
(alt. Ansley)

Scottish/Gaelic, meaning "one's own meadow." Ainsley Hayes is a character in *West Wing*. Can be used for girls or boys.

Aisha
(alt. Aeysha)

Arabic, meaning "woman"; Swahili, meaning "life." Aisha was one of the prophet Muhammad's wives.

Aishwarya

Arabic, meaning "woman." Aishwarya Rai Bachchan is a famous Bollywood actor.

Aislinn
(alt. Aislin, Aisling, Aislyn, Alene, Allene)

Irish Gaelic, meaning "dream." A tribute to aisling, which was an old poetic genre in Ireland.

Aiyanna
(alt. Aiyana)

Native American, meaning "forever flowering."

Aja

Hindi, meaning "goat."

Akela
(alt. Akilah)

Hawaiian, meaning "noble"; Hindi, meaning "alone." Akela is the wolf leader from *The Jungle Book*.

Akilina

Greek or Russian, meaning "eagle."

Akiva

Hebrew, meaning "protect and shelter."

Alaina
(alt. Alana, Alane, Alani, Alanna, Alayna, Aleena, Allannah, Allyn)

Feminine form of Alan, originating from the Greek for "rock" or "comely." Also a spelling alternative for Eleanor.

Alana
(alt. Alanna, Allannah)

Gaelic, meaning "beauty;" Hawaiian, meaning "beautiful offering"; Old German, meaning "precious."

Alanis
(alt. Alarice)

Greek, meaning "rock" or "comely." Associated with singer Alanis Morissette.

Alba

Latin for "white." Also the Gaelic name for Scotland.

Alberta
(alt. Albertha, Albertine)

Feminine form of Albert, from the Old German for "noble, bright, famous." Also a province in Canada.

Albina

Latin, meaning "white" or "fair." Name of an Etruscan goddess of the dawn.

Alda

German, meaning "old" or "prosperous." St. Alda was an Italian mystic in the 11th century.

Aldis

English, meaning "battle seasoned."

Aleta
(alt. Aletha)

Greek, meaning "footloose." Queen Aleta Ellis is a character from *The Legend of Prince Valiant*.

Alethea
(alt. Aletheia)

Greek, meaning "truth."

Alexandra
(alt. Alejandra, Alejandrina, Alejhandra, Aleksandra, Alessandra, Alexandrea, Alexandria, Aliandra; abbrev. Alex, Alexa, Alexi, Alexia, Alexina, Ali, Allie, Ally, Lexi, Lexie, Sandra, Sandy, Sasha, Sascha, Shura, Sondra, Xandra, Zandra)

Feminine form of Alexander, from the Greek interpretation of "man's defender." Also one of the ancient Greek goddess Hera's names. Perhaps the name with the most short forms, from many languages, which are often used as names in their own right.

Alexis
(alt. Alexus, Alexys)

Greek, meaning "helper." Alexis was an ancient Greek poet of comedy.

Aleydis

Variant of Alice, meaning "nobility." Alternative name for St. Alice of Scharbeek, the patron saint of the blind and paralyzed.

Alfreda

Old English, meaning "elf power." The modern spelling of AElfthryth of Crowland.

Alibeth

Variant of Elizabeth, meaning "pledged to God." Popular name during the Middle Ages.

Alice
(alt. Alika, Aliki, Alize, Alyce, Alys, Alyse)
English, meaning "noble" or "nobility." Made famous by the novel Alice in Wonderland.

Alicia
(alt. Ahlicia, Alecia, Alesha, Alesia, Alessia, Alizia, Alisha, Alycia, Alysha, Alysia)
Latin, originally derived from Alice, meaning "nobility." Famous Alicias include singer Alicia Keys, actor Alicia Silverstone, and the birth name of singer Pink.

Alida
(alt. Aleida)
Latin, meaning "small-winged one."

Alima
Arabic, meaning "cultured."

Alina
(alt. Alena, Aleana)
Slavic form of Helen, meaning "light."

Alison
(alt. Allison, Allisyn, Allyson, Alyson; abbrev. Ali, Allie, Ally)
Variant of Alice, meaning "nobility." Originally the name was Alis in the Middle Ages, with the suffix "on," which means "little."

Alivia
Variant of Olivia, meaning "olive tree."

Aliya
(alt. Aaliyah, Aleah, Alia, Aliah, Aliyah)
Arabic, meaning "exalted" or "sublime." Aliya bint Ali was the last queen consort of Iraq.

Alla
Variant of Ella or Alexandra. Also a possible reference to Allah.

Allegra
Italian, meaning "joyous."

Allura
French, from the word for entice, meaning "the power of attraction."

Alma
Latin for "giving nurture"; Italian for "soul"; Arabic for "learned." Also commonly written as Alma Mater, meaning "nourishing mother" or "fostering mother."

Almeda
(alt. Almeta)
Latin, meaning "ambitious."

Almera
(alt. Almira)
Feminine form of Elmer, from the Arabic for "aristocratic"; Old English meaning "noble."

Alohi
Variant of the Hawaiian greeting Aloha, meaning "love and affection."

Alona
(alt. Alora)

Hebrew, meaning "oak tree."

Alpha

The first letter of the Greek alphabet, usually given to a firstborn daughter.

Alta

Latin, meaning "elevated."

Altagracia

Spanish, meaning "grace." Alta Gracia is also a city in Argentina.

Althaea
(alt. Altea, Altha, Althea)

Greek, meaning "healing power." Althaea was a prominent character in ancient Greek mythology.

Alva

Spanish, meaning "blonde" or "fair-skinned." In Norway and Sweden it is considered the female form of Alf, which means "elf."

Alvena
(alt. Alvina)

Old English, meaning "elf friend." In Old German it is the feminine form of Adelwin, meaning "noble friend."

Alvia
(alt. Alyvia)

Variant of Olivia, meaning "olive tree," or Elvira, from the ancient Spanish city.

Alyssa
(alt. Alisa, Alissa, Allyssa, Alysa)

Greek, meaning "rational." Associated with the alyssum flower.

Amadea

Feminine form of Amadeus, meaning "God's love."

Amalia

German, meaning "work"; Hebrew, meaning "labor of love."

Amana

Hebrew, meaning "loyal and true." Also a genus of tulips.

Amanda
(alt. Amandine; abbrev. Mandy)

Latin, meaning "much loved." Famous Amandas include actors Amanda Bynes and Amanda Seyfried.

Amara
(alt. Amani)

Greek, meaning "lovely forever." Actor Amara Miller is known for her role in TV show *The Descendants*.

Amarantha

Contraction of Amanda and Samantha, meaning "much loved listener."

Amari
(alt. Amaris, Amasa, Amata, Amaya)

Hebrew, meaning "pledged by God."

Amaryllis
(alt. Ameris)
Greek, meaning "fresh." Also a flower.

Amber
French, from the semiprecious stone of the same name. Famous Ambers include actor Amber Heard and model Amber Rose.

Amberly
Contraction of Amber and Leigh, meaning "stone" and "meadow."

Amberlynn
Contraction of Amber and Lynn, meaning "stone" and "waterfall."

Amelia
(alt. Aemilia, Amelie)
Greek, meaning "industrious." Famous Amelias include flying legend Amelia Earhart and two Princess Amelias of Great Britain. Amelie is the French variant and the title of a movie.

America
From the country and continents of the same name. Associated with *Ugly Betty* actor America Ferrera.

Amethyst
Greek, from the precious, mulberry-colored stone of the same name.

Amina
Arabic, meaning "honest and trustworthy."

Aminta
Greek, meaning "defender."

Amira
(alt. Amiya, Amiyah)
Arabic, meaning "a high-born girl"; Hebrew, meaning "rich princess."

Amity
Latin, meaning "friendship and harmony." Also a name of a faction in the *Divergent* series.

Amory
Variant of the Spanish name Amor, meaning "love."

Amy
(alt. Aimee, Amee, Ami, Amie, Ammie, Amya)
Latin, meaning "beloved." Famous Amys include actor Amy Adams and singer Amy Winehouse. Aimee is the French form, used by actor Aimee Garcia, singer Aimee Mann, and Aimee Osbourne of the Osbourne family.

Ana-Lisa
Contraction of Anna and Lisa, meaning "grace" or "consecrated to God."

Anafa
Hebrew, meaning "heron."

Ananda

Hindi, meaning "bliss." One of Buddha's disciples.

Anastasia
(alt. Athanasia)

Greek, meaning "resurrection." Grand Duchess Anastasia of Russia was killed in 1918, following the Russian Revolution.

Anat

Jewish, meaning "water spring." Anat is an important Semitic goddess.

Anatolia

Greek, meaning "east sunrise." From the eastern Greek town of the same name.

Andrea
(alt. Andreia, Andria, Andrine, Andrina)

Feminine form of Andrew, from the Greek term for "a man's woman." Famous Andreas include writers Andrea Levy and Andrea Dworkin.

Andromeda

Greek, meaning "leader of men." From the heroine of an ancient Greek legend.

Anemone

Greek, meaning "breath." Also a flowering plant.

Angela
(alt. Angel, Angeles, Angelia, Angelle, Angie)

Greek, meaning "messenger from God" or "angel." Famous Angelas include actors Angela Lansbury and Angela Bassett.

Angelica
(alt. Angelina, Angeline, Angelique, Angelise, Angelita, Anjelica, Anjelina)

Latin, meaning "angelic." Famous Angelicas include actor Anjelica Huston and *Rugrats* character Angelica Pickles.

Anise
(alt. Anisa, Anissa)

French, from the licorice-flavored plant of the same name.

Aniston

English, meaning "town of Agnes."

Anita
(alt. Anitra)

Derived from Ann, Hannah, or Anahita (the Iranian water goddess), depending on the language. Famous Anitas include singer Anita Baker and *West Side Story* character Anita.

Anna
(alt. Ana)

Derived from Hannah, meaning "grace." A prophetess in the Bible.

Annabel

(alt. Anabel, Anabelle, Annabell, Annabella, Annabelle, Amabel)

Contraction of Anna and Belle, meaning "grace" and "beauty."

Annalise

(alt. Annalee, Annalisa, Anneli, Annelie, Annelise)

Contraction of Anna and Lise, meaning "grace" and "pledged to God."

Anne

(alt. Ann)

Originally a French form of Anna, meaning "grace," but used in England for many hundreds of years. Famous Annes include actor Anne Hathaway and two wives of Henry VIII.

Annemarie

(alt. Annamae, Annamarie, Annelle, Annmarie)

Contraction of Anna and Mary, meaning "grace" and "star of the sea." The name of actor Anne-Marie Duff.

Annette

(alt. Annetta)

Hebrew, derived from Hannah, meaning "grace." Associated with actors Annette Funicello and Annette Bening.

Annis

Greek, meaning "finished or completed." The Black Annis is a blue-faced witch in English mythology.

Annora

Latin, meaning "honor."

Anoushka

(alt. Anousha)

Russian variation of Ann, meaning "grace."

Anthea

(alt. Anthi)

Greek, meaning "flower-like." Also another name for the ancient Greek goddess Hera.

Antigone

In ancient Greek mythology, Antigone was the daughter of Oedipus.

Antoinette

(alt. Antonetta, Antonette, Antonietta; abbrev. Toni)

Feminine form of Anthony, meaning "invaluable grace." French queen consort Marie Antoinette was executed during the French Revolution fo 1789.

Antonia

(alt. Antonella, Antonina)

Latin, meaning "invaluable." A very popular name in ancient Rome.

Anwen

Welsh, meaning "very fair."

Anya

(alt. Aanya, Aniya, Aniyah, Aniylah, Anja)

Russian, meaning "grace."

Aoife

Gaelic, meaning "beautiful joy." Associated with goddess Esuvia.

Apollonia

Feminine of Apollo, the Greek god of the sun. St. Apollonia is the patron saint of dentistry.

Apple

From the name of the fruit. Famous Apples include technology company Apple Inc., and Gwyneth Paltrow's daughter.

April

(alt. Avril)

Latin, meaning "opening up." Also the fourth month, which has associations with the goddess Venus.

Aquilina

(alt. Aqua, Aquila)

Spanish, meaning "like an eagle." Associated with St. Aquilina.

Ara

Arabic, meaning "brings rain." Also a star constellation. Can be used for girls or boys.

Arabella

(alt. Arabelle; abbrev. Bel, Bella)

Latin, meaning "answered prayer." The name of an opera by Richard Strauss.

Araceli

(alt. Aracely)

Spanish, meaning "altar of Heaven."

Araminta

Contraction of Arabella and Aminta, meaning "answered prayer" and "defender."

Arcadia

Greek, meaning "paradise." The daughter of ancient Roman Emperor Arcadius.

Ardelle

(alt. Ardell, Ardella)

Latin, meaning "burning with enthusiasm." Ardelle Kloss is a figure skater.

Arden

(alt. Ardis, Ardith)

Latin, meaning "burning with enthusiasm." Made famous by the cosmetics company Elizabeth Arden.

Arella

(alt. Areli, Arely)

Hebrew, meaning "angel."

Aretha

Greek, meaning "woman of virtue."
Aretha Franklin was a legendary soul
singer.

Aria

(alt. Ariah, Arya)

Italian, meaning "melody." Arya Stark
is a character in *Game of Thrones*.

Ariadne

Both Greek and Latin, meaning "the
very holy one." In ancient Greek
mythology, Ariadne was the daughter
of King Minos.

Ariana

(alt. Ariane, Arianna, Arienne)

Welsh, meaning "silver."

Ariel

(alt. Ariela, Ariella, Arielle)

Hebrew, meaning "lioness of
God." Ariel is the main character in
Disney's *The Little Mermaid*.

Arlene

(alt. Arleen, Arline; abbrev. Arlie, Arly)

Gaelic, meaning "pledge." Associated
with actor Arlene Dahl.

Armida

Latin, meaning "little armed one."
Taken from the character of Armida
in *Gerusalemme liberata* by Italian
poet Torquato Tasso.

Artemisia

(alt. Artemis, Arti, Artie)

Greek/Spanish, meaning "perfect."
Artemisia was a legendary female
ancient Persian naval commander.

Arwen

Welsh, meaning "fair" or "fine."
Arwen is a key Elven figure in *The
Lord of the Rings*.

Ashanti

Geographical area in Africa. Also
the name of the popular R&B singer
Ashanti.

Ashby

English, meaning "ash tree farm."

Ashley

*(alt. Ashlee, Ashleigh, Ashli, Ashlie,
Ashly)*

English, meaning "ash tree meadow."
Famous Ashleys include actor Ashley
Judd, and singers Ashley Tisdale and
Ashlee Simpson. Can be used for girls
or boys.

Ashlynn

(alt. Ashlyn)

Irish Gaelic, meaning "dream."

Ashton

(alt. Ashtyn)

Old English, meaning "ash tree
town." Can be used for girls or boys.

Asia

Name of the continent. Also a name for an Oceanid in ancient Greek mythology.

Asma
(alt. Asmara)

Arabic, meaning "highstanding."

Aspen
(alt. Aspynn)

Name of the tree. Also the Colorado city famous for its ski resort.

Assumpta
(alt. Asumpta, Assunta)

Italian, meaning "raised up."

Asta
(alt. Asteria, Astor, Astoria)

Greek or Latin, meaning "starlike."

Astrid

Old Norse, meaning "beautiful like a God." Astrid Lundgren is the author of *Pippi Longstocking*.

Atara

Hebrew, meaning "diadem" or "crown." Also a genus of butterfly.

Athena
(alt. Athenais)

Greek, meaning "wise." Athena was the ancient Greek goddess of wisdom, mathematics, and arts and crafts.

Aubrey
(alt. Aubree, Aubriana, Aubrie)

French, meaning "elf ruler."

Audrey
(alt. Audra, Audrie, Audrina, Audry)

English, meaning "noble strength." St. Etheldreda was known as St. Audrey, and was a seventh-century English princess. Made famous by Hollywood icon Audrey Hepburn.

Augusta
(alt. August, Augustine)

Latin, meaning "worthy of respect."

Aura
(alt. Aurea)

Greek or Latin, meaning either "soft breeze" or "gold." An aura is the perceived field of energy surrounding people and objects in various spiritual beliefs.

Aurelia
(alt. Aurelie)

Latin, meaning gold. The mother of Julius Caesar.

Aurora
(alt. Aurore)

Latin, meaning "dawn." In ancient Roman mythology, Aurora was the goddess of sunrise.

Austine
(alt. Austen, Austin)

Latin, meaning "worthy of respect."

Autumn

Latin, from the name of the harvest season.

Ava

(alt. Avia, Avie)

Latin, meaning "like a bird."
Associated with actor Ava Gardner.

Avalon

(alt. Avalyn, Aveline)

Celtic, meaning "island of apples."
Avalon is the mythological island in the King Arthur legend.

Axelle

Greek, meaning "father of peace."

Aya

(alt. Ayah)

Hebrew, meaning "bird."

Ayanna

(alt. Ayana)

Yoruba, meaning "beautiful flower."

Ayesha

(alt. Aisha, Aysha)

Persian, meaning "small one."

Azalea

Latin, meaning "dry earth." Also the name of a flowering shrub.

Names of First Ladies

Barbara (Bush)
Edith (Roosevelt)
Elizabeth (Ford)
Grace (Coolidge)
Hillary (Clinton)
Jacqueline (Kennedy)
Martha (Washington)
Mary (Lincoln)
Melania (Trump)
Michelle (Obama)
Nancy (Reagan)

Azalia

Hebrew, meaning "aided by God."

Aziza

Hebrew, meaning "mighty"; Arabic meaning "precious." Female variation of Aziz.

Azure

(alt. Azaria)

French, meaning "sky-blue." Refers to the bright blue color of the sky on a clear day.

B

Girls' names

Babette
(alt. Babe)

French version of Barbara; Greek meaning "foreign." Babette Cole is the author of children's books *Mommy Laid an Egg* and *Princess Smartypants*.

Bailey
(alt. Baeli, Bailee)

English, meaning "law enforcer."

Bambi
(alt. Bambina)

Shortened version of the Italian "bambina," meaning "child." Made famous by the Disney movie *Bambi*.

Barbara
(alt. Barbra; abbrev. Barb, Barbie)

Greek, meaning "foreign." Famous Barbaras include journalist Barbara Walters, and singer and actor Barbra Streisand.

Basma
Arabic, meaning "smile."

Bathsheba
Hebrew, meaning "daughter of the oath." Bathsheba was a key biblical figure, and mother of King Solomon.

Bay
(alt. Bae, Baya)

From the edible plant the bay leaf, or the geographical name for a large inlet of water.

Beata
Latin, meaning "blessed."

Beatrice
(alt. Beatrix, Beatriz, Bee, Bellatrix; abbrev. Bea)

Latin, meaning "bringer of gladness." Beatrice is a character in Shakespeare's *Much Ado About Nothing*. Princess Beatrice is ninth in line to the British throne.

Belinda
(alt. Belen, Belina)

Contraction of Belle and Linda, meaning "beautiful." Well-known Belindas include singer Belinda Carlisle.

Bella
(alt. Béla)

Latin, meaning "beautiful." Bella (Isabella) Swan is the main female character in the *Twilight* series.

Belle
(alt. Bell)

French, meaning "beautiful." Popularized by the Disney princess in *Beauty and the Beast*.

Belva

Latin, meaning "beautiful view." The inspiration for one of the characters in the musical *Chicago* was real-life murderer Belva Gaertner.

Bénédicta
(alt. Benedetta; abbrev. Bennie)

Latin, the feminine form of Benedict, meaning "blessed." Associated with Benedicta Henrietta of the Palatinate.

Benita
(alt. Bernita; abbrev. Bennie)

Spanish, meaning "blessed."

Berit
(alt. Beret)

Scandinavian, meaning "splendid" or "gorgeous."

Bernadette
(alt. Bernadine; abbrev. Bernie)

French, meaning "courageous." St. Bernadette was known for her visions of the Virgin Mary.

Bernice
(alt. Berenice, Berniece, Burnice)

Greek, meaning "she who brings victory." The name of Herod's daughter in the Bible.

Bertha
(alt. Berta, Berthe, Bertie)

German, meaning "bright." There are four saints called Bertha, all from the Middle Ages.

Beryl

Greek, meaning "pale, green gemstone." The name of a precious mineral.

Bess
(alt. Bessie)

Shortened form of Elizabeth, meaning "consecrated to God." Queen Elizabeth I's nickname was Good Queen Bess.

Beth

Hebrew, meaning "house." Also shortened form of Elizabeth, meaning "consecrated to God."

Bethany
(alt. Bethan)

Hebrew, referring to a geographical location in the Bible.

Bethel

Hebrew, meaning "house of God."
A city in the Bible.

Bettina

(alt. Battina, Betiana, Betina, Bettine; abbrev. Betty, Ina, Tina)

Latin, derived from Benedetta or German derived from Elizabeth. Bettina Bush was the voice for *Rainbow Brite*.

Betty

(alt. Betsy, Bette, Bettie, Bettye)

Originally a shortened version of Elizabeth, meaning "consecrated to God," now often used as a name in its own right. Famous Bettys include cartoon character Betty Boop, actor Betty Grable, and glamor model Bettie Page.

Beulah

Hebrew, meaning "married."
The name of the place that exists between Earth and Heaven.

Beverly

(alt. Beverlee, Beverley)

English, meaning "beaver stream." Made famous by Beverly Hills, CA, and actor Beverley Mitchell.

Beyoncé

American English, made popular by the singer.

Bianca

(alt. Blanca)

Italian, meaning "white." Bianca is a character from Shakespeare's *Othello*.

Bijou

French, meaning "precious ring."

Billie

(alt. Bill, Billy, Billye)

Originally used for girls as a shortened version of Wilhelmina, meaning "determined." Now used almost universally as a standalone name, made popular by jazz singer Billie Holiday who chose it as her stage name, and tennis legend Billie Jean King.

Bina

Hebrew, meaning "knowledge."

Birdie

(alt. Birdy)

English and Swedish, meaning "little bird."

Birgit

(alt. Birgitta)

German, meaning "power and strength." Used as a variation of Bridget.

Blaer

Icelandic, meaning "light breeze."

Blair

Scottish Gaelic, meaning "flat, plain area." Well-known Blairs include actor Blair Underwood.

Blake
(alt. Blakely, Blakelyn)

English, meaning either "pale skinned" or "dark." Associated with actor Blake Lively. Can be used for girls or boys.

Blanche
(alt. Blanch)

French, meaning "white or pale." Famous Blanches include the characters of Blanche Devereaux in *The Golden Girls*, and Blanche DuBois in *A Streetcar Named Desire*.

Bliss

English, meaning "intense happiness."

Blithe

English, meaning "joyous."

Blodwen

Welsh, meaning "white flower." The name of a Welsh opera.

Blossom

English, meaning "flowerlike." *Blossom* was a 1990s sitcom.

Blythe
(alt. Bly)

English, meaning "happy and carefree." Blythe Danner starred in sitcom *Will and Grace* and is the mother of actor Gwyneth Paltrow.

Bobbi
(alt. Bobbie, Bobby)

Shortened version of Roberta, meaning "bright fame." Associated with cosmetics brand Bobbi Brown.

Bonita
(alt. Bo)

Spanish, meaning "pretty." "La Isla Bonita" is a song by Madonna.

Bonnie
(alt. Bonny)

Scottish, meaning "fair of face." One half of the outlaw duo Bonnie and Clyde.

Brandy
(alt. Brandee, Brandi, Brandie)

Dutch, meaning "burnt wine." Name of the liquor.

Brea
(alt. Bree, Bria)

Shortened form of Brianna, meaning "strong." Also the name of an ancient Irish god.

Brenda

Old Norse, meaning "sword."

Brianna
(alt. Breana, Breann, Breanna, Breanne, Brenna, Brenyn, Briana, Brianne, Bryanna)

Irish Gaelic, meaning "strong."

Bridget
(alt. Bridgett, Bridgette, Brigette, Brigid, Brigitta, Brigitte)

Irish Gaelic, meaning "strength and power." Famous Bridgets include actors Bridget Fonda and Brigitte Bardot, and the novel and movie *Bridget Jones's Diary*.

Brier
(alt. Briar)

French, meaning "heather." Sleeping Beauty's pseudonym is Briar Rose in the Disney movie.

Brit
(alt. Britt, Britta)

Celtic, meaning "spotted" or "freckled." Name of actor Britt Ekland.

Britannia

Latin, meaning "Britain." Britannia is the female personification of Great Britain.

Brittany
(alt. Britany, Britney, Britni, Brittani, Brittanie, Brittney, Brittni, Brittny)

Latin, meaning "from Britain." Famous Brittanys include the French province, singer Britney Spears, and actor Brittany Murphy.

Bronwen
(alt. Bronwyn)

Welsh, meaning "fair breast." The spelling of Bronwen is more common for girls, and Bronwyn for boys.

Brooke
(alt. Brook)

English, meaning "small stream." Brooke Shields is an actor and model. Can be used for girls or boys.

Brooklyn
(alt. Brooklynn)

Name of a New York borough. Associated with model Brooklyn Decker.

Brunhilda
(alt. Brunhilde, Brynhildr)

German, meaning "armor-wearing fighting maid." Brynhildr was an important character in Old German mythology.

Bryn
(alt. Brynn)

Welsh, meaning "mount" or "hill."

Bryony
(alt. Briony)

English, from bryonia, the name of a European vine.

Buffy

American English alternative of Elizabeth, meaning "consecrated to God." The protagonist of the sci-fi series *Buffy the Vampire Slayer*.

C

Girls' names

Cadence
(alt. Candenza)

Latin, meaning "with rhythm." Also used beginning with K.

Cai

Vietnamese, meaning "feminine."

Caitlin
(alt. Cadyn, Caitlann, Caitlyn, Caitlyn, Kaitlin)

Greek, meaning "pure." Catelyn Stark is a central character from *Game of Thrones*. Caitlyn Jenner is a former Olympian athlete and member of the Jenner/Kardashian clan. Also spelt with a K, as for Kaitlin Doubleday.

Calandra

Greek, meaning "lark." A small Mediterranean bird.

Calantha
(alt. Calanthe)

Greek, meaning "lovely flower."

Caledonia

Latin, meaning Scotland.

Calla

Greek, meaning "beautiful." Associated with the calla lily.

Callie
(alt. Caleigh, Cali, Calleigh, Cally)

Greek, meaning "beauty." Callie Khouri is a screenwriter.

Calliope
(alt. Kalliope)

Greek, meaning "beautiful voice." From the muse of epic poetry in Greek mythology.

Callista
(alt. Calista, Callisto, Kallista)

Greek, meaning "most beautiful." Best-known as the name of actor Calista Flockhart.

Camas

Native American, from the root and bulb of the same name.

Cambria

Welsh, from the alternate name for Wales.

Camden
(alt. Camdyn)

English, meaning "winding valley." Also an area of London, England.

Cameo

Italian, meaning "skin." Associated with the notion of a cameo role in film or television.

Cameron
(alt. Camryn)

Scottish Gaelic, meaning "bent nose." Used for boys and girls. Actor Cameron Diaz has starred in many Hollywood hits.

Camilla
(alt. Camelia, Camellia, Camila, Camille, Camillia)

Latin, meaning "spiritual serving girl." Made famous by model Camilla Alves, and Camilla, Duchess of Cornwall, who is married to Prince Charles.

Candace
(alt. Candice, Candis, Kandace)

Latin, meaning "brilliant white." Famous Candaces include basketball player Candace Parker, and Candace Bushnell, author of *Sex and the City*.

Candida

Latin, meaning "white."

Candra

Latin, meaning "glowing."

Candy
(alt. Candi, Kandy)

Shortened form of Candace, meaning "brilliant white." Also a name for sweets or confectionery.

Caoimhe

Celtic, meaning "gentleness." Has many different pronounciations, including "Kyva" and "Keeva," depending on where in Ireland you hear it.

Caprice

Italian, meaning "ruled by whim." Made famous by model and actor Caprice.

Cara

Latin, meaning "darling." Cara Delevingne is a model and Cara Black a bestselling mystery novelist.

C

Carey

(alt. Cari, Carie, Carri, Carrie, Cary)

Welsh, meaning "near the castle." Famous Careys include actor Carey Mulligan and singer Mariah Carey.

Carina

(alt. Corina)

Italian, meaning "dearest little one." Also the name of a star constellation.

Carissa

(alt. Carisa)

Greek, meaning "grace."

Carla

(alt. Charl, Karla)

Feminine of the Old Norse Carl, meaning "free man." Supermodel and singer-songwriter Carla Bruni-Sarkozy is married to former French president Nicolas Sarkozy.

Carlin

(alt. Carleen, Carlene)

Gaelic, meaning "little champion."

Carlotta

(alt. Carlota)

Italian, meaning "free man." Carlotta is a character from *The Phantom of the Opera*.

Carly

(alt. Carlee, Carley, Carli, Carlie, Karly, Karlie)

Feminine form of the German Charles, meaning "man." Famous Carlys include singers Carly Simon and Carly Rae Jepson, and model Karlie Kloss.

Carmel

(alt. Carmela, Carmelita, Carmella)

Hebrew, meaning "garden." American Carmelita Jeter is an Olympic medal-winning 100-meter sprinter.

Carmen

(alt. Carma, Carmina)

Latin, meaning "song." The opera *Carmen* was composed by Georges Bizet.

Carol

(alt. Carole, Carrol, Carroll, Caryl, Karol)

Originally the short form of Caroline, meaning "man." Famous Carols include actor Carol Burnett.

Caroline

(alt. Carolann, Carolina, Carolyn, Carolynn)

German, meaning "man." A feminine form of Charles. Caroline Kennedy is the daughter of John F. Kennedy.

Carrington

English, meaning "Charles's town."

Carys
(alt. Cerys)
Welsh, meaning "love."

Casey
(alt. Casy, Casie, Kasey)
Irish Gaelic, meaning "watchful."
Used for girls and boys.

Cassandra
(alt. Casandra, Cassandre, Kassandra;
abbrev. Cassie)
Greek, meaning "one who
prophesies doom" or "entangler
of men." Cassandra was a seer in
ancient Greek mythology.

Cassia
(alt. Casia, Casie, Cassie)
Greek, meaning "cinnamon."

Cassidy
Irish, meaning "clever."

Catherine
(alt. Catalina, Catarina, Caterina,
Catharine, Cathleen, Cathrine,
Cathryn; abbrev. Cate, Cathy, Cathie,
Caity, Caty)
Greek, meaning "pure." Famous
Catherines include Catherine,
Duchess of Cambridge, actor
Catherine Zeta Jones, and Russia's
Catherine the Great. Cathleen is the
Irish variant of Catherine, and Catalina
the Spanish version. All variations and
abbreviations can also be spelled with
an initial K.

Cayley
(alt. Cayla, Caylee, Caylen)
Gaelic, meaning "slim" and "fair."

Cecilia
(alt. Cecelia, Cecile, Cecilie, Cecily,
Cicely, Cicily)
Latin, meaning "blind one."

Celena
Greek, meaning "goddess of the
moon." Also a spelling variation for
Selena.

Celeste
(alt. Celestina, Celestine)
Latin, meaning "heavenly."
Associated with actor Celeste Holm.

Celine
(alt. Celia, Celina)
French version of Celeste, meaning
"heavenly." Associated with singer
Celine Dion.

Cerise
French, meaning "cherry." The color
cerise is a deep, pink-red shade.

Chanah
(alt. Chana)
Hebrew, meaning "grace." Also a
spelling variation for Hannah.

Chance
Middle English, meaning "good
fortune."

Chandler
(alt. Chandell)
English, meaning "candle maker."
Can be used for girls or, more
commonly, boys.

Chandra
(alt. Chanda, Chandry)
Sanskrit, meaning "like the moon."
Chandra is a god of the moon in
Hinduism.

Chanel
(alt. Chanelle)
French, meaning "pipe." Name of
the French fashion house founded by
designer Coco Chanel.

Chantal
(alt. Chantel, Chantelle, Chantilly)
French, meaning "stony spot."

Chardonnay
French, from the wine variety of the
same name.

Charis
(alt. Charice, Charissa, Charisse)
Greek, meaning "grace." One of the
graces in ancient Greek mythology.

Charity
Latin, meaning "brotherly love."

Charlene
(alt. Charleen, Charline)
German, meaning "man." Associated
with actor Charlene Tilton.

Charlize
French form of Charlotte, meaning
"little and feminine". Made famous
by actor Charlize Theron.

Charlotte
(alt. Charnette, Charolette; abbrev.
Charlie, Charley, Charly, Lottie)
French, meaning "little and
feminine." Famous Charlottes include
Princess Charlotte, author Charlotte
Bronte, and the novel Charlotte's
Web by E. B. White.

Charmaine
Latin, meaning "clan." Derived
from Charmain, a favorite servant of
Cleopatra.

Chastity
Latin, meaning "purity."

Chava
(alt. Chaya)
Hebrew, meaning "beloved."

Chelsea
(alt. Chelsee, Chelsey, Chelsi, Chelsie)
English, meaning "port or landing
place." Famous Chelseas include
comedian Chelsea Handler and
advocate Chelsea Clinton.

Cher
French, meaning "beloved." Made
famous by the singer Cher.

Cherie
(alt. Cheri, Cherise)
French, meaning "dear."

Cherish
(alt. Cherith)
English, meaning "to treasure." The title of a song by Madonna.

Chermona
Hebrew, meaning "sacred mountain."

Cherry
(alt. Cherri)
French, meaning "cherry fruit."

Cheryl
(alt. Cheryle)
English, meaning "little and womanly." Famous Cheryls include dancer Cheryl Burke from *Dancing With The Stars*.

Chesney
English, meaning "place to camp." More commonly used for boys.

Cheyenne
(alt. Cheyanne)
Native American, from the tribe of the same name in Wyoming.

Chiara
(alt. Ceara, Chiarina, Ciara)
Italian, meaning "light." Associated with the singer Ciara.

China
From the country of the same name.

Chiquita
Spanish, meaning "little one."

Chloe
(alt. Cloe)
Greek, meaning "pale green shoot." Famous Chloes include actors Chloe Grace Moretz and Chloe Sevigny, and author Toni Morrison—whose birth name was Chloe Wofford.

Chloris
(alt. Cloris)
Greek, meaning "pale." Made famous by actor and comedian Cloris Leachman.

Christabel
(alt. Christobel)
Latin and French, meaning "fair Christian." The title of a poem by Samuel Taylor Coleridge.

Christina
(alt. Christine, Christen, Christene, Christian, Christiana, Christiane, Christin, Cristina; abbrev. Chris, Chrissy, Christa, Christie, Christy, Crissy, Cristy)
Greek, meaning "anointed Christian." Famous Christinas include singer Christina Aguilera and actors Christina Ricci and Christine Taylor.

Chuma
Aramaic, meaning "warmth."

Cierra
(alt. Ciera)

Irish, meaning "black."

Cinderella

French, meaning "little ashgirl."
Subject of the children's fairy tale.

Cinnamon

Greek, from the exotic spice of the
same name.

Citlali
(alt. Citlalli)

Nahuatl, meaning "star." An ancient
Aztec name.

Citrine

Latin, from the gemstone of the same
name.

Claire
(alt. Clara, Clare, Claira)

Latin, meaning "bright." Associated
with actor Claire Danes.

Clarabelle
(alt. Claribel)

Contraction of Clare and Isobel,
meaning "bright" and "consecrated
to God." Clarabelle is a Disney cow
cartoon character.

Clarissa
(alt. Clarice, Clarisse)

Variation of Claire, meaning "bright."
The title character from the 1990s'
sitcom Clarissa Explains It All.

Clarity

Latin, meaning "lucid."

Claudia
(alt. Claudetta, Claudette, Claudie,
Claudine)

Latin, meaning "lame." The first
female president of Haiti was
Claudette Werleigh. Claudia Schiffer
is a German supermodel.

Clematis

Greek, meaning "vine." A type of
flowering plant.

Clementine
(alt. Clemency, Clementina, Clemmie)

Latin, meaning "mild and merciful."
Also the small orange fruit.

Cleopatra

Greek, meaning "her father's
renown." Famed as an ancient
Egyptian queen.

Clio
(alt. Cleo, Cliona)

Greek, from the ancient Greek muse
of the same name.

Clodagh

Irish, meaning "river."

Clotilda
(alt. Clothilda, Clothilde, Clotilde)

German, meaning "renowned
battle." St. Clotilde was known for
her works of charity.

Clover

English, from the flower of the same name.

Coby

Diminutive of Jacob, meaning "supplanter." More commonly used as a boy's name.

Coco

Spanish, an abbreviation of *socorro*, meaning "help." Name of the French fashion designer Coco Chanel.

Cody

English, meaning "pillow."

Colleen
(alt. Coleen)

Irish Gaelic, meaning "girl." Colleen Camp is an actor.

Collette
(alt. Colette)

Greek/French, meaning "people of victory." Sidonie-Gabrielle Colette was the author of *Gigi*.

Constance
(alt. Constanza, Constantina, Konstance; abbrev. Connie)

Latin, meaning "steadfast." Oscar Wilde's wife was Constance Lloyd. Famous Connies include actors Connie Britton and Connie Nielsen, and journalist Connie Chung.

Consuelo
(alt. Consuela)

Spanish, meaning "comfort." Originally from the Virgin Mary, who was known as Our Lady of Consolation in Spanish.

Cora
(alt. Kora)

Greek, meaning "maiden."

Coral
(alt. Coralie, Coraline, Corelia, Corene)

Latin, from the marine life of the same name.

Corazon

Spanish, meaning "heart" or "darling."

Cordelia
(alt. Cordia, Cordie)

Latin, meaning "heart." Famous fictional Cordelias include characters in Shakespeare's *King Lear* and TV's *Buffy the Vampire Slayer*.

Corey
(alt. Cori, Corrie, Cory)

Irish Gaelic, meaning "the hollow."

Corin
(alt. Corine)

Latin, meaning "spear."

Corinne
(alt. Corinna, Corrine)

French version of Cora, meaning "maiden." Associated with singer Corinne Bailey Rae.

Corliss

English, meaning "cheery."

Cornelia

Latin, meaning "like a horn." The name of several influential women of ancient Rome.

Corona

Latin, meaning 'crown'.

Cosette

French, meaning "people of victory." Name of a key character in Victor Hugo's *Les Misérables*.

Cosima
(alt. Cosmina)

Greek, meaning "order." One of the clones in *Orphan Black*.

Courtney
(alt. Cortney)

English, meaning "court-dweller." Famous Courtneys include actor Courtney Cox and singer Courtney Love.

Creola

French, meaning "American-born, English descent." Associated with the Creole language and people.

Crescent

French, meaning "increasing."

Cressida

From the Trojan heroine in Greek mythology of the same name.

Crystal
(alt. Christal, Chrystal, Cristal, Krystal)

Greek, meaning "ice." A kind of manufactured precious stone.

Csilla

Hungarian, meaning "defenses."

Cyd

Shortened form of Sidney, meaning "wide island." Cyd Charisse was a dancer and actor.

Cynara

Greek, meaning "thistly plant."

Cynthia
(abbrev. Cinda, Cindi, Cindy, Cyndi)

Greek, meaning "goddess from the mountain." Famous Cynthias include actor Cynthia Nixon and designer Cynthia Rowley. Famous Cindys include 1980s supermodel Cindy Crawford and singer Cindi Lauper.

Cyra

Persian, meaning "sun." Also a genus of ladybugs.

Cyrilla

Latin, meaning "lordly." Also a type of flowering plant.

D

Girls' names

Dacey

Irish Gaelic, meaning "from the south."

Dada

Yoruba, meaning "curly haired." Also associated with the art movement Dadaism.

Daenerys

Literary, created by author George R. R. Martin in book series *A Song of Ice and Fire*, and TV series *Game of Thrones*.

Dagmar

German, meaning "day's glory." Dagmar was the stage name of Virginia Egnor.

Dagny

Nordic, meaning "new day."

Dahlia

Scandinavian, from the flowering plant of the same name.

Daisy

(alt. Daisey, Dasia)

English, meaning "eye of the day." A flowering plant.

Dakota

Native American, meaning "allies." Associated with actor Dakota Fanning, and the states of North and South Dakota.

Dalia

(alt. Daliah, Dalila)

Hebrew, meaning "delicate branch." A Lithuanian goddess.

Dallas

Scottish Gaelic, from the village of the same name. Also the city in Texas.

Damaris

Greek, meaning "calf." Found in the Bible.

Damita

Spanish, meaning "little noblewoman."

Dana

(alt. Dania, Danna, Dayna)

English, meaning "from Denmark"; Persian, meaning "a perfect and valuable pearl."

Danae

Greek, from the mythological heroine of the same name.

Danica

(alt. Danika)

Latin, meaning "from Denmark." Famous Danicas include racing driver Danica Patrick, and actor and author Danica McKellar.

Danielle

(alt. Danelle, Daniela, Daniella, Danila, Danita, Danyell; abbrev. Dani, Danni)

The feminine form of the Hebrew Daniel, meaning "God is my judge." Famous Danielle's include actor Danielle Fischel.

Daphne

(alt. Dafne, Daphna)

Greek, meaning "laurel tree." Daphne was a water nymph in Greek mythology.

Dara

Hebrew/Persian, meaning "wisdom." Found in the Bible.

Darby

(alt. Darbi, Darbie)

Irish, meaning "park with deer."

Darcy

(alt. Darcey, Darci, Darcie)

Irish Gaelic, meaning "dark." Famous Darcys include ballerina Dame Darcey Bussell.

Daria

Greek, meaning "rich." Associated with cartoon series *Daria*.

Darla

English, meaning "darling." Made famous by the child star Darla Hood.

Darlene

(alt. Darleen, Darline)

American English, meaning "darling." Darlene Gillespie is a member of the *Mickey Mouse Club*.

Daryl

(alt. Darryl)

Old English, and possibly also Old French, meaning "loved." Daryl Hannah is an actor.

Davina

Hebrew, meaning "loved one." Davina Claire is a character in *The Vampire Diaries*.

Dawn
(alt. Dawna)

English, meaning "to become day."

Daya

Hebrew, meaning "bird of prey." A form of teaching in the Sikh religion.

Deanna
(alt. Dayana, Deana, Deanna, Deanne, Deena, Dena)

English, meaning "girl from the valley." Famous Deannas include singer and actor Deanna Durbin.

Deborah
(alt. Debbra, Debra, Debrah; abbrev. Debbi, Debbie, Debby, Debi)

Hebrew, meaning "bee." A prophetess in the Bible.

December

Latin, meaning "tenth month."

Dee
(alt. Dea)

Welsh, meaning "swarthy." Also a shortened form of many names beginning with "De-."

Deidre
(alt. Deidra, Deirdre)

Irish, meaning "raging woman."

Deja
(alt. Dejah)

French, meaning "already." The French term for "already seen" is "déjà vu."

Delaney
(alt. Delany)

Irish Gaelic, meaning "offspring of the challenger."

Delia

Greek, meaning "from Delos." Associated with the ancient Greek island of Delos.

Delilah
(alt. Delina)

Hebrew, meaning "seductive." Famous Delilahs include the lover of Samson in the Bible, and the songs "Delilah" by Tom Jones and "Hey There Delilah" by Plain White T's.

Della
(alt. Dell)

Shortened form of Adele, meaning "nobility." Donald Duck's twin sister is called Della Duck.

Delores
(alt. Deloris)

Spanish, meaning "sorrows."

Delphine
(alt. Delpha, Delphia, Delphina, Delphinia)

Greek, meaning "dolphin."

Delta

Greek, meaning "fourth child." Also the fourth letter of the Greek alphabet.

Demelza

Cornish, from the hamlet of the same name in Cornwall in the UK. Made popular by the *Poldark* character.

Demetria

(alt. Demetrice, Dimitria)

Greek, from the mythological heroine of the same name.

Demi

French, meaning "half." Famous Demis include actor Demi Moore.

Denise

(alt. Denice, Denisa, Denisse)

French, meaning "to be devoted to Bacchus." Name of the actor Denise Richards.

Desdemona

Greek, meaning "wretchedness." Desdemona is Othello's love interest in Shakespeare's *Othello*.

Desiree

(alt. Desirae, Des'ree)

French, meaning "much desired." Associated with singer Des'ree.

Desma

Greek, meaning "blinding oath."

Destiny

(alt. Destany, Destinee, Destiney, Destini)

French, meaning "fate." Associated with the former girl group Destiny's Child.

Deva

Hindi, meaning "God-like." Deva is also a name for several Buddhist, Hindu, and New Age spiritual entities or people.

Devin

(alt. Devinne)

Irish Gaelic, meaning "poet." More commonly used as a boys' name.

Devon

English, from the county of the same name. Also feminine variant of Devin, meaning "poet."

Diamond

English, meaning "brilliant." One of the hardest and most valuable substances on Earth.

Diana

(alt. Dian, Diane, Dianna, Dianne)

Roman, meaning "divine." Made famous by the late Diana, Princess of Wales.

Diandra

Greek, meaning "two males."

Dilys

Welsh, meaning "reliable."

Dimona

Hebrew, meaning "south." A town in the Bible.

> ## Names for triplets
> Abel, Bela, Elba (anagrams)
> Aidan, Diana, Nadia (anagrams)
> Amber, Jade, Ruby (jewels)
> Amy, May, Mya (anagrams)
> April, May, June (months)
> Ava, Eva, Iva (similar)
> Daisy, Lily, Rose (flowers)
> Jay, Raven, Robin (birds)
> Leah, Lianne, Liam (similar)
> Olive, Violet, Sage (colors)
> River, Rain, Summer (nature)

Dinah
(alt. Dina)
Hebrew, meaning "justified." Found in the Bible.

Dionne
Greek, from the mythological heroine of the same name. Famous Dionnes include singers Dionne Warwick and Dionne Bromfield, and the infamous Dionne quintuplets.

Divine
Italian, meaning "heavenly." Associated with divinity or Dante's *Divine Comedy*.

Dixie
French, meaning "tenth." Also an old term for the South.

Dodie
Hebrew, meaning "well-loved." Dodie Smith was the author of *101 Dalmations*.

Dolores
(alt. Doloris)
Spanish, meaning "sorrows."

Dominique
(alt. Domenica, Dominica, Domonique)
Latin, meaning "Lord." The name of a song by Soeur Sourire.

Donata
Latin, meaning "given."

Donna
(alt. Dona, Donnie)
Italian, meaning "lady." Famous Donnas include singer Donna Summer and actor Donna Reed.

Dora
Greek, meaning "gift." The title character in *Dora the Explorer*.

Doran
Irish Gaelic, meaning "fist" or "stranger."

Dorcas
Greek, meaning "gazelle." Found in the Bible.

Doreen
(alt. Dorene, Dorine)

Irish Gaelic, meaning "brooding"; Greek, meaning "gift."

Doris
(alt. Dorris)

Greek, from the place of the same name. Made famous by singer and actor Doris Day.

Dorothy
(alt. Dorathy, Doretha, Dorotha, Dorothea, Dorthy; abbrev. Dolly, Dottie, Dotty)

Greek, meaning "gift of God." Most commonly associated with Dorothy from *The Wizard of Oz*.

Dorrit
(alt. Dorit)

Greek, meaning "gift of God." *Little Dorrit* is a novel by Charles Dickens.

Dory
(alt. Dori)

French, meaning "gilded." Associated with Dory from *Finding Nemo* and its sequel *Finding Dory*.

Dove
(alt. Dovie)

English, from the bird of the same name. Used as a symbol of peace.

Dream

English, meaning "rejoice."

Drew

Greek, meaning "masculine." Can be used for girls or boys (as a nickname for Andrew). Made famous by actor Drew Barrymore.

Drusilla
(alt. Drucilla)

Latin, meaning "of the Drusus clan."

Dulcie
(alt. Dulce, Dulcia)

Latin, meaning "sweet."

Dusty
(alt. Dusti)

Old German, meaning "brave warrior." Famous as the name of singer Dusty Springfield.

E Girls' names

Earla

English, meaning "leader."

Eartha

English, meaning "earth." Associated with singer Eartha Kitt.

Easter

Egyptian, from the festival and Pacific island of the same name.

Ebba

English, meaning "fortress of riches." A Top 10 name for girls in Sweden.

Ebony
(alt. Eboni)

Latin, meaning "deep, black wood." Made famous by the song "Ebony and Ivory" by Paul McCartney and Stevie Wonder.

Echo

Greek, meaning "reflected sound." Echo was the name of a nymph in Greek mythology.

Eda
(alt. Edda)

English, meaning "wealthy and happy." An ancient goddess of time and wealth.

Edelmira

Spanish, meaning "admired for nobility."

Eden
(alt. Edie, Eddie)

Hebrew, meaning "pleasure."

Edina

Scottish, meaning "from Edinburgh."

Edith
(alt. Edyth)

English, meaning "prosperity through battle." Edith Wharton was a Pulitzer Prize-winning author.

Edna

Hebrew, meaning "enjoyment."

Edrea

English, meaning "wealthy and powerful." Edrea Vorsal is an opera singer.

Edwina

English, meaning "wealthy friend." Associated with 20th-century socialite Edwina Mountbattten.

Effie

Greek, meaning "pleasant speech." Effie Trinket is a character in *The Hunger Games* series.

Eglantine

French, from the flowering shrub of the same name.

Eileen
(alt. Eibhlín)

Irish, meaning "shining and brilliant." Associated with the song "Come on Eileen" by Dexys Midnight Runners.

Ekaterina
(alt. Ekaterini)

Slavic, meaning "pure."

Elaine
(alt. Elaina, Elayne)

French, meaning "bright, shining light." Elaine Stritch is an actor and singer.

Elba

Italian, from the island of the same name.

Elberta

English, meaning "high-born."

Eldora

Spanish, meaning "covered with gold."

Eleanor
(alt. Alienor, Aliana, Elana, Elanor, Eleanora, Eleanore, Elena, Eleni, Elenor, Elenora, Elina, Elinor, Elinore; abbrev. Elie, Ellie)

Greek, meaning "light." Queen Eleanor of Aquitane was married to England's Henry II and was one of the most influential, wealthy, and powerful women of the Middle Ages.

Electra
(alt. Elektra)

Greek, meaning "shining." Famous as a character in ancient Greek myth.

Elfrida
(alt. Elfrieda)

English, meaning "elf power." Elfrida Andree is a composer.

Eliane
(alt. Eliana)

Hebrew, meaning "Jehovah is God."

Elissa
(alt. Elise)

French, meaning "pledged to God." The other name of Dido, the ancient Roman Queen of Carthage.

Eliza
(alt. Elisha, Elise)

Hebrew, meaning "pledged to God." Made famous by the character Eliza Doolittle from the play *Pygmalion* and film adaptation *My Fair Lady*.

Elizabeth
(alt. Elisabet, Elisabeth, Elizabella, Elsbeth, Elspet; abbrev. Bess, Bessie, Bet, Beth, Betty, Libby, Liz, Lizzie)

Hebrew, meaning "pledged to God." The name of the current Queen of England, Elizabeth II. The previous Queen Elizabeth I was also known as "Good Queen Bess."

Elke

German, meaning "nobility."

Ella

German, meaning "completely."

Elle
(alt. Ellie)

French, meaning "she." Elle Macpherson was one of the original 1980s supermodels, known as "The Body."

Ellen
(alt. Elin, Eline, Ellyn)

Greek, meaning "shining." Associated with comedian and TV host Ellen DeGeneres.

Ellice
(alt. Elyse)

Greek, meaning "the Lord is God."

Elma
(alt. Elna)

Latin, meaning "soul." Elma Napier was an author and pioneering Caribbean politician.

Elmira
(alt. Elmyra)

Arabic, meaning "aristocratic lady." Elmyra Duff is a cartoon character.

Elodie

French, meaning "marsh flower."

Eloise
(alt. Elois, Eloisa, Elouise)

French, meaning "renowned in battle."

Elsa
(alt. Else, Elsie)

Hebrew, meaning "pledged to God." Elsa is a character from Disney's *Frozen*.

Elula

Hebrew, meaning "August."

Elva
Irish, meaning "noble."

Elvina
English, meaning "noble friend."

Elvira
(alt. Elvera)
Spanish, from the place of the same name. Associated with the 1980s film Elvira, Mistress of the Dark.

Ember
(alt. Embry)
English, meaning "spark."

Emeline
German, meaning "industrious."

Emerald
English, meaning "green gemstone." A precious stone.

Emery
(alt. Emory)
German, meaning "ruler of work." A dark rock used in the manufacture of nail files.

Emilia
Latin, meaning "rival, eager." Associated with Game of Thrones actor Emilia Clarke.

Emily
(alt. Emelie, Emilee, Emilie, Emlyn)
Latin, meaning "rival, eager." Famous Emilys include actor Emily Blunt and author Emily Dickinson.

Emma
(alt. Emme, Emmi, Emmie, Emmy)
German, meaning "embraces everything." Made famous by Jane Austen's novel Emma.

Emmanuelle
Hebrew, meaning "God is among us."

Emmeline
(alt. Emmelina; abbrev. Emi, Emme, Emmie, Emmy)
German, meaning "embraces everything." Emmeline Pankhurst was a British activist and suffragette, named by Time magazine as "One of the 100 Most Important People of the Twentieth Century."

Ena
Shortened form of Georgina, meaning "farmer."

Enid
(alt. Eneida)
Welsh, meaning "life spirit." Enid Blyton was an English children's novelist.

Enola
Native American, meaning "solitary." Associated with the song "Enola Gay."

Ensley
English, meaning "one's own meadow."

Enya

Irish Gaelic, meaning "fire." Irish singer Enya's birth name was Eithne.

Erica
(alt. Ericka, Erika)

Scandinavian, meaning "ruler forever." Erica Durance is an actor.

Erin
(alt. Eryn)

Irish Gaelic, meaning "from the isle to the west." An old name for Ireland. Erin Brockovich is a legal clerk and activist who was portrayed by Julia Roberts in the eponymous film.

Eris

Greek, from the mythological heroine of the same name. Eris is responsible for chaos, strife, and discord.

Erlinda

Hebrew, meaning "spirited."

Erma

German, meaning "universal."

Ermine

French, meaning "weasel." The fur of a stoat or weasel is known as ermine.

Erna

English, meaning "sincere." A character in Norse mythology.

Ernestine
(alt. Ernestina)

English, meaning "sincere." Ernestine Gilbreth Carey is the author of *Cheaper By the Dozen*.

Esme

French, meaning "esteemed." Esme Cullen is a character in the *Twilight* series.

Esmeralda

Spanish, meaning "emerald." Esmeralda is a lead character in *The Hunchback of Notre Dame*.

Esperanza

Spanish, meaning "hope."

Estelle
(alt. Estela, Estell, Estella)

French, meaning "star." Associated with R&B singer Estelle.

Esther
(alt. Esta, Ester, Etha, Ethna, Ethne)

Persian, meaning "star." A character in the biblical Book of Esther.

Eternity

Latin, meaning "forever."

Ethel
(alt. Ethyl)

English, meaning "noble." Ethel Merman was an actor and singer, best known for rousing musical theater.

Etta
(alt. Etter, Ettie)
Shortened form of Henrietta, meaning "ruler of the house." Famous Ettas include singer Etta James (real name Janesetta), and DC Comic character Etta Candy.

Eudora
Greek, meaning "generous gift." Eudora is a character in Disney's *Princess and the Frog.*

Eugenia
(alt. Eugenie)
Greek, meaning "well born." Princess Eugenie is a granddaughter of Queen Elizabeth II.

Eulalia
(alt. Eula, Eulah, Eulalie)
Greek, meaning "sweetspeaking." Associated with Spanish St. Eulalia.

Eunice
(alt. Unice)
Greek, meaning "victorious." Eunice Kennedy Shriver was JFK's sister and the founder of the Special Olympics.

Euphemia
Greek, meaning " favorable speech."

Eva
Hebrew, meaning "life." Eva Peron was the real-life inspiration for the musical *Evita.*

Evadne
Greek, meaning "pleasing one."

Evangeline
(alt. Evangelina)
Greek, meaning "good news." The very first musical comedy was called *Evangeline*, in 1874.

Evanthe
Greek, meaning "good flower."

Eve
(alt. Evie)
Hebrew, meaning "life." The biblical Eve was the first woman.

Evelina
(alt. Evelia)
German, meaning "hazelnut." An 18th-century novel by Fanny Burney.

Evelyn
(alt. Evalyn, Evelin, Eveline, Evelyne)
German, meaning "hazelnut." Famous Evelyns include singer Evelyn "Champagne" King and deaf virtuoso percussionist Evelyn Glennie.

Everly
(alt. Everleigh, Everley)
English, meaning "grazing meadow."

Evette
French, meaning "yew wood."

Evonne
(alt. Evon)
French, meaning "yew wood." Made famous by Australian tennis pro Evonne Goolagong.

F

Girls' names

Fabia
(alt. Fabiana, Fabienne, Fabiola, Fabriana)
Latin, meaning "from the Fabian clan."

Fabrizia
Italian, meaning "works with hands."

Faith
English, meaning "loyalty." Famous Faiths include singers Faith Hill and Faith Evans.

Faiza
Arabic, meaning "victorious."

Fallon
Irish Gaelic, meaning "descended from a ruler."

Fanny
(alt. Fannie)
Latin, meaning "from France." The heroine of Jane Austen's Mansfield Park is Fanny Price.

Farica
German, meaning "peaceful ruler."

Farrah
English, meaning "lovely and pleasant." Associated with actor Farrah Fawcett and reality TV star Farrah Abraham.

Fatima
Arabic, meaning "baby's nurse."

Faustine
Latin, meaning "fortunate."

Fawn
(alt. Fawne)
French, meaning "young deer." Also the light brown color.

Fay
(alt. Fae, Faye)
French, meaning "fairy." Famous Fays include author Fay Weldon and original King Kong actor Fay Wray.

Felicia

(alt. Felecia, Felice, Felicita, Felisha)

Latin, meaning "lucky and happy." Famous Felicias include actors Felicia Day and Felicia Farr, and *American Idol*'s Felicia Barton.

Felicity

Latin, meaning "fortunate."

Fenella

Irish Gaelic, meaning "white shoulder." Made famous by actor Fenella Fielding.

Fenia

Scandinavian, from the mythological giantess of the same name.

Fern

(alt. Fearn, Fearne, Ferne, Ferrin)

English, from the plant of the same name.

Fernanda

German, meaning "peace and courage."

Ffion

(alt. Fion)

Irish Gaelic, meaning "fair and pale" or "foxglove." Very popular name for baby girls in Wales.

Fia

Italian, meaning "flame." Also a nickname for Fiona.

Fifi

Hebrew, meaning "Jehovah increases."

Filomena

Greek, meaning "loved one."

Finlay

(alt. Finley)

Irish Gaelic, meaning "fair-headed courageous one." More commonly used for boys.

Finola

(alt. Fionnula)

Irish Gaelic, meaning "fair shoulder." Associated with actor Finola Hughes.

Fiona

(alt. Fiora)

Irish Gaelic and Scottish, meaning "fair and pale." Princess Fiona is a character in *Shrek*.

Flanna

(alt. Flannery)

Irish Gaelic, meaning "russet hair" or "red hair."

Flavia

Latin, meaning "yellow hair."

Fleur

(alt. Flor)

French, meaning "flower." Fleur Delacour is a character in the *Harry Potter* series.

Flora

Latin, meaning "flower." A fairy godmother in Disney's *Sleeping Beauty* (she was the red one).

Florence

(alt. Florencia, Florene, Florine; abbrev. Flo, Florrie, Flossie, Floy)

Latin, meaning "in bloom." Associated with the Italian city of the same name.

Florida

Latin, meaning "flowery." Also the southern state.

Frances

(alt. Francine, Francis; abbrev. Fanny, Fran, Frankie, Frannie, Franny)

Latin, meaning "from France." Famous Franceses include actor Frances McDormand and playwright Frances Hodgson Burnett.

Francesca

(alt. Franchesca, Francisca)

Latin, meaning "from France." Francesca Simon is a children's author.

Freda

(alt. Freida, Frida, Frieda)

German, meaning "peaceful." Associated with artist Frida Kahlo.

Frederica

German, meaning "peaceful ruler." Popular name for modern European princesses.

Fuchsia

German, from the flower of the same name.

G Girls' names

Gabrielle
(alt. Gabriel, Gabriela, Gabriella; abbrev. Gabbi, Gabby)
Hebrew, meaning "heroine of God."
A character in *Xena: Warrior Princess*.

Gaia
(alt. Gaea)
Greek, meaning "the earth." Gaia was the ancient Greek Mother Goddess.

Gail
(alt. Gale, Gayla, Gayle)
Hebrew, meaning "my father rejoices." Gail O'Grady is an actor and producer.

Gal
Hebrew, meaning "wave." Made famous by *Wonder Woman* actor Gal Gadot.

Gala
French, meaning "festive merrymaking."

Galiena
German, meaning "high one."

Galina
Russian, meaning "shining brightly."

Garnet
(alt. Garnett)
English, meaning "red gemstone." Can be used as a twin name alongside Ruby.

Gay
(alt. Gaye)
French, meaning "glad and lighthearted."

Gaynor
Welsh, meaning "white and smooth." Associated with singer Gloria Gaynor.

Gemini

Greek, meaning "twin." The third astrological sign in the Zodiac.

Gemma
(alt. Jemma)

Italian, meaning "precious stone." Well-known Gemmas include actor Gemma Arterton.

Gene

Greek, meaning "well born." Usually a boys' name.

Genesis

Greek, meaning "beginning." Associated with the first book of the Old Testament, and the band Genesis.

Geneva
(alt. Genevra)

French, meaning "juniper tree." A city in Switzerland.

Genevieve
(alt. Genie)

German, meaning "white wave." St. Genevieve is said to have saved Paris.

Georgia
(alt. Georgie)

Greek, meaning "farmer." Also the southern US state and a European country.

Georgina
(alt. Georgene, Georgette, Georgiana, Georgianna, Georgine, Giorgina; abbrev. Giget, Gigi)

Greek, meaning "farmer." Georgina Chapman is an actor and fashion designer. Gigi is a novel and a musical.

Geraldine
(abbrev. Geri)

German, meaning "spear ruler." Geraldine Chaplin is an actor and Geri Halliwell is "Ginger Spice" of the Spice Girls.

Gerda

Nordic, meaning "shelter." A character from Hans Christian Andersen's Snow Queen.

Germaine

French, meaning "from Germany." Germaine Greer is an author and activist.

Gertrude
(alt. Gertie)

German, meaning "strength of a spear." Made famous by author Gertrude Stein.

Gia
(alt. Ghia)

Italian, meaning "God is gracious."

Gianina
(alt. Giana)

Hebrew, meaning "God's graciousness."

Gilda

English, meaning "gilded." A character from Verdi's opera *Rigoletto*.

Gilia

Hebrew, meaning "joy of the Lord." Also a genus of flowering plants.

Gillian

Latin, meaning "youthful." Famous Gillians include actor Gillian Anderson and author Gillian Cross.

Ginger

Latin, from the root of the same name.

Giovanna

Italian, meaning "God is gracious."

Giselle
(alt. Gisela, Gisele, Giselle, Gisselle)

German, meaning "pledge." Famous Giselles include the romantic ballet, and supermodel Gisele Bündchen.

Gita
(alt. Geeta)

Sanskrit, meaning "song." The *Bhagavad Gita* is an important part of Hindu scripture, and is often simply known as the Gita.

Giulia
(alt. Giuliana)

Italian, meaning "youthful." Associated with TV host Giuliana Rancic.

Gladys
(alt. Gladyce)

Welsh, meaning "lame." Gladys Knight is a singer.

Glenda

Welsh, meaning "fair and good."

Glenna
(alt. Glennie)

Irish Gaelic, meaning "glen."

Gloria
(alt. Glory)

Latin, meaning "glory." Famous Glorias include singers Gloria Estefan and Gloria Gaynor.

Glynda
(alt. Glinda)

Welsh, meaning "fair." Name of the good witch in *The Wizard of Oz*.

Glynis

Welsh, meaning "small glen." Glynis Nunn is a heptathlon athlete.

Golda
(alt. Goldia, Goldie)

English, meaning "gold." Golda Meir is the former Israeli Prime Minister.

Grace
(alt. Graça, Gracie, Gracin, Grayce)

Latin, meaning "grace." The actor Grace Kelly became Princess Grace of Monaco.

Grainne
(alt. Grania)

Irish Gaelic, meaning "love." Also an ancient goddess of corn.

Gratia
(alt. Grasia)

Latin, meaning "blessing." Gratia was the ancient Greek goddess of charm, beauty, and fertility.

Greer
(alt. Grier)

Latin, meaning "alert and watchful."

Gregoria

Latin, meaning "alert."

Greta
(alt. Gretel)

Greek, meaning "pearl." One of the characters in the fairy tale *Hansel and Gretel*.

Gretchen

German, meaning "pearl." Gretchen Mol is an actor.

Griselda
(alt. Griselle)

German, meaning "gray fighting maid."

Gudrun

Scandinavian, meaning "battle."

Guinevere

Welsh, meaning "white and smooth." The legendary Queen consort of King Arthur.

Gwenda

Welsh, meaning "fair and good."

Gwendolyn
(alt. Gwen, Gwendolen, Gwenel)

Welsh, meaning "fair bow." Gwendolyn Brooks is a poet.

Gwyneth
(alt. Gwynneth, Gwynyth)

Welsh, meaning "happiness." Made famous by actor Gwyneth Paltrow.

Gwynn
(alt. Gwyn)

Welsh, meaning "fair blessed."

Gypsy

English, meaning "of the Roman tribe."

H Girls' names

Hadassah

Hebrew, meaning "myrtle tree." The Hebrew name for Esther in the Bible.

Hadley

English, meaning "heather meadow." Hadley Richardson was the wife of Ernest Hemingway.

Hadria

Latin, meaning "from Hadria." The name of two ancient cities in Italy.

Hala

Arabic, meaning "halo." A female weather demon in Serbian mythology.

Haley

(alt. Hailee, Hailey, Hailie, Haleigh, Hali, Halie, Haylee, Hayleigh, Hayley, Haylie)

English, meaning "hay meadow." Famous Haleys include singer Haley Reinhart and singer Hayley Mills.

Halima

(alt. Halimah, Halina)

Arabic, meaning "gentle." The prophet Mohammad's foster mother was called Halimah.

Hallie

(alt. Halle, Halley)

German, meaning "ruler of the home or estate." Associated with actor Halle Berry.

Hannah

(alt. Haana, Hana, Hanna)

Hebrew, meaning "grace." Famous Hannahs include actor Hannah Gordon and TV musical comedy Hannah Montana.

Harley

(alt. Harlene)

English, meaning "the long field." Used for girls and boys. Made famous by the Harley-Davidson motorbike company.

Harlow

English, meaning "army hill."

Harmony

Latin, meaning "harmony."

Harper

English, meaning "minstrel." Has risen in popularity after its use by Victoria and David Beckham for their daughter Harper Seven.

Harriet
(alt. Harriett, Harriette, Hattie)

German, meaning "ruler of the home or estate." Famous Harriets include activist Harriet Tubman and author Harriet Beecher Stowe.

Haven

English, meaning "a place of sanctuary."

Hayden

Old English, meaning "hedged valley."

Hazel
(alt. Hazle)

English, from the tree of the same name. Also an eye color.

Heather

English, from the flower of the same name. Famous Heathers include actors Heather Graham and Heather Locklear, and model Heather Mills.

Heaven

English, meaning "everlasting bliss."

Hedda

German, meaning "warfare." *Hedda Gabler* is a play by Henrik Ibsen.

Hedwig

German, meaning "warfare and strife." Also Harry Potter's constant owl companion.

Heidi
(alt. Heidy)

German, meaning "nobility." The title of a children's book *Heidi* by Johanna Spyri.

Helen
(alt. Halen, Helena, Helene, Hellen)

Greek, meaning "light." In Greek mythology Helen of Troy was considered to be the most beautiful woman in the world.

Helga

German, meaning "holy and sacred."

Heloise

French, meaning "renowned in war." Heloise d'Argenteuil was a nun and writer.

Henrietta
(alt. Henriette)

German, meaning "ruler of the house." Henrietta Maria of France was queen consort to England's King Charles I.

Long names

Alexandria

Bernadette

Christabelle

Constantina

Evangeline

Gabrielle

Henrietta

Jacqueline

Marguerite

Wilhelmina

Hephzibah

Hebrew, meaning "my delight is in her." Found in the Bible.

Hera

Greek, meaning "queen." Hera is the ancient Greek Queen of the Gods and the goddess of marriage, women, and births.

Hermia
(alt. Hermina, Hermine, Herminia)

Greek, meaning "messenger." A character from Shakespeare's
A Midsummer Night's Dream.

Hermione

Greek, meaning "earthly." Harry Potter's closest (and smartest) female friend.

Hero

Greek, meaning "brave one of the people."

Hertha

English, meaning "earth." Another name for Nerthus, the goddess of fertility in ancient German mythology.

Hesper
(alt. Hesperia)

Greek, meaning "evening star." The first evening star in ancient Greece.

Hester
(alt. Hestia)

Greek, meaning "star." Hester Prynne is a character from The Scarlet Letter.

Hilary
(alt. Hillary)

Greek, meaning "cheerful and happy." Famous Hilarys include actor Hilary Swank and politician Hillary Rodham Clinton.

Hilda
(alt. Hildur)

German, meaning "battle woman." The first female pilot to own a license was Hilda Hewlett.

Hildegarde
(alt. Hildegard)

German, meaning "battle stronghold."

Hildred

German, meaning "battle counselor."

Hilma

German, meaning "helmet."

Hollis

English, meaning "near the holly bushes."

Holly
(alt. Holli, Hollie)

English, from the tree of the same name. Famous Hollys include writer Holly Black and actor Holly Hunter.

Honey

English, meaning "sweet nectar."

Honor
(alt. Honora, Honoria, Honour)

Latin, meaning "woman of worth and respect." Actor Honor Blackman played Bond girl Pussy Galore in *Goldfinger*.

Hope

English, meaning "desire and expectation." One of the three virtues: faith, hope, and charity.

Hortense
(alt. Hortencia, Hortensia)

Latin, meaning "of the garden." The name of Napoleon Bonaparte's mother.

Hulda

German, meaning "loved one." A prophetess in the Bible.

Hyacinth

Greek, from the flower of the same name. A hero in ancient Greek mythology.

I Girls' names

Ianthe
(alt. Iantha)

Greek, meaning "purple flower."

Ida
(alt. Idell, Idella)

English, meaning "prosperous." Ida B. Wells was a prominent African-American civil rights activist and journalist.

Idona

Nordic, meaning "renewal."

Ignacia

Latin, meaning "ardent."

Ila

French, meaning "island." In Hindu mythology, Ila is a character able to change sexes at will.

Ilana

Hebrew, meaning "tree." Famous Ilanas include pianist Ilana Vered and a character in TV series Lost.

Ilaria

Italian, meaning "cheerful."

Ilene

American English, meaning "light." Ilene Woods was the voice of Disney's Cinderella.

Iliana
(alt. Ileana)

Greek, meaning "Trojan."

Ilona

Hungarian, meaning "light." The name of the Queen of the Fairies in Magyar mythology.

Ilsa

German, meaning "pledged to God." The character played by Ingrid Bergman in Casablanca.

Ima

German, meaning "embraces everything."

Iman

Arabic, meaning "faith." Associated with the model, actor and entrepreneur known simply as Iman.

Imelda

German, meaning "all-consuming fight." Imelda Staunton is an Oscar-nominated British actor.

Imogen
(alt. Imogene)

Latin, meaning "last-born."

Ina

Latin, meaning "to make feminine." Famous Inas include author and presenter Ina Garten, childbirth pioneer Ina May Gaskin, and the Ina language of Brazil.

Inaya

Arabic, meaning "taking care."

India
(alt. Indie)

Hindi, from the country of the same name. India Arie is a singer.

Indiana

Latin, meaning "from India." Also the Midwestern state.

Indigo

Greek, meaning "deep blue dye." One of the seven colors of the rainbow.

Indira
(alt. Inira)

Sanskrit, meaning "beauty." Indira Gandhi was the first and only female prime minister of India.

Inez
(alt. Ines)

Spanish, meaning "pure."

Inga
(alt. Inge, Ingeborg, Inger)

Scandinavian, meaning "guarded by Ing."

Ingrid

Scandinavian, meaning "beautiful." Made famous by actor Ingrid Bergman.

Io
(alt. Eye)

Greek, from the mythological priestess and heroine of the same name.

Ioanna

Greek, meaning "grace."

Iola
(alt. Iole)

Greek, meaning "cloud of dawn." Iola Leory by Frances Harper is one of the first published novels by a black female author.

Iolanthe

Greek, meaning "violet flower." The title of a comic opera by Gilbert and Sullivan.

Iona

Greek, from the island of the same name.

Ione

Greek, meaning "violet." Also a genus of orchid.

Iphigenia

Greek, meaning "sacrifice." The ancient Greek victim of slaughter, who became known as the mother of all strong children.

Ira

(alt. Iva)

Hebrew, meaning "watchful."

Irene

(alt. Irelyn, Irena, Irina, Irini)

Greek, meaning "peace." Singer Irene Cara won an Academy Award for Best Original Song.

Iris

Greek, meaning "rainbow." Also a flower and the Greek goddess who travels with the speed of wind from one end of the rainbow to the other, and from sea to sky, and connects the gods with humanity.

Irma

German, meaning "universal."

Isabel

(alt. Isabela, Isabell, Isabella, Isabelle, Isobel, Izabella, Izabelle; abbrev. Izzie, Izzy)

Spanish, meaning "pledged to God." The name of various historical members of European royal families, including Queen Isabella I of Spain. Isabella Swan is the lead character in the *Twilight* series.

Isadora

Latin, meaning "gift of Isis."

Ishana

Hindi, meaning "desire." One of the names for Shiva in the Hindu faith.

Isis

Egyptian, from the goddess of the same name. She was worshipped as the ideal mother and wife, and the goddess of nature and magic.

Isla

(alt. Isa, Isela, Isley)

Scottish Gaelic, meaning "river." Isla Fischer is an actor.

Isolde

Welsh, meaning "fair lady." A character in Richard Wagner's opera *Tristan und Isolde*.

Istas

Native American, meaning "snow."

Ivana
(alt. Iva, Ivanka)

Slavic, meaning "Jehovah is gracious." Associated with model Ivana Trump.

Ivory

Latin, meaning "white as elephant tusks."

Ivy

English, from the plant of the same name. Beyoncé and Jay-Z's daughter is Blue Ivy.

Ixia

South African, from the flower of the same name.

Girls' names

Jacinda
(alt. Jacinta)

Spanish, meaning "hyacinth." Jacinda Barrett is an actor.

Jacqueline
(alt. Jacalyn, Jacklyn, Jaclyn, Jacquelin, Jacquelyn, Jacquline, Jaquelin, Jaqueline; abbrev. Jackie, Jacky, Jacqui)

French, meaning "he who supplants." Famous Jacquelines include actor Jacqueline Bisset, cellist Jacqueline du Pré, First Lady Jacqueline (Jackie) Kennedy Onassis, and singer Jackie Evancho.

Jade
(alt. Jada, Jaida, Jayda, Jayde)

Spanish, meaning "green stone." Associated with TV host Jade McCarthy.

Jaden
(alt. Jadyn, Jaiden, Jayden)

Contraction of Jade and Hayden, meaning "green hedged valley." Used for girls and boys.

Jael

Hebrew, meaning "mountain goat." Found in the Bible.

Jaime
(alt. Jaima, Jaimie, Jami, Jamie)

Spanish, meaning "he who supplants." J'aime is also French for "I love."

Jamila

Arabic, meaning "lovely." Jamila Gavin is a children's author.

Jan
(alt. Jana, Janae, Janay, Jann, Janna, Joana)

Hebrew, meaning "the Lord is gracious"; Arabic, meaning "dear"; Persian, meaning "life."

Jane
(alt. Jayne)

Feminine form of John, meaning "the Lord is gracious." Famous Janes include actors Jane Lynch, Jane Seymour, and Jayne Mansfield.

Janelle
(alt. Janael, Janel, Janell, Jenelle)

American English, derived from Jane, meaning "the Lord is gracious." Janelle Monae is a singer and Janell Burse is a professional basketball player.

Janet
(alt. Janette)

Scottish, meaning "the Lord is gracious." Famous Janets include singer Janet Jackson and Olympic champion swimmer Janet Evans.

Janice
(alt. Janis)

American, meaning "the Lord is gracious." Janice Dickinson is a former supermodel.

Janie
(alt. Janey, Janney, Jannie)

Derived from Jane or short form of Janet, meaning "the Lord is gracious." Famous Janies include Motown songwriter Janie Bradford, country singer Janie Frickie and Janie Hendrix, the sister of musician Jimi.

Janine
(alt. Janeen)

English, meaning "the Lord is gracious." Associated with actor Janine Turner.

Janoah
(alt. Janiya, Janiyah)

Hebrew, meaning "quiet and calm."

January

Latin, meaning "the first month." January Jones is an actor.

Jasmine
(alt. Jasmin, Jazim, Jazmine)

Persian, meaning "jasmine flower." Also the princess in Disney's *Aladdin*.

Jay

Latin, meaning "jaybird."

Jayna

Sanskrit, meaning "bringer of victory."

Jean
(alt. Jeane, Jeanie, Jeanne, Jeannie)

Scottish, meaning "the Lord is gracious." Jean Harlow was a glamorous acting star of the 1930s. Also associated with the sitcom *I Dream of Jeannie*.

Jeana
(alt. Jeanna)

Latin, meaning "queen."

Jeanette
(alt. Jeannette, Janette)
French, meaning "the Lord is gracious." Jeanette MacDonald is an actor.

Jeanine
(alt. Jeannine)
Latin, meaning "the Lord is gracious."

Jemima
Hebrew, meaning "dove." Famous Jemimas include writer Jemima Khan, actor Jemima Kirke, and the children's book character Jemima Puddle-Duck.

Jena
Arabic, meaning "little bird."

Jennifer
(alt. Jenifer; abbrev. Jenna, Jennie, Jenny)
Cornish alternative to Guinevere, meaning "white and smooth." Famous Jennifers include actors Jennifer Lawrence, Jennifer Aniston, Jenna Elfman, Jenna Dewan, and singer Jennifer Hudson.

Jerrie
(alt. Jeri, Jerri, Jerrie, Jerry)
German, meaning "spear ruler." Jerry Hall is a model and actor.

Jerusha
Hebrew, meaning "married." Jerusha Hess is a film maker.

Jeryl
English, meaning "spear ruler." Associated with actor Jeryl Prescott.

Jessamy
(alt. Jessame, Jessamine, Jessamyn)
Persian, meaning "jasmine flower." Also a children's book by Barbara Sleigh.

Jessica
(alt. Jesica, Jessika; abbrev. Jess, Jessa, Jessie)
Hebrew, meaning "He sees." Famous Jessicas include actors Jessica Alba and Jessica Lange, singer Jessie J and the character Jess from *Girls*.

Jesusa
Spanish, meaning "mother of the Lord."

Jette
(alt. Jetta, Jettie)
Danish, meaning "black as coal."

Jewel
(alt. Jewell)
French, meaning "delight." Associated with singer songwriter Jewel.

Jezebel
(alt. Jezabel, Jezabelle)
Hebrew, meaning "pure and virginal." The misbehaving wife of King Ahab in the Bible.

Short names

Bea	Jo
Bo	Kim
Fay	May
Jan	Mia
Jo	Val

Jill

Latin, meaning "youthful."

Jillian

Latin, meaning "youthful." Jillian Michaels is a personal trainer and TV personality.

Jimena

Spanish, meaning "heard."

Joan

Hebrew, meaning "the Lord is gracious." Famous Joans include St. Joan of Arc, actor Joan Collins, and comedian Joan Rivers.

Joanna

(alt. Joana, Joanie, Joann, Joanne, Johanna, Joni; abbrev. Jo)

Hebrew, meaning "the Lord is gracious." Famous Joannas include actors Joanna Lumley and Joanna Page. Author J. K. Rowling's first name is Joanne.

Jocasta

Italian, meaning "lighthearted." A character in ancient Greek mythology.

Jocelyn

(alt. Jauslyn, Jocelyne, Joscelin, Joslyn; abbrev. Joss)

German, meaning "cheerful." Famous Jocelyns include American socialite Jocelyn Wildenstein, singer Jocelyn Brown, and English soul singer-songwriter Joss Stone.

Jody

(alt. Jodee, Jodi, Jodie)

Shortened form of Judith, meaning "Jewish." Made famous by actor Jodie Foster.

Joelle

(alt. Joela)

Hebrew, meaning "Jehovah is the Lord."

Joie

French, meaning "joy."

Jolene

Contraction of Joanna and Darlene, meaning "gracious darling." The title of a song by Dolly Parton.

Jolie

(alt. Joely)

French, meaning "pretty." Made famous by actor and director Angelina Jolie.

Jonisa
(alt. Jonisha)

Hebrew and French, meaning "God is gracious."

Jordan
(alt. Jordana, Jordin, Jordyn)

Hebrew, meaning "descend." Made famous by singer Jordan Sparks.

Jorgina

Dutch, meaning "farmer."

Josephine
(alt. Josefina, Josephina; abbrev. Jo, Josie, Joss)

Hebrew, meaning "Jehovah increases." Famous Josephines include actor Josephine Baker and author Josephine Bell.

Jovita
(alt. Jovie)

Latin, meaning "made glad." Associated with St. Jovita.

Joy

Latin, meaning "joy." Joy Behar is a comedian.

Joyce

Latin, meaning "joyous." Famous Joyces include author Joyce Carol Oates and actors Joyce Blair and Joyce DeWitt.

Juanita
(alt. Juana)

Spanish, meaning "the Lord is gracious." Associated with the ice maiden Mummy Juanita.

Jubilee

Hebrew, meaning "ram's horn" or "special anniversary." The celebration of an anniversary.

Judith
(alt. Judit; abbrev. Jude, Judi, Judy)

Hebrew, meaning "Jewish." Found in the Bible. Famous Judiths include actors Judy Garland and Judi Dench.

Jules

French, meaning "Jove's child."

Julia
(alt. Juli, Julie)

Latin, meaning "youthful." Famous Julias include actor Julia Roberts, TV chef Julia Childs, and actor and singer Julie Andrews.

Julianne
(alt. Juliana, Juliann, Julianna)

Latin, meaning "youthful." Julianne Moore and Julianna Margulies are both actors.

Juliet
(alt. Joliet, Juliette)

Latin, meaning "youthful." A character in Shakespeare's play *Romeo and Juliet*.

June
(alt. Juna)

Latin, after the month of the same name. The name of several American actors famous in the period 1930–60, and country singer June Carter Cash.

Juniper

Dutch, from the shrub of the same name used in the production of gin.

Juno
(alt. Juneau)

Latin, meaning "queen of heaven." Juno was an ancient Roman goddess of marriage and Rome.

Justice

English, meaning "to deliver what is just." The female spirit of Justice is depicted with balance scales, a blindfold, and a sword.

Justine
(alt. Justina)

Latin, meaning "fair and righteous." Famous Justines include the Christian saint and actor Justine Bateman.

K Girls' names

Kady
(alt. Kadi, Kadie)
Irish Gaelic, meaning "a rhythmic flow of sounds."

Kailani
(alt. Kehlani)
Hawaiian, meaning "sea and sky."

Kala
(alt. Kaela, Kaiala, Kaila)
Sanskrit, meaning "black one." The great ape that saved Tarzan as a baby.

Kali
(alt. Kailey, Kaleigh, Kaley, Kalie, Kalli, Kally, Kaylee, Kayleigh)
Sanskrit, meaning "black one." Also the Hindu goddess of time and change.

Kalila
Arabic, meaning "beloved."

Kalina
Slavic, meaning "flower."

Kama
Sanskrit, meaning "love." Associated with the Hindu goal of intellectual fulfillment.

Kami
Japanese, meaning "lord."

Kamilla
(alt. Kamilah)
Slavic, meaning "serving girl."

Kana
Hawaiian, from the demi-god of the same name who could take the form of a rope that could stretch from Molokai to Hawaii.

Kara
Latin, meaning "dear one." The bracelet worn by Sikhs.

Karen

(alt. Caren, Carin, Caron, Caryn, Karan, Karin, Karina, Karon, Karren; abbrev. Kari)

Greek, meaning "pure." Famous Karens include singer Karen Carpenter, actor Karen Gillan, and TV host and scientist Kari Byron.

Karimah

Arabic, meaning "giving."

Karishma

(alt. Karisma)

Sanskrit, meaning "miracle." Karisma Kapoor is an actor.

Karissa

(alt. Carissa, Korissa)

Greek, meaning "very dear."

Karma

Hindi, meaning "destiny." Karma is the principle of good and bad deeds being returned to you.

Kate

(alt. Kat, Katie, Kathi, Kathie, Kathy, Kati, Katy)

Derived from Catherine or Katherine, meaning "pure." Famous Kates include Princess Kate Middleton and actors Kate Winslet and Kate Hudson.

Katherine

(alt. Katharine, Kathrine, Kathryn, Katrina, Katya, Katyea; abbrev. Kate, Kathy, Katie, Katy, Kay, Kitty)

Greek, meaning "pure." Enduringly popular spelled with either a C or a K.

Kathleen

(alt. Kathlyn)

Greek, meaning "pure." Kathleen Robertson is an actor.

Katniss

From one of the common names of the aquatic plant genus *Sagittaria*. Made famous by the character Katniss Everdeen from *The Hunger Games* trilogy.

Kaya

Sanskrit, meaning "nature"; Turkish, meaning "rock." Also a sweet coconut jam.

Kayla

(alt. Kaylah)

Greek, meaning "pure"; Gaelic, meaning "slim" and "fair."

Kaylee

(alt. Kayley, Kayleigh, Kayli, Kaylin)

Derived from Kayla, meaning "pure." Kayley is a character from *The Magic Sword: Quest for Camelot*.

Keeley

(alt. Keely)

Irish, meaning "battle maid." Keeley Hawes is a British actor.

Keila

Hebrew, meaning "citadel."

Keira

Irish Gaelic, meaning "dark." Name of actor Keira Knightley.

Keisha
(alt. Keesha)
Arabic, meaning "woman." Name of actor Keisha Pulliam.

Kelila
Hebrew, meaning "crown of laurel."

Kelis
American English, meaning "beautiful." Kelis is an R&B singer.

Kelly
(alt. Keli, Kelley, Kelli, Kellie)
Irish Gaelic, meaning "battle maid." Famous Kellys include singer Kelly Clarkson and TV personality Kelly Osbourne.

Kelsey
(alt. Kelcie, Kelsea, Kelsi, Kelsie)
English, meaning "island."

Kendall
(alt. Kendal)
English, meaning "the valley of the Kent."

Kendra
English, meaning "knowing." Kendra Wilkinson is a reality TV star.

Kenna
Irish Gaelic, meaning "handsome."

Kennedy
(alt. Kenadee, Kennedi)
Irish Gaelic, meaning "helmet head." Made famous by the Kennedy family.

Kenya
African, from the eponymous country.

Kenzie
Shortened form of Mackenzie, meaning "son of the wise ruler."

Kerensa
Cornish, meaning "love." Also used as a spelling variation of Karen.

Kerrigan
Irish, meaning "black haired."

Kerry
(alt. Keri, Kerri, Kerrie)
Irish, from the eponymous county.

Khadijah
(alt. Khadejah)
Arabic, meaning "premature baby." Khadija bint Khuwaylid was the first wife of Muhammad and known as the "Mother of Islam."

Khaleesi
Dothraki, meaning "queen." Royal title from *Game of Thrones*.

Kiana
(alt. Kia, Kianna)
American English, meaning "fibre." Associated with TV personality Kiana.

Kiara
Italian, meaning "light." St. Kiara saved an Irish town from a fire through prayer.

Kiki

Spanish, meaning "home ruler." "Let's Have a Kiki" is a song by the Scissor Sisters. Kiki Dee was the stage name of a pop singer from the 1970s.

Kimberly

(alt. Kimberleigh, Kimberley; abbrev. Kim, Kimmy)

Old English, meaning "royal forest." Also a town in South Africa. Famous Kimberlys include reality star Kim Kardashian and singer Lil' Kim.

Kingsley

(alt. Kinsley, Kynslee)

English, meaning "king's meadow." Used for boys as well as girls.

Kinsey

English, meaning "king's victory."

Kira

Greek, meaning "lady." The antagonist in the popular Japanese anime *Death Note*.

Kiri

Maori, meaning "tree bark." Dame Kiri Te Kanawa is an opera singer.

Kirsten

(alt. Kirstin; abbrev. Kirstie, Kirsty)

Scandinavian, meaning "Christian." Kirsten Dunst and Kirstie Alley are actors and Kirsten Gillibrand is a politican.

Kizzy

Hebrew, meaning the plant cassia.

Klara

Hungarian, meaning "bright."

Komal

Hindi, meaning "soft and tender."

Kristen

(alt. Kristan, Kristin, Kristine; abbrev. Kri, Krista, Kristi, Kristie, Kristy)

Greek, meaning "Christian." Famous Kristens include actor Kristen Stewart and reality TV star Kris Jenner.

Kwanza

(alt. Kwanzaa)

African, meaning "beginning." Also the name of the African-American festival in December and January.

Kyla

(alt. Kya, Kylah, Kyle)

Scottish, meaning "narrow spit of land." The name of actor Kyla Pratt.

Kylie

(alt. Kiley, Kylee)

Irish Gaelic, meaning "graceful." Associated with the singer Kylie Minogue.

Kyra

Greek, meaning "lady."

Kyrie

Greek, meaning "the Lord." Also a prayer sung at the beginning of Christian masses.

L

Girls' names

Lacey
(alt. Laci, Lacie, Lacy)

French, from the town of the same name. Famous Laceys include dancer Lacey Schwimmer.

Ladonna

Italian, meaning "lady." A spelling alternative to Madonna.

Lady

English, meaning "bread kneader." A character from Disney's *Lady and the Tramp*.

Laila
(alt. Layla, Leila, Lejla, Lela, Lelah, Lelia)

Arabic, meaning "night." Famous Lailas include boxer Laila Ali, and the song "Layla" by Eric Clapton.

Lainey
(alt. Laine, Laney)

French, meaning "bright light."

Lakeisha
(alt. Lakeshia)

American English, meaning "woman." A contraction of La and Keisha.

Lakshmi
(alt. Laxmi)

Sanskrit, meaning "good omen." The Hindu goddess of wealth.

Lana

Greek, meaning "light." Famous Lanas include singer Lana Del Rey, and actor Lana Turner.

Lani
(alt. Lanie)

Hawaiian, meaning "heaven and sky."

Lara

Latin, meaning "famous." Famous Laras include actor Lara Flynn Boyle, Tomb Raider star Lara Croft, and an ancient Roman nymph.

Laraine

French, meaning "from Lorraine."

Larissa

(alt. Larisa)

Greek, meaning "light-hearted." Larissa was a nymph in ancient Greek mythology.

Lark

(alt. Larkin)

English, meaning "playful songbird."

Larsen

(alt. Larsan)

Scandinavian, meaning "son of Lars."

Latifa

(alt. Latifah)

Arabic, meaning "gentle and pleasant." Queen Latifah is a rapper and actor.

Latika

(alt. Lotika)

Hindi, meaning "a plant." Also a character in *Slumdog Millionaire*.

Latisha

Latin, meaning "happiness."

Latona

(alt. Latonia)

Latin, from the mythological ancient Roman heroine of the same name who had twin boys with Zeus.

Latoya

Spanish, meaning "victorious one." Name of singer LaToya Jackson.

Latrice

(alt. Latricia)

Latin, meaning "noble."

Laura

(alt. Lora)

Latin, meaning "laurel." Famous Lauras include actor Laura Dern, author Laura Ingalls Wilder, and designer Laura Ashley.

Laurel

Latin, meaning "laurel tree." Also a term used for young women in the Mormon Church.

Lauren

(alt. Lauran, Lauryn Hill, Loren)

Latin, meaning "laurel." Famous Laurens include actors Lauren Bacall and Lauran Grace, and singer-songwriter Lauryn Hill.

Laveda

(alt. Lavada)

Latin, meaning "cleansed."

Lavender

Latin, from the plant of the same name. A character from the *Harry Potter* series.

Laverne

(alt. Lavern, Laverna)

Latin, from the goddess of the same name. Famous Lavernes include Laverne Andrews, of the Andrews Sisters, and sitcom *Laverne & Shirley*.

Lavinia

(alt. Lavina)

Latin, meaning "woman of Rome." In Roman mythology Lavinia is a heroine whose hair caught fire, creating a prophecy.

Lavonne

(alt. Lavon)

French, meaning "yew wood."

Leah

(alt. Lea, Leia)

Hebrew, meaning "weary." Name of musical actor Lea Michele.

Leandra

Greek, meaning "lion man." A character in *Don Quixote*.

Leanne

(alt. Leann, Leanna, Leeann)

Contraction of Lee and Ann, meaning "meadow grace." Famous Leannes include singers LeAnn Rimes and Lee Ann Womack.

Leda

Greek, meaning "gladness." The ancient Greek heroine Leda was seduced by Zeus in the form of a swan.

Lee

(alt. Leigh)

English, meaning "pasture or meadow."

Leilani

Hawaiian, meaning "flower from heaven." Name of actor Leilani Jones.

Leith

Scottish Gaelic, meaning "broad river."

Lena

(alt. Leena, Lina)

Latin, meaning "light." Famous Lenas include actors and filmmakers Lena Dunham and Lena Headey.

Lenna

(alt. Lennie)

German, meaning "lion's strength." The Lenna photograph is a standard test image used in image processing.

Léonie

(alt. Leona, Leone)

Latin, meaning "lioness." Léonie Adams was a 20th-century American poet.

Leonora

(alt. Lenora, Lenore, Leonor, Leonore, Leora)

Greek, meaning "light." Leonora Braham is an opera singer.

Lesley

(alt. Leslee, Leslie)

Scottish Gaelic, meaning "the gray castle." Famous Leslies include actor and dancer Leslie Caron, and singer Leslie Feist. Lesley is more commonly the female spelling and Leslie the male.

Leta

Latin, meaning "glad and joyful." Leta Hollingworth was a pioneering child psychologist.

Letha

Greek, meaning "forgetfulness." Also a type of butterfly.

Letitia

(alt. Leticia, Lettice, Lettie)

Latin, meaning "joy and gladness." St. Leticia was a Spanish virgin martyr.

Lexia

(alt. Lexi, Lexie)

Greek, meaning "defender of mankind." Also a genus of butterfly.

Lia

Italian, meaning "bringer of the gospel." Lia Williams is an actor.

Liana

French, meaning "to twine around."

Libby

(alt. Libbie)

Originally a shortened form of Elizabeth, meaning "pledged to God." Name of singer Libby Holman.

Liberty

English, meaning "freedom." Made famous by the Statue of Liberty in New York, NY.

Lida

Slavic, meaning "loved by the people."

Liese

(alt. Liesel, Liesl)

German, meaning "pledged to God." Liesl is a character in *The Sound of Music*.

Lila

(alt. Lilah)

Arabic, meaning "night." In the Hindu faith, Lila refers to playtime or pastimes.

Lilac

Latin, from the flower of the same name. Also the pale purple color.

Lilia

(alt. Lilias)

Scottish, meaning "lily."

Lilith

Arabic, meaning "ghost." In Jewish mythology Lilith was thought to be a female demon.

Lillian

(alt. Lilian, Liliana, Lilla, Lillianna)

Latin, meaning "lily." Famous Lillians include actor Lillian Gish, playwright Lillian Hellman, and nursing pioneer Lillian Wald.

Lily
(alt. Lili, Lillie, Lilly)

Latin, from the flower of the same name. Famous Lilys include singer Lily Allen, actor Lily Collins, and model Lily Cole.

Linda
(alt. Lynda)

Spanish, meaning "pretty." Famous Lindas include actor Linda Blair and singer Linda Ronstadt.

Linden
(alt. Lindie, Lindy)

European, from the tree of the same name.

Lindsay
(alt. Lindsey, Linsey, Lynsey)

English, meaning "island of linden trees." Famous Lindsays include actor Lindsay Lohan and skier Lindsay Vonn. Can be used for both girls and boys.

Linette
(alt. Lynette)

Welsh, meaning "idol."

Linnea
(alt. Linnae, Linny)

Scandinavian, meaning "lime or linden tree." An extremely popular name for baby girls in Sweden.

Liora
(alt. Lior)

Hebrew, meaning "I have a light." Also a spelling alternative to Leora.

Lisa
(alt. Leesa, Lise, Liza)

Hebrew, meaning "pledged to God." Famous Lisas include singer Lisa Bonet, actor Lisa Kudrow, and *The Simpsons* character Lisa Simpson.

Lish

Shortened form of Elisha, meaning "my God is salvation."

Lissa

Greek, meaning "bee." Also a shortened form of Melissa.

Lissandra
(alt. Lisandra)

Greek, meaning "man's defender."

Liv

Nordic, meaning "defense." Also a short form of Olivia. Actor Liv Tyler is an original Liv.

Livia

Latin, meaning "olive." Livia Drusilla was the wife of Roman Emperor Augustus.

Logan

Irish Gaelic, meaning "small hollow." Used more commonly for boys.

Lois

German, meaning "renowned in battle." Made famous by *Superman* heroine Lois Lane.

Lolita
(alt. Lola; abbrev. Lollie)

Spanish, meaning "sorrows." The title of a novel by Vladimir Nabokov.

Lona

Latin, meaning "lion." Lona is a moon deity in Hawaiian mythology.

Lorelei
(alt. Loralai, Loralie)

German, meaning "dangerous rock." Associated with the Lorelei myth in Germany.

Lorenza

Latin, meaning "from Laurentium."

Loretta
(alt. Loreto)

Latin, meaning "laurel." Loretta Devine is an actor.

Lori
(alt. Laurie, Lorie, Lorri)

Latin, meaning "laurel." Name of actor Lori Petty.

Lorna

Scottish, from the place of the same name. The title character in R. D. Blackmore's novel *Lorna Doone*.

Lorraine
(alt. Loraine)

French, meaning "from Lorraine." Famous Lorraines include actor Lorraine Bracco, paranormal investigator Lorraine Warren, and playwright Lorraine Hansberry.

Lottie
(alt. Lotta, Lotte)

French, meaning "little and womanly." Also a shortened form of Charlotte.

Lotus

Greek, meaning "lotus flower."

Louise
(alt. Lou, Louie, Louisa, Luisa)

German, meaning "renowned in battle." Famous Louises include actors Louise Fletcher and Louise Lasser.

Lourdes

French, from the town of the same name. Chosen by Madonna for her eldest daughter.

Love

English, meaning "deep affection and attraction."

Lowri

Welsh, meaning "crowned with laurels."

Luanne
(alt. Luann, Luanna)

German, meaning "renowned in battle"; Hawaiian, meaning "enjoyment." Famous Luannes include author Luanne Rice and *Real Housewife* LuAnn de Lesseps.

L

Lucia
(alt. Luciana)
Italian, meaning "light."

Lucille
(alt. Lucile, Lucilla)
French, meaning "light." Name of actor Lucille Ball.

Lucinda
English, meaning "light." Famous Lucindas include actor Lucinda Jenney and singer Lucinda Williams.

Lucretia
(alt. Lucrece)
Spanish, meaning "light." Important figure in ancient Roman history.

Lucy
(alt. Lucie)
Latin, meaning "light." Associated with the sitcom I Love Lucy.

Ludmilla
Slavic, meaning "beloved of the people."

Luella
(alt. Lue)
English, meaning "renowned in battle." Luella Bartley is an English fashion designer.

Lulu
(alt. Lula)
German, meaning "renowned in battle." Name of the singer.

Luna
Latin, meaning "moon." Luna was the personification of the moon in ancient Roman mythology.

Lupita
Spanish, from the town of the same name. Lupita Nyong'o is an Academy Award-winning actor.

Luz
Spanish, meaning "light."

Lydia
(alt. Lidia)
Greek, meaning "from Lydia." Lydia Bennet is one of the five sisters in Jane Austen's Pride and Prejudice.

Lynn
(alt. Lyn, Lynna, Lynne)
Spanish, meaning "pretty"; English, meaning "waterfall." Name of the actor Lynn Redgrave.

Lyla
Hebrew, meaning "night."

Lyra
Latin, meaning "lyre." The main female character in Philip Pullman's trilogy His Dark Materials.

M Girls' names

Mab
(alt. Mabe)

Irish Gaelic, meaning "joy."
Queen Mab is a character from
Shakespeare's *Romeo and Juliet*.

Mabel
(alt. Mabelle, Mable)

Latin, meaning "loveable." Dates
from the fifth century.

Macaria

Spanish, meaning "blessed."

Mackenzie
(alt. Mackenzy, McKenzie)

Irish Gaelic, meaning "son of the
wise ruler." Used for girls and boys.

Macy
(alt. Macey, Maci, Macie)

French, meaning "Matthew's estate."
Famous Macys include department
store Macy's and reality TV star Maci
Bookout.

Mada

English, meaning "from Magdala."
In Hindu mythology, Mada is an
enormous monster who is able to
swallow the universe.

Madden
(alt. Maddyn)

Irish, meaning "little dog." Associated
with the video game series.

Madeline
(alt. Madaline, Madalyn, Madeleine,
Madelyn, Madilyn; abbrev. Maddi,
Maddie, Madie)

Greek, meaning "from Magdala."
Associated with Ludwig Bemelmans's
"Madeline" novels.

Madge

Greek, meaning "pearl." Also the
short form of Marjorie and the
nickname of singer Madonna.

Madhuri

Hindi, meaning "sweet girl."

Madison

(alt. Maddison, Madisen, Madisyn)

English, meaning "son of the mighty warrior." Made famous by *Splash* character Madison and President James Madison.

Madonna

Latin, meaning "my lady." Made famous by pop legend Madonna and the Virgin Madonna.

Maeve

Irish Gaelic, meaning "intoxicating." Queen Maeve appears in Irish mythology and Maeve Binchy was an Irish author.

Mafalda

Spanish, meaning "battlemighty." Mafalda Hopkirk is a character in the *Harry Potter* series.

Magali

Greek, meaning "pearl."

Magdalene

(alt. Magdalen, Magdalena)

Greek, meaning "from Magdala." Associated with Mary Magdalene from the Bible.

Maggie

Shortened form of Margaret, meaning "pearl." Famous Maggies include actors Maggie Gyllenhaal and Maggie Grace, and *The Simpsons* character Maggie Simpson.

Magnolia

Latin, from the flowering plant of the same name. Also the name of a movie.

Mahala

(alt. Mahalia)

Hebrew, meaning "tender affection."

Maia

(alt. Maja)

Greek, meaning "mother." An important character in ancient Greek mythology.

Maida

English, meaning "maiden."

Maisie

(alt. Maisey, Maisy, Maizie, Masie, Mazie)

Greek, meaning "pearl." Name of actor Maisie Williams.

Malin

(alt. Maline)

Hebrew, meaning "of Magda." Famous Malins include actor Malin Akerman, singer Malin Berggren, and infamous alleged Swedish witch Malin Matsdotter.

Maliyah
(alt. Malia)

Hawaiian, meaning "beloved." Also the name of one of former President Barack Obama's daughters.

Malka

Hebrew, meaning "queen."

Mallory
(alt. Malorie)

French, meaning "unhappy." The name of children's author Malorie Blackman.

Malvina

Gaelic, meaning "smooth brow."

Mamie
(alt. Mammie)

Shortened form of Margaret, meaning "pearl." Famous Mamies include former First Lady Mamie Eisenhower, actor Mamie Gummer, and infamous midwife Mamie Cadden.

Mandy
(alt. Mandie)

Shortened form of Amanda, meaning "much loved." Famous Mandys include actor Mandy Moore, performer Mandy Miller, and the song "Mandy" by Barry Manilow.

Manisha

Sanskrit, meaning "desire." Manisha is the goddess of wisdom in the Hindu faith.

Mansi

Hopi, meaning "plucked flower."

Manuela

Spanish, meaning "the Lord is among us."

Mara

Hebrew, meaning "bitter." Famous Maras include actors Mara Wilson and Rooney Mara, and author Mara Bergman.

Marcy
(alt. Marci, Marcie, Marcia, Marcela, Marceline, Marcella, Marcelle)

Latin, meaning "war-like." Famous Marcias include actor Marcia Cross and voice actor Marcia Wallace.

Margaret
(alt. Margarete, Margaretta, Margarette, Margret, Margarita, Margeurite; abbrev. Maggie, Margot, Meg)

Greek, meaning "pearl." Famous Margarets include author Margaret Atwood, actor Margaret Rutherford, and former Prime Minister of Great Britain Margaret Thatcher. Margot is the abbreviation of the French form, Marguerite, used by dancer Margot Fonteyn.

Maria
(alt. Mariah)

Latin, meaning "bitter." Famous Marias include tennis pro Maria Sharapova, performer Maria Von Trapp, and singer Mariah Carey.

Marian
(alt. Marianne, Mariam, Mariana, Marion)

French, meaning "bitter grace." Maid Marian is a character from the Robin Hood legend.

Maribel
Hebrew, meaning "beautiful."

Marie
French, meaning "bitter." Famous Maries include French Queen consort Marie Antoinette, physicist Marie Curie, and singer Marie Osmond.

Mariel
(alt. Mariela, Mariella, Marika)

Dutch, meaning "bitter."

Marietta
(alt. Marieta)

French, meaning "bitter." Marietta Stow was a suffragist.

Marigold
English, from the flowering plant of the same name. Associated with the movie *The Best Exotic Marigold Hotel*.

Marilyn
(alt. Marilee, Marilene, Marilynn)

English, meaning "bitter." Made famous by actor and singer Marilyn Monroe.

Marin
American English, from the county of the same name.

Marina
(alt. Marine)

Latin, meaning "from the sea."

Mariposa
Spanish, meaning "butterfly."

Marisa
(alt. Maris, Marissa)

Latin, meaning "of the sea." Famous Marisas include actors Marisa Tomei, Marissa Ribisi, and Marissa Jaret Winokur.

Marisol
Spanish, meaning "bitter sun." Associated with Maria de la Soledad, which is a Spanish title for the Virgin Mary.

Marjolaine
French, meaning "marjoram."

Marjorie
(alt. Margery, Marjory; abbrev. Madge, Marge, Margie, Margit, Margy)

French, meaning "pearl." Famous Marjories include actors Marjorie Reynolds and Marjorie Main, socialite Marjorie Bridges, and autobiographer Margery Kempe.

Marlene
(alt. Marla, Marlen, Marlena)

Hebrew, meaning "bitter." Name of the actor Marlene Dietrich.

Marley
(alt. Marlee)

American English, meaning "bitter." Made famous by singer Bob Marley.

Marlo
(alt. Marlowe)

American English, meaning "bitter."

Marnie
(alt. Marney)

Scottish, meaning "from the sea." Famous Marnies include the character of Marnie from *Girls*, the movie *Marnie* by Alfred Hitchcock, and the birth name of ballerina Dame Darcey Bussell.

Marseille

French, from the city of the same name.

Marsha

English, meaning "war-like." Famous Marshas include singer Marsha Hunt, playwright Marsha Norman, and *Brady Bunch* character Marsha.

Martha
(alt. Marta)

Aramaic, meaning "lady." Found in the Bible.

Martina
(alt. Martine)

Latin, meaning "war-like." Famous Martinas include singer Martina McBride, and tennis pros Martina Hingis and Martina Navratilova.

Marvel

French, meaning "something to wonder at." Also a comic book brand.

Mary

Hebrew, meaning "bitter." Famous Marys include the Virgin Mary and Mary Magdalene from the Bible, and author Mary Shelley.

Masada

Hebrew, meaning "foundation."

Matilda
(alt. Mathilda, Mathilde; abbrev. Tilly)

German, meaning "battlemighty." *Matilda* is a novel by Roald Dahl, and a movie from the book.

Mattea

Hebrew, meaning "gift of God."

Maude
(alt. Maud)

German, meaning "battlemighty." Maude Flanders is a character from *The Simpsons*.

Maureen
(alt. Maura, Maurine)

Irish, meaning "bitter."

Mavis

French, meaning "thrush." Mavis is a character in *Hotel Transylvania*.

Maxine
(abbrev. Maxie)

Latin, meaning "greatest." Maxine Andrews was one of the singing group the Andrews Sisters.

May
(alt. Mae, Maya, Maye, Mayra)

Hebrew, meaning "gift of God." Also the fifth month.

Mckenna
(alt. Mackenna)

Irish Gaelic, meaning "son of the handsome one." Used more commonly for boys.

Medea
(alt. Madea, Meda)

Greek, meaning "ruling." Associated with the Tyler Perry character Madea.

Meg

Shortened form of Margaret, meaning "pearl." Famous Megs include actor Meg Ryan, and the characters of Meg from Disney's *Hercules* and Meg Griffin from *Family Guy*.

Megan
(alt. Meagan, Meghan)

Welsh, meaning "pearl." Famous Megans include actor Megan Fox and the Duchess of Sussex, Meghan Markle.

Mehitabel

Hebrew, meaning "benefited by God."

Mehri

Persian, meaning "kind."

Melanie
(alt. Melania, Melany, Melonie; abbrev. Mel)

Greek, meaning "dark-skinned." Famous Melanies include actor Melanie Griffith and singers Melanie Brown and Melanie Chisholm of the Spice Girls.

Melba

Australian, meaning "from Melbourne." Made famous by Melba toast and the dessert Peach Melba.

Melia
(alt. Meliah)

German, meaning "industrious."

Melina

Greek, meaning "honey." Name of actor Melina Kanakaredes.

Melinda

Latin, meaning "honey."
Philanthropist Melinda Gates is the
wife of Microsoft founder Bill Gates.

Melisande

(alt. Melisende, Melisandre)

French, meaning "bee." Melisandre
is a character from *Game of Thrones*.

Melissa

(alt. Melisa, Mellissa; abbrev. Missy)

Greek, meaning "bee." Famous
Melissas include singer Melissa
Etheridge and actor Melissa Joan Hart.

Melody

(alt. Melodie)

Greek, meaning "song."

Melvina

Celtic, meaning "chieftain."

Menora

(alt. Menorah)

Hebrew, meaning "candlestick."
A Menorah is a candalabrum with
seven branches, used in Jewish
worship; a symbol of Judaism.

Mercedes

Spanish, meaning "mercies."
Made famous by the car company
Mercedes-Benz.

Mercy

English, meaning "mercy."

Meredith

(alt. Meridith)

Welsh, meaning "great ruler."
Meredith Brooks is a singer. Also the
name of the title character Meredith
Grey in *Grey's Anatomy*.

Merle

French, meaning "blackbird." Also
the term for the patterning on the
coat of a dog.

Merry

English, meaning "lighthearted."

Meryl

(alt. Merrill)

Irish Gaelic, meaning "seabright."
The name of actor Meryl Streep and
ice dancer Meryl Davis.

Meta

German, meaning "pearl."

Mia

Italian, meaning "mine." Famous
Mias include actors Mia Farrow
and Mia Wasikowskaa.

Michaela

*(alt. Makaela, Makaila, Makayla,
McKayla, Micaela, Mikaela, Mikaila,
Mikala, Mikayla)*

Hebrew, meaning "who is like
the Lord." The name of gymnast
McKayla Maroney.

Michelle

(alt. Machelle, Mechelle, Michaele, Michal, Michele; abbrev. Micki, Mickie, Micky)

French, meaning "who is like the Lord." Famous Michelles include former First Lady Michelle Obama, and actor Michelle Rodriguez.

Migdalia

Greek, meaning "from Magdala."

Mignon

French, meaning "cute." Also a cut of steak.

Mika

(alt. Micah)

Hebrew, meaning "who resembles God."

Milada

Czech, meaning "my love."

Milagros

Spanish, meaning "miracles." Also a type of Mexican folk charm.

Milan

Italian, from the city of the same name.

Mildred

English, meaning "gentle strength." The title character from the movie and TV series *Mildred Pierce*.

Milena

Czech, meaning "love and warmth."

Miley

American English, meaning "smiley." Name of singer and actor Miley Cyrus.

Millicent

(alt. Milicent; abbrev. Millie, Milly)

German, meaning "high-born power." Famous Millicents include suffragist Millicent Fawcett, British spy Milicent Bagot, and the musical *Thoroughly Modern Millie*.

Mimi

Italian, meaning "bitter." Mimi is a character from Giacome Puccini's opera *La boheme*.

Mina

(alt. Mena)

German, meaning "love"; Persian, meaning "colored glass."

Mindy

(alt. Mindi)

Latin, meaning "honey." Famous Mindys include comedian Mindy Kaling, singer Mindy McCready, and actor Mindy Sterling.

Minerva

Roman, from the goddess of the same name. Minerva was the goddess of wisdom, arts, and defense.

Ming

Chinese, meaning "bright." Associated with the Ming Dynasty in China.

Minnie
(alt. Minna)

German, meaning "helmet." Made famous by Disney's Minnie Mouse.

Mira
(alt. Meera)

Latin, meaning "admirable."

Mirabel
(alt. Mirabella, Mirabelle)

Latin, meaning "wonderful." Also a type of plum.

Miranda
(alt. Meranda)

Latin, meaning "admirable." Famous Mirandas include actors Miranda Richardson and Miranda Hart, and model Miranda Kerr.

Mirella
(alt. Mireille, Mirela)

Latin, meaning "admirable." Mirella Freni is an opera singer.

Miriam

Hebrew, meaning "bitter." A prophetess in the Bible.

Mirta

Spanish, meaning "crown of thorns."

Missy
(alt. Missie)

Shortened form of Melissa, meaning "bee." The name of singer and producer Missy Elliot.

Misty
(alt. Misti)

English, meaning "mist." Associated with Misty from Pokémon.

Mitzi

German, meaning "bitter." Name of actor Mitzi Gaynor.

Miu

Japanese, meaning "beautiful feather."

Moira
(alt. Maira)

Irish, meaning "bitter." Associated with actor Moira Kelly.

Molly
(alt. Mollie)

American English, meaning "bitter." Famous Mollys include actors Molly Ringwald and Molly Sims.

Mona

Irish Gaelic, meaning "aristocratic." The vampire from *Mona the Vampire*.

Monica
(alt. Monika, Monique)

Latin, meaning "advisor." Famous Monicas include intern Monica Lewinsky, tennis pro Monica Seles, and *Friends* character Monica Geller.

Monroe

Gaelic, meaning "mouth of the river Rotha." Made famous by singer and actor Marilyn Monroe.

Montserrat
(alt. Monserrate)

Spanish, from the town of the same name. Montserrat Caballe is an opera singer.

Morag

Scottish, meaning "star of the sea." Also the name of the Loch Morar monster in Scotland.

Morgan
(alt. Morgann)

Welsh, meaning "great and bright." Used for girls and boys.

Moriah

Hebrew, meaning "the Lord is my teacher."

Morwenna

Welsh, meaning "maiden." St. Morwenna is the patron saint of Cornwall, England.

Moselle
(alt. Mozell, Mozella, Mozelle)

Hebrew, meaning "savior."

Mulan

Chinese, meaning "wood orchid." Also a Disney movie.

Muriel

Irish Gaelic, meaning "seabright." Name of the novelist Muriel Spark.

Mya
(alt. Maya, Myah)

Greek, meaning "mother." Famous Myas include author Maya Angelou, comedian Maya Rudolph, and the Mayan people of Central America.

Myfanwy

Welsh, meaning "my little lovely one."

Myla

English, meaning "merciful."

Myleene

English, from the Latin Melaine meaning "dark as night."

Myra

Latin, meaning "scented oil." Name of the pioneering lawyer Myra Bradwell.

Myrna
(alt. Mirna)

Irish Gaelic, meaning "tender and beloved." Associated with actor Myrna Fahey.

Myrtle

Irish, from the shrub of the same name. Myrtle Wilson is a character from The Great Gatsby.

N

Girls' names

Nadia
(alt. Nadya)

Russian, meaning "hope." Nadia Comaneci was the first gymnast to be awarded a perfect score of ten in an Olympic event.

Nadine

French, meaning "hope." Name of the socialite Nadine Caridi.

Nahara

Aramaic, meaning "light."

Naima

Arabic, meaning "water nymph."

Nalani

Hawaiian, meaning "serenity of the skies."

Nancy
(alt. Nanci, Nancie; abbrev. Nan, Nanna, Nannie)

Hebrew, meaning "grace." Famous Nancys include former First Lady Nancy Reagan and figure skater Nancy Kerrigan.

Nanette
(alt. Nannette)

French, meaning "grace." Associated with musical *No, No, Nanette*.

Naomi
(alt. Naoma, Noemi)

Hebrew, meaning "pleasant." Found in the Bible. Famous Naomis include actor Naomi Watts, author Naomi Wolf, and supermodel Naomi Campbell.

Narcissa

Greek, meaning "daffodil." Narcissa Malfoy is a character in the *Harry Potter* series.

Girls' names N

Nastasia

Greek, meaning "resurrection."
Can also refer to a baby born on
Christmas Day.

Natalie

(alt. Natalia, Natalya, Nathalie)

Latin, meaning "birth day." Natalie
Wood was an actor.

Natasha

(alt. Natasa; abbrev. Nat, Tasha)

Russian, meaning "birth day." A
character from Leo Tolstoy's *War
and Peace*.

Neda

English, meaning "wealthy."
An ancient Greek nymph.

Nedra

English, meaning "underground."

Neema

Swahili, meaning "born of
prosperity."

Neka

Native American, meaning "goose."

Nell

(alt. Nelda, Nella, Nellie, Nelly)

Originally a shortened form of
Eleanor, meaning "light." The title of
a movie. Singer Nelly Furtado was
given the name at birth, but Nell
Gwynn, mistress of King Charles II,
was an Eleanor.

Nemi

Italian, from the lake of the same
name.

Neoma

Greek, meaning "new moon."

Nereida

Spanish, meaning "sea nymph."

Nerissa

Greek, meaning "sea nymph."
A character in Shakespeare's play
The Merchant of Venice.

Nettie

(alt. Neta)

Shortened form of Henrietta,
meaning "ruler of the house."

Neva

Spanish, meaning "snowy."

Nevaeh

American English, meaning "heaven"
(and spelled that way backwards).

Neytiri

Na'vi, meaning "princess." From the
Avatar film series.

Niamh

(alt. Neve)

Irish, meaning "brightness."
An Irish goddess.

265

Nicola
(abbrev. Nicki, Nicky, Nikki)

Greek, meaning "victory of the people." Famous Nicolas include actor Nicola Peltz and singer Nicola Roberts.

Nicole
(alt. Nichol, Nichole, Nicolette, Nicolle, Nikole)

Greek, meaning "victory of the people." Famous Nicoles include actor Nicole Kidman, socialite Nicole Richie, and singer Nicole Scherzinger.

Nidia
Spanish, meaning "graceful."

Nigella
Irish Gaelic, meaning "champion." Name of British chef Nigella Lawson.

Nikita
Greek, meaning "unconquered." Also a song by Elton John.

Nila
Egyptian, meaning "Nile." Associated with Nila wafers.

Nilda
German, meaning "battle woman."

Nina
Spanish, meaning "girl." Nina Simone was a singer-songwriter and civil rights activist.

Old name, new fashion

Bella	Hazel
Carolyn	Matilda
Clara	Nora
Dorothy	Penelope
Emmeline	Rosalie

Nissa
Hebrew, meaning "sign."

Nita
Spanish, meaning "gracious."

Nixie
German, meaning "water sprite."

Noelle
(alt. Noel)

French, meaning "Christmas." Noelle is usually the feminine form and Noel the masculine form.

Nola
(alt. Nuala)

Irish Gaelic, meaning "white shoulder." Often refers to someone with white or very blonde hair.

Nona
Latin, meaning "ninth."

Nora
(alt. Norah)

Shortened form of Eleanor, meaning "light." The name of screenwriter Nora Ephron, singer Norah Jones, and author Nora Roberts.

Noreen
(alt. Norine)

Irish, meaning "light." Noreen Murray was a scientist who helped develop the vaccine against hepatitis B.

Norma

Latin, meaning "pattern." Marilyn Monroe's birth name was Norma Jean Mortenson.

Normandie
(alt. Normandy)

French, from the province of the same name.

Novia
(alt. Nova)

Latin, meaning "new."

Nydia

Latin, meaning "nest."

Nysa
(alt. Nyssa)

Greek, meaning "ambition." A district in ancient Greek mythology.

O

Girls' names

Oaklyn
(alt. Oaklynn)
English, meaning "from the oak meadow."

Oceana
(alt. Ocean, Océane, Ocie)
Greek, meaning "ocean."

Octavia
Latin, meaning "eighth." Famous Octavias include actor Octavia Spencer, and Octavia in Shakespeare's *Antony and Cleopatra*.

Oda
(alt. Odie)
Shortened form of Odessa, meaning "long voyage"; German, meaning "wealth" or "inheritance."

Odele
(alt. Odell)
English, meaning "woad hill." Woad is a dye for the color indigo.

Odelia
Hebrew, meaning "I will praise the Lord." Associated with St. Odelia.

Odessa
Greek, meaning "long voyage."

Odette
(alt. Odetta)
French, meaning "wealthy." Name of the "good" swan in *Swan Lake*.

Odile
(alt. Odilia)
French, meaning "prospers in battle." Name of the "bad" swan in *Swan Lake*.

Odina
Feminine form of Odin, meaning "creative inspiration," from the Nordic god of the same name.

Odyssey

Greek, meaning "long journey."
Title of the epic poem by Homer.

Oksana

Russian, meaning "praise to God."

Ola
(alt. Olie)

Greek, meaning "man's defender."

Olena
(alt. Olene)

Russian, meaning "light."

Olga

Russian, meaning "holy." Name of
the model and actor Olga Kurylenko,
and gymnast Olga Korbut.

Olivia
(alt. Olivev, Oliviana, Olivié, Ollie;
abbrev. Liv, Livia)

Latin, meaning "olive." Famous
Olivias include actors Olivia Munn
and Olivia Wilde, and Scandal
character Olivia Pope.

Olwen

Welsh, meaning "white footprint."

Olympia
(alt. Olimpia)

Greek, meaning "from Mount
Olympus." Name of actor Olympia
Dukakis.

Oma
(alt. Omie)

Arabic, meaning "leader." In some
communities, Oma refers to a
grandmother.

Omyra

Latin, meaning "scented oil."

Oneida
(abbrev. Ona, Onnie)

Native American, meaning "long
awaited." The name of a tribe.

Onyx

Latin, meaning "veined gem." Also
a semiprecious stone.

Oona
(alt. Oonagh)

Irish, meaning "unity."

Opal

Sanskrit, meaning "gem." Also a
precious stone.

Ophelia
(alt. Ophélie)

Greek, meaning "help." A character
in Shakespeare's Hamlet.

Oprah

Hebrew, meaning "young deer."
Name of the legendary TV host
Oprah Winfrey.

Ora

Latin, meaning "prayer." Also a platinum metal.

Orabela

Latin, meaning "prayer."

Oralie
(alt. Oralia)

French, meaning "golden."

Orane

French, meaning "rising."

Orchid

Greek, from the flower of the same name.

Oriana
(alt. Oriane)

Latin, meaning "dawning." One of the many nicknames of Queen Elizabeth I.

Orla
(alt. Orlaith, Orly)

Irish Gaelic, meaning "golden lady."

Orlean

French, meaning "plum." The city of New Orleans in Louisiana.

Orsa
(alt. Osia, Ossie)

Latin, meaning "bear."

Otthid

Greek, meaning "prospers in battle."

Ottilie
(alt. Ottie)

French, meaning "prospers in battle." Name of the opera singer Ottilie Metzger.

Ouida

French, meaning "renowned in battle."

Ozette

Native American, from the village of the same name.

P

Girls' names

Padma

Sanskrit, meaning "lotus." Padma Lakshmi is an Indian-born American cookery book writer, actor, and TV host.

Paige
(alt. Page)

French, meaning "serving boy." Paige Turco is an actor.

Paisley

Scottish, from the town of the same name. The name of a fabric pattern.

Palma
(alt. Palmira)

Latin, meaning "palm tree."

Paloma

Spanish, meaning "dove." Famous Palomas include singer Paloma Faith and designer Paloma Picasso.

Pamela
(alt. Pamala, Pamella; abbrev. Pam, Pammie)

Greek, meaning "all honey." Famous Pamelas include actors Pamela Anderson and Pamela Adlon, and author Pamela (P. L.) Travers.

Pandora

Greek, meaning "all gifted." Associated with the myth of Pandora's box in ancient Greek mythology.

Pangiota

Greek, meaning "all is holy."

Pansy

French, from the flower of the same name.

Paradisa
(alt. Paradis)

Greek, meaning "garden orchard."

Paris
(alt. Parisa)

Greek, from the mythological hero of the same name. Famous Parises include the French capital and socialite Paris Hilton.

Parker

English, meaning "park keeper." Parker Posey is an actor.

Parthenia

Greek, meaning "virginal."

Parthenope

Greek, from the mythological Siren of the same name. Parthenope Nightingale was sister of nurse Florence Nightingale.

Parvati

Sanskrit, meaning "daughter of the mountain." The Hindu goddess of love and devotion.

Pascale

Latin, meaning "Easter child." Also a boys' name, usually spelt Pascal.

Patience

French, meaning "the state of being patient."

Patricia
(abbrev. Pat, Patsy, Patti, Pattie, Patty, Trisha)

Latin, meaning "noble." Famous Patricias include actors Patricia Arquette and Patricia O'Neal.

Paula

Latin, meaning "small." Famous Paulas include singer Paula Abdul, actor Paula Patton, and chef Paula Deen.

Pauline
(alt. Paulette, Paulina)

Latin, meaning "small."

Paxton

Latin, meaning "peaceful town."

Paz

Spanish, meaning "peace."

Pazia

Hebrew, meaning "golden."

Peace

English, meaning "peace."

Pearl
(alt. Pearle, Pearlie, Perla)

Latin, meaning "pale gemstone."

Peggy
(alt. Peggie)

Greek, meaning "pearl." The name of actor Peggy Lipton and figure skater Peggy Fleming; also associated with the movie *Peggy Sue Got Married*.

Pelia

Hebrew, meaning "marvel of God."

Penelope
(abbrev. Penni, Pennie, Penny)

Greek, meaning "bobbin worker."
Penelope was also the loyal wife of
Odysseus in Greek mythology.

Peony

Greek, from the flower of the same
name.

Perdita

Latin, meaning "lost." A character
in William Shakespeare's play *The
Winter's Tale*.

Peri
(alt. Perri)

Hebrew, meaning "outcome."
Associated with Peri spirits in Persian
mythology.

Perry

French, meaning "pear tree."

Persephone

Greek, meaning "bringer of
destruction." The Queen of the
Underworld in ancient Greek
mythology.

Petra
(alt. Petrina)

Greek, meaning "rock."

Petula

Latin, meaning "to seek." Name of
the singer Petula Clark.

Petunia

Greek, from the flower of the same
name.

Peyton
(alt. Payton)

Old English, meaning "fighting man's
estate." Associated with TV series
Peyton Place.

Phaedra

Greek, meaning "bright."

Philippa
(abbrev. Pippa)

Greek, meaning "horse lover."
Philippa Gregory is an author.

Philomena
(alt. Philoma)

Greek, meaning "loved one." Title of
the book and movie *Philomena*.

Phoebe

Greek, meaning "shining and
brilliant." Famous Phoebes include
actor Phoebe Cates, and *Friends*
character Phoebe Buffay.

Phoenix

Greek, meaning "red as blood." The
city in Arizona and the mythical bird.

Phyllis
(alt. Phillia, Phyllida, Phylis)

Greek, meaning "leafy bough."
Name of the groundbreaking
comedian Phyllis Diller.

Pia

Latin, meaning "pious."

Pilar

Spanish, meaning "pillar."

Piper

English, meaning "pipe player." Piper Laurie is an actor. Piper Kerman was the real-life inspiration behind the character Piper Chapman in Netflix hit *Orange is the New Black*.

Plum

Latin, from the fruit.

Polly

Hebrew, meaning "bitter." Associated with the classic Polly Pocket toy.

Pomona

Latin, meaning "apple." The goddess of fruitful abundance in ancient Roman mythology.

Poppy

Latin, from the flower of the same name. Poppy Delevingne is a model.

Portia
(alt. Porsha)

Latin, meaning "from the Portia clan." Portia de Rossi is an actor.

Posy
(alt. Posie)

English, meaning "small flower."

Precious

Latin, meaning "of great worth." Title of the movie *Precious*.

Priela

Hebrew, meaning "fruit of God."

Primrose

English, meaning "first rose."

Princess

English, meaning "daughter of the monarch."

Priscilla
(alt. Priscila)

Latin, meaning "ancient." Actor Priscilla Presley was married to Elvis.

Priya

Hindi, meaning "loved one."

Prudence
(abbrev. Pru, Prudie)

Latin, meaning "caution." Prudence is the mother of all virtues.

Prunella

Latin, meaning "small plum." Prunella Scales is a British actor.

Psyche

Greek, meaning "breath." The name of TV show *Psyche*.

Girls' names

Qianru

Chinese, meaning "pretty."

Qiturah

Arabic, meaning "incense."

Queen
(alt. Queenie)

English, meaning "queen." The name of rapper and actor Queen Latifah.

Quiana

American English, meaning "silky." Name of the model Quiana Grant.

Quincy
(alt. Quincey)

French, meaning "estate of the fifth son."

Quinn
(alt. Quinnie)

Irish Gaelic, meaning "counsel." Quinn is a character from *Glee*.

Quinnlan

Gaelic, meaning "strong and well-made."

R Girls' names

Rachel

(alt. Rachael, Rachelle, Raquel; abbrev. Rach)

Hebrew, meaning "ewe." Found in the Bible. Famous Rachel's include actors Rachel Weisz and Rachel Bilson, and the *Friends* character Rachel Green.

Radhika

Sanskrit, meaning "prosperous."

Rae

(alt. Ray)

Feminine form of Ray, meaning "ray," or shortened form of Rachel, meaning "ewe." Rae Armantrout is a poet.

Rahima

Arabic, meaning "compassionate." Name of smallpox survivor Rahima Banu.

Raina

(alt. Rain, Raine, Rainey, Rayne)

Latin, meaning "queen."

Raissa

(alt. Raisa)

Yiddish, meaning "rose." Name of former Russian First Lady Raisa Gorbacheva.

Raleigh

(alt. Rayleigh)

English, meaning "meadow of roe deer."

Rama

(alt. Ramey, Ramya)

Hebrew, meaning "exalted." Associated with the Vishnu's avatars in the Hindu faith.

Ramona

(alt. Romona)

Spanish, meaning "wise guardian." Associated with the "Ramona" books, and the movie *Ramona and Beezus*.

Ramsey
(alt. Ramsay)
English, meaning "raven island."

Rana
(alt. Rania, Rayna)
Arabic, meaning "beautiful thing."

Randy
(alt. Randi)
Shortened form of Miranda, meaning "admirable." More commonly used for boys, as a short form of Randall.

Rani
Sanskrit, meaning "queen."

Raphaela
(alt. Rafaela, Raffaella)
Spanish, meaning "healing God."

Rashida
Turkish, meaning "righteous." Name of actor Rashida Jones.

Raven
(alt. Ravyn)
English, from the bird of the same name. Raven-Symoné is an actor.

Razia
Arabic, meaning "contented."

Reagan
(alt. Reagen, Regan)
Irish Gaelic, meaning "descendant of Riagán." Associated with former President and First Lady Ronald and Nancy Reagan.

Reba
Shortened form of Rebecca, meaning "joined." Name of singer and actor Reba McEntire.

Rebecca
(alt. Rebekah; abbrev. Reb, Reba, Becca, Bex)
Hebrew, meaning "joined." Found in the Bible. Famous Rebeccas include designer Rebecca Minkoff, and actor Rebecca Hall.

Reese
(alt. Reece)
Welsh, meaning "fiery and zealous." Name of actor Reese Witherspoon.

Regina
(abbrev. Geena, Gena, Gina)
Latin, meaning "queen." Famous Reginas include actors Regina Hall and Regina King, and singer Regina Spektor. Geena Davis is an actor.

Reina
(alt. Reyna, Rheyna)
Spanish, meaning "queen."

Rena
(alt. Reena, Rina)
Hebrew, meaning "serene."

Renata
Latin, meaning "reborn." Renata Tebaldi was an Italian opera singer.

Rene

Greek, meaning "peace." Rene Russo is an actor.

Renée
(alt. Renae)

French, meaning "reborn." Name of actor Renée Zellweger.

Renita
(alt. Renira)

Latin, meaning "resistant."

Reshma
(alt. Resha)

Sanskrit, meaning "silk."

Reta
(alt. Retha, Retta)

Portuguese, meaning "straight." Also a shortened form of Margaret.

Rhea

Greek, meaning "earth." Also a type of ostrich-like bird. Name of actor Rhea Perlman.

Rheta

Greek, meaning "eloquent speaker." Flora Rheta Schreiber is an author.

Rhiannon
(alt. Rhian)

Welsh, meaning "witch." A prominent figure in Welsh mythology.

Rhoda

Greek, meaning "rose." Title of the sitcom *Rhoda*.

Rhona

Nordic, meaning "rough island." Rhona Mitra is a model and actor.

Rhonda
(alt. Ronda)

Welsh, meaning "noisy." "Help Me Rhonda" is a song by the Beach Boys.

Ría
(alt. Rie, Riya)

Shortened form of Victoria, meaning "victor."

Ricki
(alt. Rieko, Rika, Rikki)

Shortened form of Frederica, meaning "peaceful ruler." Name of the TV host Ricki Lake.

Rihanna
(alt. Reanna, Rhianna)

Welsh, meaning "witch." Robyn Rihanna fenty is a Barbadian singer and businesswoman.

Riley

Irish Gaelic, meaning "courageous."

Rilla

German, meaning "small brook."

Rima

Arabic, meaning "antelope." Name of the comic book character *Rima the Jungle Girl*.

Riona

Irish Gaelic, meaning "like a queen."

Ripley

English, meaning "shouting man's meadow."

Risa

Latin, meaning "laughter."

Rita

Shortened form of Margaret, meaning "pearl." Famous Ritas include actors Rita Hayworth and Rita Moreno, and singer Rita Ora.

River
(alt. Riviera)

English, from the body of water of the same name.

Roberta
(abbrev. Bobbi, Bobby, Robbie, Robi, Roby)

English, meaning "bright fame." Name of singer Roberta Flack.

Robin
(alt. Robbin, Robyn)

English, meaning "bright fame." Famous Robins include actor Robin Wright Penn, and singers Robyn and Robin Thicke. Used for both girls and boys.

Rochelle
(alt. Richelle, Rochel)

French, meaning "little rock." Name of actor Rochelle Aytes.

Rogue

French, meaning "beggar." Also an "X-Men" character.

Rohina
(alt. Rohini)

Sanskrit, meaning "sandalwood."

Roisin

Irish Gaelic, meaning "little rose."

Rolanda

German, meaning "famous land." Rolanda Watts is a voice actor.

Roma

Italian, meaning "Rome." Also the name of an ancient Roman deity, and a group of nomadic people.

Romaine
(alt. Romina)

French, meaning "from Rome."

Romola
(alt. Romilda, Romily)

Latin, meaning "Roman woman." Name of the actor Romola Garai.

Romy

Shortened form of Rosemary, meaning "dew of the sea." Famous Romys include actor Romy Rosemont and the movie *Romy and Michele's High School Reunion*.

Rona
(alt. Ronia, Ronja, Ronna)

Nordic, meaning "rough island."

Ronnie
(alt. Roni, Ronnie)

English, meaning "strong counsel."

Rosa

Italian, meaning "rose." Made famous by Civil Rights activist Rosa Parks.

Rosabel
(alt. Rosabella)

Contraction of Rose and Belle, meaning "beautiful rose."

Rosalie
(alt. Rosale, Rosalia, Rosalina)

French, meaning "rose garden." Actor Andie MacDowell's birth name is actually Rosalie.

Rosalind
(alt. Rosalinda)

Spanish, meaning "pretty rose." A character in Shakespeare's play *As You Like It*.

Rosalyn
(alt. Rosaleen, Rosaline, Roselyn)

Contraction of Rose and Lynn, meaning "pretty rose."

Rosamund
(alt. Rosamond)

German, meaning "renowned protector." Famous Rosamunds include actor Rosamund Pike and author Rosamunde Pilcher.

Rose
(alt. Rosie, Rosia)

Latin, from the flower of the same name. Famous Roses include actors Rose Byrne and Rose McGowan, and the character of Rose DeWitt Bukater from *Titanic*.

Roseanne
(alt. Rosana, Rosanna, Rosanne, Roseann, Roseanna)

Contraction of Rose and Anne, meaning "graceful rose."

Rosemary
(alt. Rosemarie; abbrev. Rosie, Rosy)

Latin, meaning "dew of the sea." Famous Rosemarys include the late actor Rosemary Clooney and the film *Rosemary's Baby*.

Rosita

Spanish, meaning "rose." Also a character on *Sesame Street*.

Rowena
(alt. Rowan)

Welsh, meaning "slender and fair." Rowena was a powerful and beautiful seductress in ancient Welsh mythology.

Roxanne
(alt. Roxana, Roxane, Roxanna; abbrev. Roxie)

Persian, meaning "dawn." Also a song by The Police. Famous Roxies include the character of Roxie Hart from the musical *Chicago*, and the band Roxy Music.

Rubina
(alt. Rubena)

Hebrew, meaning "behold, a son."

Ruby
(alt. Rubi, Rubie)

English, meaning "red gemstone." Made famous by the song "Ruby Tuesday" by the Rolling Stones.

"Bad girl" names

Delilah	Roxy
Desdemona	Salome
Jezebel	Scarlett
Lilith	Tallulah
Pandora	Trixie

Ruth
(alt. Ruthe, Ruthie)

Hebrew, meaning "friend and companion." Found in the Bible. Famous Ruths include Supreme Court Justice Ruth Bader Ginsburg.

Ryan
(alt. Riaan)

Gaelic, meaning "little king." More commonly used for boys.

S Girls' names

Saba
(alt. Sabah)

Greek, meaning "from Sheba."

Sabina
(alt. Sabine)

Latin, meaning "from the Sabine tribe." The title given to political women in ancient Rome.

Sabrina

Latin, meaning "the River Severn." Famous Sabrinas include the movie *Sabrina*, the sitcom *Sabrina, the Teenage Witch*, and the character from *Charlie's Angels*.

Sadie
(alt. Sade, Sadye)

Hebrew, meaning "princess." Sadie Frost is British designer and actor.

Saffron

English, from the reddish-yellow spice of the same name.

Safiyya
(alt. Safiya)

Arabic, meaning "sincere friend." One of Muhammad's wives in the Qur'an.

Sage
(alt. Saga, Saige)

Latin, meaning "wise and healthy." Also an aromatic herb.

Sahara

Arabic, meaning "desert."

Sakura

Japanese, meaning "cherry blossom."

Sally
(alt. Sallie)

Hebrew, meaning "princess." Actor Sally Field has had a long and successful career.

Salome
(alt. Salma)

Hebrew, meaning "peace." A seductress in the Bible.

Samantha
(abbrev. Sam, Sammie, Sammy)

Hebrew, meaning "told by God." Famous Samanthas include TV host Samantha Brown and actors Samantha Lewes and Samantha Morton.

Samara
(alt. Samaria, Samira)

Hebrew, meaning "under God's rule."

Sanaa

Arabic, meaning "brilliance." Also the capital of Yemen.

Sandra
(alt. Saundra; abbrev. Sandy)

Shortened form of Alexandra, meaning "defender of mankind." Famous Sandras include actor Sandra Bullock and the character Sandy from *Grease*.

Sangeetha
(alt. Sangeeta)

Hindi, meaning "musical."

Sanna
(alt. Saniya, Sanne, Sanni)

Hebrew, meaning "lily."

Santana
(alt. Santina)

Spanish, meaning "holy."

Saoirse

Irish Gaelic, meaning "freedom."

Sapphire
(alt. Saphira)

Hebrew, meaning "blue gemstone." Associated with *Push* (or *Precious*) author Sapphire.

Sarah
(alt. Sara, Sarai, Sariah)

Hebrew, meaning "princess." Famous Sarahs include actors Sarah Michelle Gellar and Sarah Hyland, and politician and reality TV star Sarah Palin.

Sasha
(alt. Sacha, Sascha)

Russian, meaning "man's defender." Name of former President Barack Obama's daughter.

Saskia
(alt. Saskie)

Dutch, meaning "the Saxon people"; Danish, meaning "valley of light."

Savannah
(alt. Savanah, Savanna, Savina)

Spanish, meaning "treeless."

Scarlett
(alt. Scarlet)

English, meaning "scarlet." Scarlett O'Hara is the protagonist of Margaret Mitchell's novel *Gone With The Wind*.

Scout

French, meaning "to listen." Also the lead character in Harper Lee's novel *To Kill a Mockingbird*.

Sedona
(alt. Sedonia, Sedna)

Spanish, from the city of the same name.

Selah
(alt. Sela)

Hebrew, meaning "cliff"; Hebrew, meaning "stop and listen."

Selby

English, meaning "manor village."

Selena
(alt. Salena, Salima, Salina, Selene, Selina)

Greek, meaning "moon goddess." Famous Selenas include singers Selena Gomez and Selena Quintanilla-Perez (known simply as Selena), and actor Selena Royle.

Selma

German, meaning "Godly helmet." Name of actor Selma Blair.

Seneca

Native American, meaning "from the Seneca tribe."

Sephora

Hebrew, meaning "bird"; Greek, meaning "beauty."

September

Latin, meaning "seventh month." The ninth month.

Seraphina
(alt. Serafina, Seraphia, Seraphine)

Hebrew, meaning "ardent." St. Serafina was known for her strong faith despite illness and suffering.

Serena
(alt. Sarina, Sereana)

Latin, meaning "tranquil." Name of tennis pro Serena Williams.

Serenity

Latin, meaning "serene." Also a sci-fi movie.

Shakira

Arabic, meaning "thankful." Name of the singer Shakira.

Shania
(alt. Shaina, Shana, Shaniya)

Hebrew, meaning "beautiful." Name of the singer Shania Twain.

Shanice

American English, meaning "from Africa." Name of the singer Shanice.

Shaniqua
(alt. Shanika)

African, meaning "warrior princess."

Shanna

English, meaning "old."

Shannon
(alt. Shannan, Shanon)

Irish Gaelic, meaning "old and ancient." Shannon Elizabeth is an actor.

Shantal
(alt. Shantel, Shantell)

French, from the place of the same name.

Shanti
(alt. Shantih)

Hindi, meaning "peaceful."

Sharlene

German, meaning "man."

Sharon
(alt. Sharen, Sharona, Sharron)

Hebrew, meaning "a plain." Famous Sharons include reality TV star Sharon Osbourne and actors Sharon Stone and Sharon Tate.

Shasta

American English, from the mountain and Native American tribe of the same name.

Shauna
(alt. Sharna, Shawna)

Irish, meaning "the Lord is gracious." Sharna Burgess is a dancer.

Shayla
(alt. Shaylie, Shayna, Sheyla)

Irish, meaning "blind."

Shea

Irish Gaelic, meaning "from the fairy fort." The tree and nut of the same name.

Sheena

Irish, meaning "the Lord is gracious." Name of the singer Sheena Easton.

Sheila
(alt. Shelia, Shila)

Irish, meaning "blind." Name of singer Sheila E.

Shelby
(alt. Shelba, Shelbie)

English, meaning "estate on the ledge."

Shelley
(alt. Shellie, Shelly)

English, meaning "meadow on the ledge." Famous Shelleys include actor Shelley Fabares and Shelley Duvall, and author Mary Shelley.

Shenandoah

Native American, meaning "after an Oneida chief." Also the name of a national park.

Sheridan

Irish Gaelic, meaning "wild man."

Sheryl
(alt. Sherryl; abbrev. Sheri, Sherie, Sherri, Sherrie)

German, meaning "man." Famous Sheryls include singer Sheryl Crow, businesswoman Sheryl Sandberg, and host Sheryl Underwood. Also comedian and host Sherri Shepherd.

Shiloh

Hebrew, meaning "his gift." Name of Angelina Jolie and Brad Pitt's daughter.

Shirley
(alt. Shirlee)

English, meaning "bright meadow." Famous Shirleys include singer Dame Shirley Bassey, actor Shirley MacLaine, and child star Shirley Temple.

Shivani

Sanskrit, meaning "wife of Shiva."

Shona

Irish Gaelic, meaning "God is gracious."

Shoshana
(alt. Shoshanna)

Hebrew, meaning "lily." Shoshanna Shapiro is a character from *Girls*.

Shura

Russian, meaning "man's defender"; Arabic, meaning "consultation."

Sian
(alt. Sianna)

Welsh, meaning "the Lord is gracious."

Sibyl
(alt. Sybil)

Greek, meaning "seer and oracle." Sibyl was a prophetess in ancient Greek mythology.

Sidney
(alt. Sydney)

English, meaning "from St. Denis." Name of the city in Australia.

Sidonie
(alt. Sidonia, Sidony)

Latin, meaning "from Sidonia."

Siena
(alt. Sienna)

Latin, from the town of the same name.

Sierra

Spanish, meaning "saw."

Great female singers

Adele (Adkins)

Aretha (Franklin)

Billie (Holiday)

Dionne (Warwick)

Dolly (Parton)

Ella (Fitzgerald)

Gladys (Knight)

Jennifer (Hudson)

Judy (Garland)

Nina (Simone)

Signa
(alt. Signe)

Scandinavian, meaning "victory."

Sigrid

Nordic, meaning "fair victory." Sigrid the Haughty was an important figure in ancient Norse mythology.

Silja

Scandinavian, meaning "blind."

Simcha

Hebrew, meaning "joy."

Simone
(alt. Simona)

Hebrew, meaning "listening intently." Famous Simones include singer Nina Simone, and philosopher Simone de Beauvoir.

Sinead

Irish, meaning "the Lord is gracious." Name of singer Sinead O'Connor.

Siobhan

Irish, meaning "the Lord is gracious." Siobhan Fallon Hogan is an actor.

Siren
(alt. Sirena)

Greek, meaning "entangler." In ancient Greek mythology, sirens were beautiful and dangerous creatures who lured sailors to their deaths.

Siria

Spanish, meaning "glowing."

Skye
(alt. Sky)

Scottish, from the island of the same name in Scotland.

Skylar
(alt. Skyla, Skyler)

Dutch, meaning "giving shelter." Skylar White is a character from Breaking Bad.

Sloane
(alt. Sloan)

Irish Gaelic, meaning "man of arms." Famous Sloanes include tennis player Sloane Stephens, the infamous Sloane Rangers, and the character of Sloane Sabbith on Newsroom.

Socorro

Spanish, meaning "to aid."

Sojourner

English, meaning "temporary stay."
Name of 19th-century women's
rights and civil rights activist
Sojourner Truth.

Solana

Spanish, meaning "sunlight."

Solange

French, meaning "with dignity."
Solange Knowles is a singer.

Soledad

Spanish, meaning "solitude."

Soleil

French, meaning "sun."

Solveig

Scandinavian, meaning "woman of
the house."

Sonia
(alt. Sonja, Sonya)

Greek, meaning "wisdom." Sonia
Kasuk is a designer.

Sophia
(alt. Sofia, Sofie, Sophie)

Greek, meaning "wisdom." Famous
Sophias include director Sofia
Coppola and actors Sofia Vergara
and Sophia Loren.

Sophronia

Greek, meaning "sensible."

Soraya

Persian, meaning "princess."

Sorcha

Irish Gaelic, meaning "bright and
shining."

Sorrel

English, from the herb of the same
name.

Spirit

Latin, meaning "breath."

Stacey
(alt. Stacie, Stacy)

Greek, meaning "resurrection."
Famous Staceys include actors Stacey
Keibler and Stacey Dash,
and presenter Stacey Dales.

Star
(alt. Starla, Starr)

English, meaning "star." The name of
reality TV star Star Jones.

Stella

Latin, meaning "star." Stella
McCartney is a British designer.

Stephanie
(alt. Stefanie, Stephani, Stephany, Stephenie; abbrev. Steph)

Greek, meaning "crowned." Famous Stephanies include actor Stephanie Beacham, and author Stephenie Meyer.

Storm
(alt. Stormi, Stormy)

English, from the weather feature. Kylie Jenner's daughter is Stormi.

Sukey
(alt. Sukey, Sukie)

Derived from Susan, meaning "lily."

Sula

American English, meaning "peace" or "little she-bear." Also the novel *Sula* by Toni Morrison.

Summer

English, from the season of the same name. Summer Glau is an actor.

Sunday

English, meaning "the first day." Nicole Kidman and Keith Urban's daughter is Sunday Rose.

Sunny
(alt. Sun)

English, meaning "of a pleasant temperament."

Suri

Persian, meaning "red rose." Tom Cruise and Katie Holmes's daughter is Suri.

Surya

Hindi, from the sun god of the same name.

Susan
(alt. Susann, Suzan; abbrev. Sue, Susie, Suzy)

Hebrew, meaning "lily." Famous Susans include actor Susan Sarandon, singer Susan Boyle, and suffragist Susan B. Anthony.

Susannah
(alt. Susana, Susanna, Susanne, Suzanna, Suzanne)

Hebrew, meaning "lily."

Svetlana

Russian, meaning "star."

Swanhild

Saxon, meaning "battle swan."

Sylvia
(alt. Silvia, Sylvie)

Latin, meaning "from the forest." Famous Sylvias include authors Sylvia Plath and Sylvia Day, and singer Sylvia Robinson.

T

Girls' names

Tabitha
(alt. Tabatha, Tabetha)
Aramaic, meaning "gazelle." Found in the Bible.

Tahira
Arabic, meaning "virginal."

Tai
Chinese, meaning "big."

Taima
(alt. Taina, Tayna)
Native American, meaning "peal of thunder."

Talia
(alt. Tali)
Hebrew, meaning "heaven's dew." Talia Shire is an actor.

Taliesin
Welsh, meaning "shining brow." The name of Welsh poet Taliesin.

Talise
(alt. Talisa, Talyse)
Native American, meaning "lovely water." Talisa Stark is a character from *Game of Thrones*.

Talitha
Aramaic, meaning "young girl."

Tallulah
(alt. Taliyah)
Native American, meaning "leaping water." Famous Tallulahs include actors Tallulah Bankhead and Tallulah Riley, and *Bugsy Malone* character Tallulah.

Tamara
(alt. Tamera)
Hebrew, meaning "palm tree." Famous Tamaras include actors Tamara Taylor and Tamera Mowry.

Tamatha
(alt. Tametha)

American English, meaning "dear Tammy."

Tamika
(alt. Tameka)

American English, meaning "people."

Tamsin
(abbrev. Tami, Tammie, Tammy)

Hebrew, meaning "twin." Tammy Wynette is the name used by the legendary country singer—her real first name was Virginia.

Tanis

Spanish, meaning "to make famous."

Tanya
(alt. Tania, Tanya, Tonya)

Shortened form of Tatiana, meaning "from the Tatius clan." The name of actor Tanya Roberts and figure skater Tonya Harding.

Tara
(alt. Tahra, Tarah, Tera)

Irish Gaelic, meaning "rocky hill." Famous Taras include actors Tara Reid and Tara Fitzgerald.

Tatiana
(alt. Tatyana)

Russian, meaning "from the Tatius clan." Famous Tatianas include actors Tatyana Ali and Tatiana Maslany, and author Tatiana de Rosnay.

Tatum

English, meaning "lighthearted." Famous Tatums include actors Tatum O'Neal and Channing Tatum.

Tawny
(alt. Tawanaa, Tawnee, Tawnya)

English, meaning "golden brown."

Taya

Greek, meaning "poor one." In several languages the name also means "princess" or "goddess."

Taylor
(alt. Tayler)

English, meaning "tailor." Famous Taylors include singer Taylor Swift and actor Taylor Schilling.

Tea

Greek, meaning "goddess." Tea Leoni is an actor.

Teagan
(alt. Teague, Tegan)

Irish Gaelic, meaning "poet."

Teal

English, from the bird of the same name. Also the blue-green color.

Tecla

Greek, meaning "fame of God."

Temperance

English, meaning "virtue." Temperance Brennan is a character from *Bones*.

Tempest

French, meaning "storm." The Shakespeare play of the same name.

Teresa

(alt. Terese, Tereza, Theresa, Therese)

Greek, meaning "harvest." Famous Teresas include nun Mother Teresa, and the late actor Teresa Graves.

Terri

(alt. Teri, Terrie, Terry)

Derived from the short form of Teresa, meaning "harvest." Actor Teri Hatcher was given this short name at birth.

Tessa

(alt. Tess, Tessie)

Derived from the short form of Teresa, meaning "harvest." Famous Tessas include ice dancer Tessa Virtue and literary heroine *Tess of the D'Urbervilles* by Thomas Hardy.

Thais

Greek, from the mythological heroine of the same name.

Thalia

Greek, meaning "blooming." The name of numerous ancient Greek muses, nymphs, and graces.

Thandie

(alt. Thana, Thandi)

Arabic, meaning "thanksgiving." Thandie Newton is an actor.

Thea

Greek, meaning "goddess." Can be a shortened form of Theodora or Dorothea.

Theda

German, meaning "people." Name of the silent movie actor Theda Bara.

Thelma

Greek, meaning "will." Famous Thelmas include singer Thelma Houston, and the movie *Thelma & Louise*.

Theodora

Greek, meaning "gift of God." The name of numerous ancient Roman figures.

Theodosia

Greek, meaning "gift of God."

Thisbe

Greek, from the mythological heroine of the same name.

Thomasina

(alt. Thomasin, Thomasine, Thomasyn)

Greek, meaning "twin." The birth name of singer Tammi Terrell was Thomasina Montgomery.

Thora

Scandinavian, meaning "Thor's struggle." Name of the actor Thora Birch.

Tia
(alt. Tiana)

Spanish, meaning "aunt." Tia Mowry is an actor.

Tiara

Latin, meaning "jeweled headband."

Tierney

Irish Gaelic, meaning "Lord."

Tierra
(alt. Tiera)

Spanish, meaning "land."

Tiffany
(alt. Tiffani, Tiffanie)

Greek, meaning "God's appearance." Name of the one-hit-wonder singer Tiffany.

Tigris
(alt. Tiggy)

Irish Gaelic, meaning "tiger."

Tilly
(alt. Tilda, Tillie)

Shortened form of Matilda, meaning "battle-mighty."

Timothea

Greek, meaning "honoring God."

Tina
(alt. Teena, Tena)

Shortened form of Christina, meaning "anointed Christian." Famous Tinas include comedian Tina Fey and singer Tina Turner.

Tirion

Welsh, meaning "kind and gentle."

Tirzah

Hebrew, meaning "pleasantness." Found in the Bible.

Titania

Greek, meaning "giant." The Fairy Queen from Shakespeare's play *A Midsummer Night's Dream*.

Toby
(alt. Tobi)

Hebrew, meaning "God is good." Usually a boy's name.

Toni
(alt. Tony)

Latin, meaning "invaluable." Feminine version of Tony, or short form of Antoinette. Famous Tonis include singer Toni Braxton, author Toni Morrison, and choreographer Toni Basil.

Tonia
(alt. Tonja, Tonya)

Russian, meaning "praiseworthy."

Topaz

Latin, meaning "golden gemstone."

Tori
(alt. Tora)

Shortened form of Victoria, meaning "victory." Famous Toris include actor Tori Spelling and singer Tori Amos.

Tova
(alt. Tovah, Tove)
Hebrew, meaning "good."

Tracy
(alt. Tracey, Tracie)
Greek, meaning "harvest." Famous Tracys include singer Tracy Chapman, actor Tracey Ullman, and artist Tracey Emin.

Treva
Welsh, meaning "homestead."

Trilby
English, meaning "vocal trills." Also the name of a style of men's hat.

Trina
(alt. Trena)
Greek, meaning "pure."

Trinity
Latin, meaning "triad." Associated with the Christian Holy Trinity. The lead female character from the film series *The Matrix*.

Trisha
(alt. Tricia)
Shortened form of Patricia, meaning "noble." Name of singer Trisha Yearwood.

Trista
Latin, meaning "sad."

Trixie
Shortened form of Beatrix, meaning "bringer of gladness."

Trudie
(alt. Tru, Trudy)
Shortened form of Gertrude, meaning "strength of a spear."

True
English, meaning "loyal."

Tullia
Roman, meaning "bound for glory."

Twyla
(alt. Twila)
American English, meaning "star." Name of the choreographer Twyla Tharp.

Tyler
English, meaning "tiler." Used for both boys and girls.

Tyra
Scandinavian, meaning "Thor's struggle." Tyra Banks is a model.

Tzipporah
Hebrew, meaning "bird."

U Girls' names

Ula
(alt. Ulla)
Celtic, meaning "gem of the sea."

Ulrika
(alt. Urica)
German, meaning "power of the wolf."

Uma
Sanskrit, meaning "flax." Uma Thurman is an actor best known for her roles in Quentin Tarantino's *Pulp Fiction* and *Kill Bill*.

Una
Latin, meaning "one."

Undine
Latin, meaning "little wave."

Unique
Latin, meaning "only one."

Unity
English, meaning "oneness."

Uriela
(alt. Uriella)
Hebrew, meaning "God's light."

Ursula
Latin, meaning "little female bear." The villain from Disney's *The Little Mermaid*.

Uta
German, meaning "prospers in battle."

V

Girls' names

Vada
German, meaning "famous ruler."

Valdis
(alt. Valdiss, Valdys, Valdyss)
Norse, meaning "goddess of the dead," from the mythological goddess of the same name.

Valencia
(alt. Valancy, Valarece)
Latin, meaning "strong and healthy." A city in Spain.

Valentina
Latin, meaning "strong and healthy."

Valentine
Latin, from the saint of the same name.

Valerie
(alt. Valarie, Valeria, Valery, Valorie; abbrev. Val, Vale, Valia, Vallie)
Latin, meaning "to be healthy and strong." Famous Valeries include actors Valerie Bertinelli and Valerie Harper, and the song "Valerie" by The Zutons.

Vandana
Sanskrit, meaning "worship."

Vanessa
(alt. Vanesa)
Greek, meaning "butterfly." Famous Vanessas include actor Vanessa Hudgens and singer Vanessa Williams.

Vanity
Latin, meaning "self-obsessed."

Vanya
Russian, meaning 'gift of God'. Vanya is a lead character in The Umbrella Academy series.

Vashti
Persian, meaning "beauty." A Persian queen in the Bible.

Veda

Sanskrit, meaning "knowledge and wisdom."

Vega

Arabic, meaning "falling vulture."

Velda

German, meaning "ruler."

Vella

American English, meaning "beautiful."

Velma

English, meaning "determined protector." A character from *Scooby Doo*.

Venice
(alt. Venetia, Venita)

Latin, meaning "city of canals." An Italian city.

Venus

Latin, from the Roman goddess of the same name. Venus was the goddess of love, beauty, sex, and fertility.

Vera
(alt. Verla, Verlie)

Slavic, meaning "faith." Famous Veras include designer Vera Wang, actor Vera Farmiga, and singer Vera Lynn.

Verda
(alt. Verdie)

Latin, meaning "spring-like."

Verena

Latin, meaning "true." Associated with St. Verena.

Verity

Latin, meaning "truth."

Verna
(alt. Vernie)

Latin, meaning "spring green."

Verona

Latin, from the Italian city of the same name.

Veronica
(alt. Verica, Veronique)

Latin, meaning "true image." Famous Veronicas include actors Veronica Lake and Veronica Carlson, and the "Veronica Mars" series and movie.

Veruca

Latin, meaning "wart." Veruca Salt is a character from *Charlie and the Chocolate Factory*.

Vesta

Latin, from the Roman goddess of the same name.

Vicenta

Latin, meaning "prevailing."

Victoria
(abbrev. Tori, Vicki, Vicky, Vikki, Vix)

Latin, meaning "victory." Famous Victorias include designer Victoria Beckham, England's Queen Victoria, and lingerie store Victoria's Secret.

Vida
Spanish, meaning "life."

Vidya
Sanskrit, meaning "knowledge." Refers to learning and knowledge in the Hindu faith.

Vienna
Latin, from the city of the same name in Austria.

Vigdis
Scandinavian, meaning "war goddess."

Vina
(alt. Vena)

Spanish, meaning "vineyard."

Viola
Latin, meaning "violet." Name of the actor Viola Davis.

Violet
(alt. Violetta)

Latin, meaning "purple." The famed nurse and survivor Violet Jessop.

Virginia
(alt. Virgie, Virginie; abbrev. Ginnie, Ginny)

Latin, meaning "maiden." Famous Virginias include author Virginia Woolf, Raising Hope character Virginia Chance, and the eastern states of Virginia and West Virginia.

Vita
Latin, meaning "life."

Vittoria
Variation of Victoria, meaning "victory."

Viva
Latin, meaning "alive." Name of the actor Viva.

Vivian
(alt. Vivien, Vivienne, Vyvian)

Latin, meaning "lively." Famous Vivians include actor Vivian Leigh, designer Vivienne Westwood, and photographer Vivian Maier.

Vivica
(alt. Viveca)

Scandinavian, meaning "war fortress." Name of the actor Vivica A. Fox.

Vonda
Czech, meaning "from the tribe of Vandals." Vonda Shepard is a singer.

Girls' names

Waleska
Polish, meaning "beautiful."

Wallis
English, meaning "from Wales." Name of socialite Wallis Simpson, the woman held responsible for the abdication of Great Britain's King Edward VIII.

Wanda
(alt. Waneta, Wanita)
Slavic, meaning "tribe of the vandals." Name of comedian and actor Wanda Sykes.

Wava
English, meaning "way."

Waverly
(alt. Waverley)
Old English, meaning "meadow of aspens."

Wendy
English, meaning "friend." Famous Wendys include host Wendy Williams, the character of Wendy Darling in *Peter Pan*, and the hamburger chain Wendy's.

Whisper
English, meaning "whisper."

Whitley
Old English, meaning "white meadow."

Whitney
(alt. Witney)
Old English, meaning "white island." Famous Whitneys include the late singer Whitney Houston, comedian Whitney Cummings, and dancer Witney Carson.

Wilda
German, meaning "willow tree."

Wilhelmina
(abbrev. Mina, Mine, Minna, Willa, Willy, Wilma)

German, meaning "determined to protect." A popular name with the German royal family.

Willa
(alt. Willene, Willia)

German, meaning "helmet." Willa Cather is an author.

Willow

English, from the tree of the same name. Famous celebrity children called Willow include Willow Smith (Will and Jada Pinkett Smith's daughter) and Willow Hart (Pink and Carey Hart's daughter).

Winifred
(alt. Winnie)

Old English, meaning "holy and blessed." South African activist Winifred "Winnie" Madikizela-Mandela was once married to former South African President Nelson Mandela.

Winona
(alt. Wynonna)

Indian, meaning "first-born daughter." Famous Winonas include actor Winona Ryder and singer Wynonna Judd.

Winslow

English, meaning "friend's hill."

Winter

English, meaning "winter."

Wisteria

English, meaning "flower."

Wren

English, meaning "wren."

Wynne
(alt. Wynn)

Welsh, meaning "white."

Girls' names

Xanthe

Greek, meaning "blonde." The name of several ancient Greek mythological characters.

Xanthippe

Greek, meaning "nagging."

Xaverie

Greek, meaning "bright."

Xaviera

Arabic, meaning "bright."

Xena
(alt. Xenia)

Greek, meaning "foreigner." The title character from the TV sci-fi series *Xena: Warrior Princess*.

Ximena

Greek, meaning "listening."

Xiomara

Spanish, meaning "battle ready."

Xochitl

Spanish, meaning "flower." Queen Xochitl was a legendary Toltec ruler.

Xoey

Variation of Zoe, meaning "life." Spelling alternative for Zoey or Joey.

Xristina

Variation of Christina, meaning "follower of Christ." Singer Christina Aguilera often spells her name Xristina.

Xylia
(alt. Xylina, Xyloma)

Greek, meaning "from the woods."

Y

Girls' names

Yadira
Arabic, meaning "worthy."

Yael
Hebrew, meaning "mountain goat."
Found in the Bible.

Yaffa
(alt. Yahaira, Yajaira)
Hebrew, meaning "lovely."

Yamilet
Arabic, meaning "beautiful."

Yana
Hebrew, meaning "the Lord is gracious."

Yanira
Hawaiian, meaning "pretty."
A character in ancient Greek mythology.

Yara
Arabic and Persian, meaning "small butterfly." Yara Greyjoy is a character from *Game of Thrones*.

Yareli
Latin, meaning "golden."

Yaretzi
(alt. Yaritza)
Aztec, meaning "forever beloved."

Yasmin
(alt. Yasmeen, Yasmina, Yasmine)
Persian, meaning "jasmine flower."

Yelena
Greek, meaning "bright and chosen."

Yesenia
Arabic, meaning "flower."

Yetta
English, from Henrietta, meaning "ruler of the house."

Yeva

Hebrew variant of Eve, meaning "life."

Ylva

Old Norse, meaning "she wolf."

Yoki

(alt. Yoko)

Native American, meaning "rain." Yoko Ono is an artist and peace activist.

Yolanda

(alt. Yolonda)

Spanish, meaning "violet flower." Name of reality TV star Yolanda Foster.

Yoselin

English, meaning "lovely."

Yoshiko

Japanese, meaning "good child." Princess Yoshiko was an important Empress of Japan.

Ysabel

English, meaning "God's promise." Spelling alternative to Isabel.

Ysanne

Contraction of Isabel and Anne, meaning "pledged to God" and "grace."

Yuki

Japanese, meaning "lucky."

Yuliana

Latin, meaning "youthful."

Yuridia

Russian, meaning "farmer."

Yvette

(alt. Ivette, Ivonne, Yvonne)

French, meaning "yew." Yvette Nicole Brown is an actor.

Z
Girls' names

Zafira
Arabic, meaning "successful."

Zahara
(alt. Zahava, Zahra)
Arabic, meaning "flowering and shining." Name of Angelina Jolie and Brad Pitt's daughter.

Zaida
(alt. Zaide)
Arabic, meaning "prosperous"; Hebrew, meaning "loved grandfather."

Zalika
Swahili, meaning "well born."

Zaltana
Arabic, meaning "high mountain."

Zamia
Greek, meaning "pine cone."

Zaneta
(alt. Zanceta, Zanetah, Zanett, Zanetta)
Hebrew, meaning "a gracious present from God."

Zaniyah
Arabic, meaning "lily."

Zara
(alt. Zaria, Zariah, Zora)
Arabic, meaning "radiance." A fashion brand.

Zaya
(alt. Zayah)
Tibetan, meaning "victorious woman."

Zelda
German, meaning "dark battle." Associated with the hugely successful video game series Legend of Zelda.

Zelia
(alt. Zella)
Scandinavian, meaning "sunshine."

Zelma
German, meaning "helmet."

Zemira
(alt. Zemirah)
Hebrew, meaning "joyous melody."
Title of the opera *Zemira* by
Francesco Bianchi.

Zena
(alt. Zenia, Zina)
Greek, meaning "hospitable."

Zenaida
Greek, meaning "the life of Zeus."
Associated with physician
St. Zenaida.

Zenobia
Latin, meaning "the life of Zeus."
Zenobia was a queen of ancient
Roman Syria.

Zephyr
Greek, meaning "the west wind."

Zetta
Latin, meaning "seven."

Zia
Arabic, meaning "light and splendor."

Zinaida
Greek, meaning "belonging to Zeus."

Zinnia
Latin, meaning "flower."

Zipporah
Hebrew, meaning "bird." Zipporah
was one of Moses' wives in the Bible.

Zita
(alt. Ziva)
Spanish, meaning "little girl."
St. Zita is the patron saint of maids
and domestic servants.

Zizi
(alt. Zizzy)
Hungarian/Hebrew, meaning "God
is my oath."

Zoe
(alt. Zoi, Zoie, Zoey, Zoeya, Zooey)
Greek, meaning "life." Famous Zoes
include actors Zoe Saldana and
Zooey Deschanel.

Zoila
Greek, meaning "life."

Zoraida
Spanish, meaning "captivating
woman."

Zosia
(alt. Zosima)
Greek, meaning "wisdom." Zosia
Mamet is an actor.

Zoya

Greek, meaning "life." Zoya Kosmodemyanskaya was a Soviet Union heroine.

Zula

African, meaning "brilliant."

Zuleika

Arabic, meaning "fair and intelligent." Zuleika was the name of Potiphar's wife in the Bible.

Zulma

Arabic, meaning "peace."

Zuzana

Hebrew, meaning "lily."

Zuzu

Czech, meaning "flower." Susan (Zuzu) is a character in the movie *It's A Wonderful Life*.

A name for all seasons

Spring	Summer	Fall	Winter
April	August	Autumn	January
Kelda	June	Demetria	Neva
May	Persephone	September	Neve
Primavera	Soleil	Theresa	Perdita
Verda	Summer	Tracey	Rainer